What Really Matters for Struggling Readers

Designing Research-Based Programs

THIRD EDITION

Richard L. Allington

University of Tennessee, Knoxville

PEARSON

Boston   Columbus   Indianapolis   New York   San Francisco   Upper Saddle River
Amsterdam   Cape Town   Dubai   London   Madrid   Milan   Munich   Paris   Montreal   Toronto
Delhi   Mexico City   Sao Paulo   Sydney   Hong Kong   Seoul   Singapore   Taipei   Tokyo

Editor-in-Chief: Aurora Martínez Ramos
Editorial Assistant: Meagan French
Marketing Manager: Danae April
Production Editor: Annette Joseph
Editorial Production Service: Lynda Griffiths
Manufacturing Buyer: Megan Cochran
Electronic Composition: Denise Hoffman
Interior Design: Denise Hoffman
Art Director: Linda Knowles

10 9 8 7   RRD-VA 15 14

www.pearsonpd.com

ISBN-10: 0-13-705700-8
ISBN-13: 978-0-13-705700-9

Contents

chapter 6

Where to Begin:
Instruction for Struggling Readers   157

Preface

New to This Edition

In this third edition of *What Really Matters for Struggling Readers* I have brought the text up to date in several ways.

- In the first chapter, especially, I note what we learned from the federal Reading First initiative. This initiative was targeted to the school with the greatest proportion of low-income children and included more federal directives about what schools were required to do than any previous federal legislation. However, even with federal mandates to monitor reading progress and to use only core and supplemental reading programs tabbed as "evidence based," the Reading First program nationally was a failure (Gamse et al., 2009). In other words, the Reading First initiative did not improve reading achievement in the Reading First schools to any greater degree than in other schools serving low-income families and their children. In Chapter 1 I also update the reports on reading achievement in U.S. schools, pointing out that little improvement has been noted since 1988, but that U.S. students still perform relatively well in the international assessments, especially in the earlier years of schooling.

- In Chapter 2 I update on the topic of reading volume. In the past few years, since the last edition of this book was written, we have learned even more about how volume of reading predicts reading proficiency. Struggling readers too often participate in interventions that actually reduce how much reading they do! During these interventions the struggling readers do everything but read. I am more convinced today than ever before that designing interventions and classroom reading lessons that dramatically expand the amount of reading students do is the essential change that must come if we hope to have everyone reading on grade level.

- Chapter 3 includes several recent studies indicating the critical nature of the reader/text match. Struggling readers especially need huge amounts of high-success reading. But too often our lesson designs and even our intervention designs have ignored this critical aspect of lesson planning. The evidence is clearer now than ever before that any one-size-fits-all lesson design is not only ineffective but it also ignores literally hundreds of studies on effective teaching. Without differentiation all day long, struggling readers have little chance of ever catching up with their more proficient peers.

- Research on fostering fluency has made great strides in recent years and in Chapter 4 I review what the research says today about fostering fluency in struggling readers. Perhaps the most important recent finding is that simply expanding reading volume works even better than repeated readings in fluency development. Yes, and not surprisingly, simply allowing struggling readers to read appropriate-level texts for the same amount of time that they might be engaged in repeated reading of the same text produces the same fluency gains but more quickly. It also produces gains in meaning vocabulary that repeated readings do not foster. The revised Chapter 4 presents a stronger framework for promoting fluency than in earlier editions.

- Chapter 5 is about fostering comprehension growth. In this revision I expand on the topics of nurturing vocabulary growth and engaging students in literate conversations about what they have been reading. It is with the latter topic that we have seen the most research and development since the last revision of this book. But literate conversation still takes a back seat to textual interrogation when it comes to the reading lessons struggling readers receive. The evidence is now clear: If we want to foster growth in reading comprehension proficiencies, we must routinely engage students in literate conversation both during and after they read.

- I made the fewest revisions in Chapter 6 if only because little has actually changed in what we need to do to make struggling readers into proficient readers. In fact, little has changed in schools since I wrote the first edition of this book. Struggling readers are still struggling and schools are still attempting to blame the victims for this suffering. I note in this chapter that a recent study found that two-thirds of new teachers believe they are neither responsible for nor capable of providing reading lessons to pupils with disabilities! This seems to be at the core of our problems. Special education populations have been growing at a rate far greater than the growth of the total school enrollment. It seems to me that this growth in special education placements may simply signal that far too many teachers believe as these new teachers believe—that they are neither accountable for nor competent to provide high-quality reading lessons to some children. Thus, a referral for special education services follows.

We know how to teach everyone to read. We now know that the term *learning disability* is basically an excuse for not providing the sorts of intensive, expert reading instruction that eliminates the learning disability. It is classroom teachers who have the most to offer students who get labeled LD. But too often, classroom teachers believe it isn't their job and that they are unprepared to work successfully with these children.

I prepared this third edition of *What Really Matters for Struggling Readers* because we have an increasing amount of research demonstrating that we can teach every child who arrives at your school's kindergarten door to read. And we can have them all reading on level by the end of first grade! However, until we begin a substantial redesign of our schools and the programs we provide, we will always have struggling readers. These struggling readers, it is now clear, are not children with a learning disability but, rather, children we failed to teach adequately or sufficiently. Hopefully, by the time you finish reading this book you will have a clear idea of what needs attention in your school if all children are to become proficient readers.

Thank you to the following reviewers for their comments and suggestions: Sam Bommarito, Fontbonne University; Diana L. Carr, Elgin Junior High School, Green Camp, OH; Margot Kinberg, National University; Stacey Leftwich, Rowan University; and Denise Stuart, The University of Akron.

The **What Really Matters** *Series*

The past decade or so has seen a dramatic increase in the interest in what the research says about reading instruction. Much of this interest was stimulated by several recent federal education programs: the Reading Excellence Act of 1998, the No Child Left Behind Act of 2001, and the Individuals with Disabilities Education Act of 2004. The commonality shared by these federal laws is that each law restricts the use of federal funds to instructional services and support that have been found to be effective through "scientific research."

In this new series we bring you the best research-based instructional advice available. In addition, we have cut through the research jargon and at least some of the messiness and provide plain-language guides for teaching students to read and write. Our focus is helping you use the research as you plan and deliver instruction to your students. Our goal is that your lessons be as effective as we know how, given the research that has been published.

Our aim is that all children become active and engaged readers and writers and that all develop the proficiencies needed to be strong independent readers and writers. Each of the short books in this series features what we know about one aspect of teaching and learning to read and write independently. Each of these pieces is important to this goal but none is more important than the ultimate goal: active, strong, independent readers and writers who read and write eagerly

So, enjoy these books and teach your students all to read and write.

Chapter 1

Reading Achievement and Instruction in U.S. Schools

Much has changed in American schools in the decade since I penned the first edition of this book.

Most of that change was stimulated by the federal No Child Left Behind Act (NCLB) of 2001. We now know that the hundreds of millions of federal dollars spent under NCLB had one positive outcome: First-grade students from low-income homes enrolled in Reading First schools read nonsense syllables faster and more accurately than low-income first-graders in schools not benefiting from Reading First funding. In addition, children in Reading First schools received more minutes of reading instruction every day than the other poor kids and more of that reading instruction was focused on the five pillars of early reading instruction outlined in the report of the National Reading Panel. But, not surprisingly (from my point of view), at the end of first, second, and third grade there was no difference in

National Reading Panel

The National Reading Panel (NRP) was charged by Congress with recommending the scientific studies that were worthy of consideration in the design of reading instruction in the future. The NRP elected to examine only the experimental research studies in developing their report, a decision decried by many educational researchers. Based on their review of this body of research they concluded the following:

- Developing phonemic awareness and phonics skills in kindergarten and first grade was supported by the research but systematic phonics was not effective for struggling readers in grades 2 to 6.
- Providing regular guided oral reading with a focus on fluency was important.
- Silent reading was recommended for developing fluency, vocabulary, and comprehension skills (though the panel felt that the research reviewed had not adequately demonstrated the benefits of various incentive programs for increasing reading volume).
- Direct teaching of comprehension strategies was recommended and it was noted that providing good comprehension strategy instruction is a complex instructional activity. Thus, the panel recommended extensive, formal preparation in comprehension strategies teaching for all teachers.
- Little research was available to support the use of technology (e.g., computers) in teaching reading, but the few studies available suggested that it was possible that there was a potential for some benefits to students.

For further information, see Allington, R. L. (2002). *Big Brother and the national reading curriculum.* Portsmouth, NH: Heinemann.

the reading achievement posted by the children in these two types of schools, nor was there any difference in student engagement in reading (Gamse et al., 2009). Additionally, the reading gap between children from more and less economically advantaged families did not close in the past decade, even though that was the impetus behind NCLB. One could say NCLB was a failure in fostering better reading achievement.

So why did all this extra federal money and local reading instructional time not produce either better readers or narrow the rich/poor reading gap? As I have argued earlier (Allington, 2002a), I think it was because the NCLB wasn't designed to raise reading scores. Instead, it was simply part of a larger scheme intended to reduce the power of teacher unions, colleges of education, and teacher professionalism—all ultimately, I believe, in the name of greater privatization of public education in the future. If public schools cannot raise the reading achievement of poor children even when given substantial extra funding, then something else must be needed was the mindset of those who developed NCLB.

But with its focus on teacher and student accountability and penalties for schools failing to raise reading achievement and close the reading achievement gap, the No Child Left Behind Act was designed largely by politicians and policy makers, most of whom had never spent a day in a classroom as a teacher. The best you can say is they believed the hypothesis that greater accountability and sanctions for schools and educators would somehow improve reading achievement. They believed that schools were like widget factories, where such plans had improved productivity (and raised the profit margin). But as Diane Ravitch (2010) has so articulately described, there was no evidence that any of the components of NCLB had ever raised reading achievement, anywhere.

We are now entering roughly the fiftieth year of reforming American schools and attempting to close the reading achievement gap between children from economically different families while also raising the achievement of all children substantially. The NCLB Act is simply the legislative extension of the Elementary and Secondary Education Act of 1966 that was a major component of the War on Poverty declared by then-President Lyndon B. Johnson. But we have more poor families and children today than we had way back then. And we still have a large gap in the reading abilities of children from low-income and middle-class families. However, what we have today that was missing back then is reasonably clear evidence that we can teach virtually every child to read and have virtually all of them reading on grade level by the end of first grade (Mathes et al., 2005; Scanlon et al., 2005; Vellutino et al., 1996). The only children who fail to meet the grade-level criteria are those who fail to attend school regularly and those with the most severe disabilities.

In this book, then, I hope to convey to you, first, the promise of the power of effective reading lessons and, second, a solid description of just what you really have to pay attention to when designing reading lessons for struggling readers.

Why Another Book?

The rationale for writing this book is that much of the rhetoric and policy making that surrounds current efforts at "reforming" U.S. reading instruction are misguided. They are misguided because a considerable amount of the reform sentiment focuses on features of instruction that don't really matter that much in the grand scheme of things. Many of the reforms are narrowly conceived and simply cannot have the sort of impact that we might hope for given the time, money, and energy that has been spent. In this book I will refocus attention on the few things that really matter in teaching children to read (and the things over which we as teachers and administrators can actually exert a degree of control).

Why Now?

Simply, the reason for revising the book now is that we can now see the impact of the No Child Left Behind Act on the design of school reading programs. And I, for one, don't much like what I am seeing. I am writing because I am worried that, to date, "What the research says . . ." has been narrowly interpreted and focused almost wholly on the very beginning stages of reading instruction. I am writing because I am deeply worried that so much of what we have learned about teaching reading effectively—especially to children who have difficulty—is being routinely ignored. I am writing because the research is being misrepresented (see Allington, 2002b; Allington & Woodside-Jiron, 1998, 1999; Coles, 2003; Garan, 2002; Pearson, 2004; Taylor, 1998). I am writing because much of what might prove useful instructionally in first grade is being misapplied to older children and to children having difficulty. I am also writing because the scientific evidence has shown that those Reading First initiatives did not improve reading achievement even though teachers in the Reading First schools allocated more time for teaching reading than teachers in other schools.

My goal is to provide a readable, practical treatise on designing a more effective reading instruction. My long-standing concern for children who have difficulties learning to read will be evident because it is the instruction of those children that seems most often to go awry in schools.

But to begin, let me correct some of the misunderstandings about U.S. children's reading proficiency and U.S. reading instruction today.

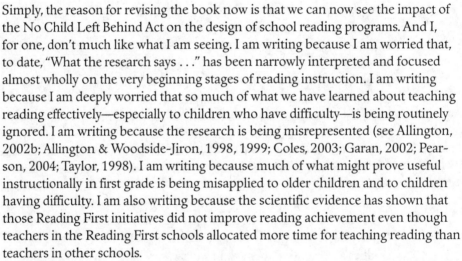

So How Bad Is the Situation in Terms of Reading Achievement?

Actually, the answer to how bad the reading achievement situation is depends on your reference point. For instance, in a recent international comparison of children's reading achievement (Bracey, 2004), U.S. fourth-graders were ranked ninth in the world. Only three nations had scores that were significantly higher (see Table 1.1). U.S. ninth-graders ranked right in the middle, at the international average. These data often surprise many people in the United States, including educators, but as they say, "You can look it up!"

On these international assessments there were separate sections on prose and informational reading. Students from the United States performed sharply better on prose reading than they did on informational text reading. They ranked third on prose reading, with only a single nation earning statistically higher scores, and twelfth on reading informational texts, with five nations statistically ahead. But the U.S. best readers performed well, with twice as many students ranking in the top 10 percent of readers (19 percent versus 10 percent), as would be expected. Students in schools enrolling fewer than 25 percent free-lunch students performed well above the average score of the top nation. But schools with more than 75 percent free-lunch students ranked twenty-eighth with the score of 485 (Bracey, 2004).

Obviously, students in many U.S. schools read quite well, whereas students in other schools, primarily schools enrolling many children from low-income families, lag far behind. On average, though, the performance of both our 9- and 15-year-olds equaled or exceeded that of students in the majority of other industrialized nations participating in these international assessments.

National Assessment of Educational Progress

Every two years, the U.S. Department of Education releases a new Report Card on Reading. This report card draws national headlines along with, typically, statements of concerns from federal and state policy makers—concerns that U.S. schools are failing their responsibility to produce a literate citizenry. The report card details the findings of the National Assessment of Educational Progress (NAEP), a series of assessments covering an array of subject areas. The NAEP reading assessments are the most frequently administered and seem to generate the most discussion. The general theme of such discussions recently has gone something like this: "We've dramatically increased education expenditures, but reading scores remain flat with huge achievement gaps between different subgroups." In this section, I will attempt to help you understand that the general interpretation of NAEP achievement data ignores important gains that have been made over the past 40 years.

TABLE 1.1   Combined Reading Literacy Scores, Ages 9 and 15

Age 9		Age 15	
Sweden	561	Finland	546
Netherlands	554	Canada	534
England	553	New Zealand	529
Bulgaria	550	Australia	528
Latvia	545	Ireland	527
Canada	544	Korea	525
Lithuania	543	England	523
Hungary	543	Japan	522
United States	**542**	Sweden	516
Italy	541	Austria	507
Germany	539	Belgium	507
Czech Republic	537	Iceland	507
New Zealand	529	Norway	505
Scotland	528	France	505
Singapore	528	**United States**	**504**
Russian Fed.	528	Denmark	497
Hong Kong	528	Switzerland	494
France	525	Spain	493
Greece	524	Czech Republic	492
Slovak Rep.	518	Italy	487
Iceland	512	Germany	484
Romania	512	Lichtenstein	483
Israel	509	Hungary	480
Slovenia	502	Poland	479
Norway	499	Greece	474
Cyprus	494	Portugal	470
Moldova	492	Russian Fed.	462
Turkey	449	Latvia	458
Macedonia	442	Luxembourg	441
Colombia	422	Mexico	422
Argentina	420	Brazil	396
Iran	419		
Kuwait	396		
Morocco	350		
Belize	327		

Source: National Center for Education Statistics. (2004). *The nation's report card: Reading highlights 2003.* Washington, DC: U.S. Department of Education, Institute for Education Sciences.

(For full information on the NAEP, including sample test items and state NAEP reports, visit http://nces.ed.gov/nationsreportcard.)

There are actually two NAEP assessments. One, the Trend Assessment, is designed to allow comparisons of reading achievement over time. The most recent Trend Assessment was completed in 2008. Figure 1.1 shows the longer-term pattern of reading achievement for each of the three grade levels tested. A quick glance suggests that scores have remained largely stable for 40 years. There is a worrisome small decline in twelfth-graders' reading performance since 1990 and similarly a small rise in fourth-graders' reading performances in that same period.

Bracey (2004) notes, however, the presence of Simpson's Paradox in the NAEP Trend Assessment data. Simpson's Paradox illustrates how average achievement data reports can obscure important findings. For instance, since 1971 the average NAEP trend reading score for fourth-grade Black students rose 34 points (from 170 to 204), Hispanic students' scores rose 24 points (from 183 to 207), and White students' scores rose 14 points (from 214 to 228). Similar gains were made at eighth and twelfth grades. In other words, across the 40-year period, much progress was made in closing the achievement gap between White and minority students. But the overall average gain in the NAEP fourth-grade trend data shows an average reading improvement of only 12 points between 1971 and 2009 (from 208 to 220) and only a 5-point gain since 1980 (from 215 to 220). How can it be that every subgroup grew by a greater amount than the average gain reported?

FIGURE 1.1   NAEP Reading Long-Term Trend Scores for the Nation

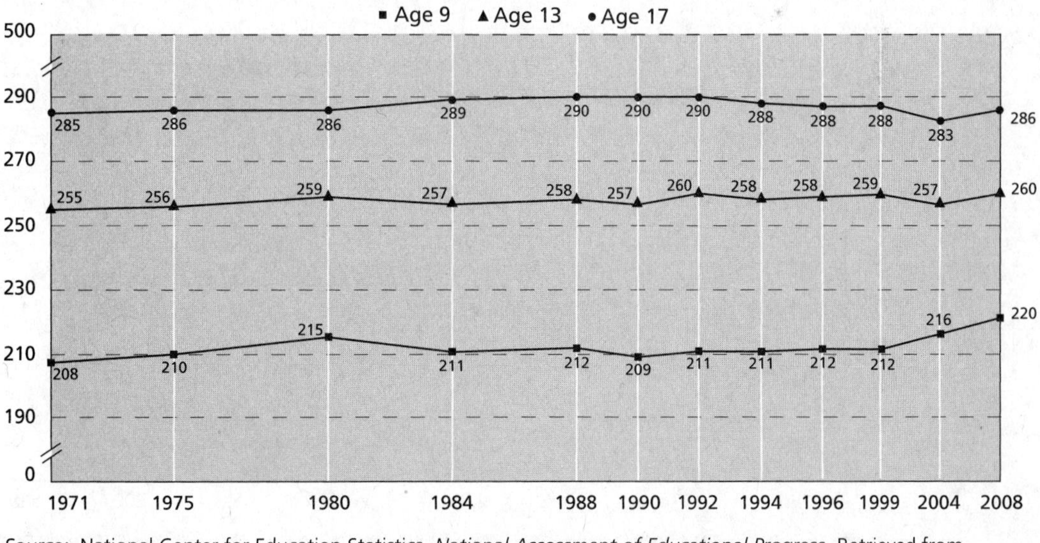

Source: National Center for Education Statistics. *National Assessment of Educational Progress.* Retrieved from http://nces.ed.gov.

This is where Simpson's Paradox comes in. The average trend score comparisons are a bit of an apples and oranges comparison. What I mean is that minority enrollment expanded rapidly in U.S. schools over the 1971 to 2008 time period, from about 15 percent to about half (44 percent) of the student population tested. Even with their improved reading performances, minority students still trail White students by a substantial margin (a gap of 20 to 30 points). Thus, the population shifts resulted in about three times as many minority students in the current NAEP assessment pool as there were in the earliest NAEP assessment pools. The overall lower achievement of this much larger group of minority students produced a trend line that looks almost flat over the 40-year period. But underneath the overall average trend line are substantial improvements by every subpopulation of students, especially minority students. A worrisome trend, however, is that although the racial and family income achievement gaps narrowed over time, those gaps are still far too large, and it was these gaps that fueled the No Child Left Behind legislation. But NCLB had no effect on closing this reading achievement gap.

The second NAEP assessment offers the Main Assessments Report (National Center for Educational Statistics, 2009). These are the ones that are commonly discussed. Because of changes in the NAEP assessment and in the administration (including accommodations for pupils with disabilities, for instance), Main Assessment Reports are more difficult to compare over time. The National Assessment Governing Board (NAGB) indicates that only NAEP Main Assessments from 1992 to 2008 can be considered equivalent (see Figure 1.2).

FIGURE 1.2   NAEP Main Report Reading Scores 1992–2009

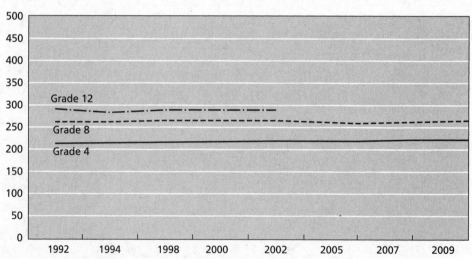

Source: National Center for Education Statistics. (2008). *The nation's report card: Reading highlights 2008.* Washington, DC: U.S. Department of Education, Institute for Education Sciences.

The NAEP scores over the past two decades have shown little change, with only small improvements across the three grades (4, 8, and 12). The percentage of students failing to achieve the basic level of reading performance dropped from 40 to 37 percent at fourth grade and from 31 to 26 percent at eighth grade. The results also indicate that, in general, the best readers are reading better and the worst readers are reading about the same or slightly worse than was the case two decades ago. The gap between White and minority students and the gap between more and less economically advantaged students have not narrowed in the past two decades. In other words, the progress noted previously in closing achievement gaps occurred between 1971 and 1990. Since then, little progress has been made in overcoming this challenge, even though this was a major goal of federal legislation.

The achievement of U.S. elementary and middle school students on nationally normed, standardized commercial tests of reading achievement have been rising since 1980. Between 1965 and 1980, the heyday of the basic skills instruction movement, these scores declined but began to rise substantially in recent years (Bracey, 2004). For instance, on the Iowa Test of Basic Skills, the average fifth-grader's achievement in 1990 roughly equaled the average sixth-grader's achievement in 1975, and the average third-grader's achievement in 1990 equaled the achievement of the average fourth-grader in 1955. Across the 40- to 50-year period (1960–2010), elementary school student achievement rose quite dramatically, whereas average middle school achievement improved only modestly. But at all grade levels children today outperform children from earlier eras of U.S. schooling.

Finally, one other indicator that might be used is the readability formulas that were created to estimate the difficulty of books. The oldest and most popular of these formulas originated in the 1940s and 1950s. However, two such stalwarts—the Dale-Chall and the Spache readability formulas—were renormed in the 1980s because they no longer accurately reflected the grade difficulty of texts. In both cases, the difficulty estimates were overestimating the complexity. So, in renorming, what had been a seventh-grade-level book became a sixth-grade-level book.

Various explanations for the wave of negative information that has filled the media have been offered, but a simple principle for educational reporting—good news is no news—may provide the simplest explanation. Of course, when advocates of privatization of education attempt to move their political agendas, bad news about U.S. schools is necessary as a lever to attempt to persuade the public to accept such a radical shift in the financing of public education (Bracey, 2004). And for three decades (since 1981), the White House has been occupied by privatization advocates. But, interestingly, the U.S. public seemed more confused than convinced by the notion that U.S. education was failing.

In one Gallup poll (Coles, 1999), half of U.S. adults awarded their local schools an A or B grade for effectiveness. However, fewer than half of these same adults awarded U.S. schools generally the same grade. In other words, lots of folks believe their children attend one of the few good schools in the country. These adults

So How Bad Is the Situation in Terms of Reading Achievement?

9

award grades to local schools based on more direct knowledge of the achievements of those schools. They award lower grades when asked to rate schools that they have little direct knowledge of. These are schools that they acquire information about only indirectly, largely through media accounts. So it seems that most U.S. adults believe that *other* schools need to improve but *their* schools are doing a creditable job of educating children.

But if Achievement Is Actually Rising, Why Another Book?

Research points to high reading achievement levels in U.S. students today—no doubt about it. But research also points to several disturbing trends in U.S. reading achievement. The first is the trend for certain groups of children to lag behind their peers in literacy learning. The more disturbing part is that these children are all too often predictable. For instance, researchers at the Rand Institute on Education and Training (Grissmer et al., 1994) found that students whose parents were not high school graduates had achievement levels significantly below the achievement levels of children whose parents were college graduates. Family income was also related to achievement, as were mother's age (with the children of older mothers achieving higher levels) and other factors. But, perhaps surprisingly, these researchers found little relationship between achievement and children from single-parent homes or homes where both parents worked. They concluded that only parent educational levels and family income were related to achievement.

There are also other group differences in achievement. The one most frequently mentioned is the Black/White achievement gap. The 2009 NAEP results (National Center for Education Statistics, 2009) show a 25-point gap between Black and White fourth-graders' reading scores and a 26-point gap at eighth grade. These are sizable differences. For instance, the gap between Black eighth-graders and White fourth-graders is 14 points (246 and 230).

But there are other gaps as well. The Hispanic/White gap is almost identical to the Black/White gap at both grade levels. There is a rich/poor gap of 28 and 26 points at the fourth- and eighth-grade levels, respectively, again similar to the Black/White gap.

Then there is the boy/girl gap. This gap is smaller, but girls outperform boys in reading by 7 and 10 points at grades 4 and 8, respectively. This gender gap was also observed in the international achievement comparisons, with girls significantly outperforming boys in reading in every nation.

There is also one additional confounding factor: Retention in grade. Flunking children with low reading scores has been mandated in several states and in a number of city school districts. This means that we can now find many children who should be in middle school still enrolled in the elementary grades. In one of our most current studies (Allington & McGill-Franzen et al., 2010) we found 13- and 14-year-old students enrolled in grades 4 and 5. Recently we had a discussion with a 17-year-old seventh-grade student! By state mandate this student had spent 3 years in third grade and 3 years in sixth grade along with having repeated two other grades. Even if this student is promoted every year onward, he will be 22 years old when he earns his high school diploma—assuming of course that he stays in school, which seems unlikely.

I mention these cases because the children taking the fourth- and eighth-grade NAEP reading assessments are getting older than they used to be. If a child has repeated grade 3 three times and is now 12 or 13 years old, shouldn't her reading scores be higher than had she been promoted and tested when she should have been in fourth grade? There are simply too many students taking the fourth-grade NAEP today who should be in grades 5, 6, or 7 for anyone to claim that fourth-grade reading scores are improving.

One way to consider these data is as additive risk factors. Being poor places you at risk of reading difficulties; being a boy or being a minority also places you at risk. One might examine local data using these broad categories. Do more boys, more poor boys, more poor minority boys struggle with reading? Is this also true for flunking a grade? If so, this seems to say more about problems in the school system than it says about these boys.

Three Challenges

The evidence indicates that U.S. schools currently work better for certain children than for others. In order to hope to fulfill the promise of public education, schools must work for all children—regardless of gender, race, or which parents the children got. One challenge for U.S. education is designing schools that are less parent dependent, where all children can expect to be successful readers and writers. Given that only about one-third of all entering kindergarten students arrive at school not knowing all the letter names of the alphabet (Zill & West, 2001) and that about one-third of all fourth-graders fail to achieve the basic level of reading proficiency, it becomes clearer that schools don't work well for some children. These are the children of low-income families where levels of parental educational attainment are also typically low. If our schools fail to teach these children to read well, how likely is it they will ever become productive citizens?

There is a second challenge for U.S. education. Although we have been largely successful in teaching children to read and write at basic levels of proficiency, the vast amount of growing technology places higher-order literacy demands on all of us. As Bill Kovach and Tom Rosenstiel point out in their hard-hitting book, *Warp*

Speed: America in the Age of Mixed Media (1999), we have entered an age of unfettered information flow. Historically, only a few large publishers could afford to provide national news and information dissemination. These authors argue that with that power came a sense of responsibility for attempting to ensure an accuracy and completeness of the information—in other words, journalistic codes of ethics and editorial decisions about the quality of the "evidence" supporting a story. They note that the modern information environment is different with its proliferation of news outlets, 24-hour news, and infotainment channels. They point to a new "journalism of assertion" as the dominant mode of delivery. This mode has fewer checks and balances and literally places far greater demands on the reader, viewer, and listener. These demands include synthesizing and evaluating information from multiple sources. These multiple information sources have fewer editorial controls and fewer filters through which information is sifted for accuracy, reliability, and civility. And Kovach and Rosenstiel hardly even mention the Internet but instead focus on the television and print media.

The Internet imposes virtually no controls on information quality and reliability. Type the word *Holocaust* into an Internet search engine and you will find many web pages denying the Holocaust ever took place. Although materials denying the Holocaust have been around since the 1950s, never have they been so widely accessible to so many people; never have they appeared so "official."

Because of the increase in the unfettered flow of information, U.S. schools need to enhance the ability of children to search and sort through information, to synthesize and analyze information, and to summarize and evaluate the information they encounter. On the one hand, the performances of U.S. students on the NAEP have been improving, having risen to historically high levels of attainment. On the other hand, only a few U.S. students seem to be able to demonstrate even minimal proficiency with higher-order literacy strategies (and the children most likely to demonstrate these are those children whose parents have high levels of educational attainment). Even a quick examination of the NAEP items that so many children and adolescents find especially difficult suggests that we have done a better job of teaching the basic literacy skills (word recognition, literal comprehension) than the higher-order thinking skills and strategies. The items attempting to assess higher-order proficiencies do not require rocket-scientist–type performances. Many, in fact, require little more than the types of judgments about information, ideas, and assertions that an adult makes nearly every day.

There is a third challenge for U.S. education that needs to be mentioned. Our schools create more students who *can* read than students who *do* read. Too many students and adults read only when they are required to. Interest in voluntary reading begins to fall in the upper-elementary grades, declines steeply in middle school, and continues to fall across high school. We seem to be producing readers who can read more difficult texts but who elect not to read even easy texts on their own time.

U.S. schools, especially elementary schools, produce children who rank among the world's best readers. The schools are improving. More children are better readers than ever before, but there are still substantial challenges that need to be confronted.

Can Educational Research Provide Support for Meeting These Challenges?

The answer to this question is *perhaps*. We have learned much about what sorts of schools, classrooms, and lessons foster reading proficiency. We have learned about how to redesign schools and classrooms and lessons to better meet the needs of children who find learning difficult (Allington & Cunningham, 2006). We have also been learning more about what sorts of classrooms and lessons foster the higher-order literacy that seems often neglected (Allington & Johnston, 2002).

And we have learned more than a little about the sorts of classrooms and lessons that foster ownership of reading and writing (Guthrie & Humenick, 2004). But with all we have learned, there still is no simple blueprint for restructuring schools, classrooms, and lessons. Perhaps that is because blueprints differ for virtually every building constructed. Perhaps the same is true of school restructuring. Because we build different buildings for different clients, we may need to build different classrooms and lessons for different students in order to meet the challenges that confront us.

In suggesting that educational research can provide no blueprint I am not suggesting that educational research can provide no guidelines—quite the contrary. But educational research is a slippery beast. There is a trove of published studies and an even greater supply of unpublished studies to be found in ERIC, in Dissertation Abstracts, and on publishers' websites. Much of the educational research available, even in the published papers, fails to meet rigorous quality criteria. Skeptics suggest that "You can prove anything with research." To some extent that is true, especially at the level of comparing particular programs, materials, or methods. Such comparisons have a long history in education even though the results are rarely consistent from study to study. Too often, proponents of a particular method, material, or program selectively review the available research and report on studies supporting their biases. A more comprehensive review often shifts the resulting conclusions.

It is not uncommon to hear someone initiate a discussion of any particular method, material, or program with the phrase "Hundreds of studies show . . . ." Truth be told, it is impossible to locate 100 studies showing the same effect for any method, material, or program. Consider that Jeanne Chall, author of *Learning to Read: The Great Debate* (1987), located fewer than 100 studies comparing different approaches to teaching beginning reading even though her review covered 80 years of research. Every approach she examined produced the best results in at least one of the comparison studies, and every approach was found less effective in some studies. Similar findings after 27 coordinated studies compared methods and materials in the largest beginning reading field experiment ever conducted led the authors of the *First Grade Studies* (Bond & Dykstra, 1967) to conclude: "Children learn to read by a variety of materials and methods. . . . No one approach is so distinctly better in all situations and respects than the others that it should be considered the one best method" (p. 75).

One useful component of NCLB was the creation of the federal What Works Clearinghouse (WWC). This agency was tasked with reviewing educational research and developing a sort of score card in different areas. They reviewed the research available on over 150 reading programs. But only one reading program received the WWC's rating as having "strong evidence" of improving reading achievement. That program was Reading Recovery, an individualized reading tutorial for first-grade students having difficulty. Only two other commercially available reading programs were rated as having "possible evidence" of positive effects. Not a single core reading program had even one study supporting its use. And almost no reading program currently available had any evidence it improved reading achievement. Some had evidence they helped children read faster or decode nonsense syllables better but only one had strong evidence it improved reading achievement. Nonetheless, commercial vendors routinely tout their programs as "research-based" and typically have glossy slides showing how well their program works. Visit the What Works Clearinghouse website (www.whatworks.ed.gov) for full details on the findings as well as plain language material on making sense from research claims.

On most educational questions there are only a handful of published studies, and often these are smallish and local. In the case of materials and programs, the number of published studies shrinks even further. Additionally, more often than not, the majority of the few published studies are authored by the developers and marketers of the materials and programs. In other words, there are few independent evaluations of most materials and programs available. Several examples come to mind.

First, there was the Waterford Early Reading program, an expensive, computer-based package designed for kindergarten and primary-grade classrooms. Although the publisher provided data from a number of local unpublished evaluation studies, the only independent experimental field trial found no effect on early reading achievement. The authors (Patterson et al., 2003) concluded:

> It is clear from the present results that the Waterford Early Literacy Program had relatively little overall effect on the participants' literacy development. . . . [T]o the extent there was an effect, it was in a negative direction. . . . On the other hand, teacher variables had a consistently strong effect on reading success. (p. 198)

Then there is the heavily promoted Success for All (SFA) program and the highly publicized Direct Instruction (DI) materials. In both these cases there exists a substantial set of studies, often published in professional journals (with fewer studies published in peer-reviewed research journals). In both programs there are some independent research studies that have also been published. The sets of SFA studies generally find that the program produces statistically significant achievement effects when SFA schools are compared to control schools (schools without SFA). The independent studies report the same sort of effects, though often reporting smaller differences in achievement between schools than the studies by the SFA developers. There exists, then, published evidence that implementing the SFA program improves achievement.

However, as Venezky (1998) points out in his reanalysis of the SFA data, the program continues to produce large numbers of children with dismayingly low reading achievement. He reported that fifth-grade students in the SFA schools had reading achievement levels at the middle–third-grade level compared to the beginning–third-grade reading levels of fifth-graders in the control schools. Venezky does not question whether SFA produced higher achievement levels—it did. Rather, he asks whether we are willing to accept *so little* improvement in reading as sufficient evidence that the SFA program should be recommended for wide implementation.

In the case of the DI materials, the body of research extends back 40 years, and the evidence has been controversial across that period of time (e.g., House et al., 1978; Jordan, 2005; Schweinhart & Weikart, 1998). The majority of the DI research has been done by the developers, with much of it reported in *Effective School Practices,* the in-house magazine of the Association for Direct Instruction edited by one of the DI program authors. This research was summarized in a self-published selective review (Adams & Englemann, 1996)—a review that omitted a number of DI studies that did not report positive effects. There are so few independent studies published in peer-reviewed research journals that some scholars largely discount the evidence available (Stahl et al., 1998).

This sort of criticism could just as easily be offered on Wilson Phonics, whole language, and the Houghton Mifflin (or any other major publisher) reading program. The important point here is that "What the research says . . ." is currently an almost meaningless phrase. In other words, virtually every proponent of any method, material, or program can find some sort of evidence to prove what they have to offer works somewhere, some of the time. By selectively reviewing the evidence, by creating magazines to publish their own supportive data (because no peer-reviewed journal would accept it as unbiased), and by controlling the design of the evaluation and the implementation of their favorite method, material, or program, almost anyone can create the impression that "research shows" positive effects for their product or pedagogy.

Ideally, research studies would demonstrate the longer-term impact of interventions as well as report the shorter-term effects. Unfortunately, rather few studies report effects over periods greater than one year, and many report the effects after only a few months. Longer-term studies are more complicated and more expensive but they are also essential.

There is a long-standing federal enthusiasm for packaged reading reform. Unfortunately, we also have 50 years of research showing that packaged reforms simply do not seem reliable in improving student achievement (Allington & Nowak, 2004). Nonetheless, federal and state education policy makers ignore these studies and attempt to reform from the top down. Sometimes the push is for a particular method of teaching children to read. Other times the push is for particular commercial reading programs. Much of the recent focus on so-called proven programs can be traced back to the early 1990s, when Congress passed the Comprehensive School Reform Development Act of 1990 (Berends et al., 2002). This legislation provided funds for adopting one of several national school reform models (e.g.,

Success for All, Accelerated Schools, America's Choice). These were supposed to be "proven programs" that supported schoolwide reform. The RAND research group produced a 10-year evaluation of this federal effort. It concluded, "The initial hypothesis, that by adopting a whole-school design a school could improve its performance was largely unproved" (Berends et al., 2002, p. 173). In other words, while there were some schools that adopted one of the national designs and then saw student achievement rise, there were at least as many schools that adopted one of the designs in which achievement did not improve.

Publishers and promoters of packages and products have simply modified their advertising and advocacy campaigns to include the message that "research shows" that their product works. The education marketplace is a "buyers beware" market. Little scientific research exists that demonstrates any package or program works consistently and reliably. For instance, none of the "proven programs" that generated so much excitement more than a decade ago has withstood the independent research review. None of the commercial reading series has either. There is a lot of money to be made in the education marketplace, but that means convincing administrators and teachers to buy your stuff (including this book and my consulting services).

There is one final problem with research available today. In most cases, the available studies evaluated the effects of a literacy intervention on assessments of basic literacy, not on thoughtful literacy assessments. In other words, most studies use word lists, tests of subskill knowledge, or assessments of low-level comprehension found on traditional standardized tests with their multiple-choice items. We have only a handful of studies that have evaluated interventions against student attainment of the new, higher-order literacy standards. But it is against student achievement of these new, higher standards that schools are typically now being evaluated.

For years, no one actually paid much attention to "research" evidence on various methods, materials, and programs. Yes, marketing departments often created some flyer or glossy brochure designed to convince the occasionally wary buyer that there was a research base for the product. (And none of this is to suggest that research did not influence the design of educational methods, materials, and products—it did.) But today there are greater demands on publishers and promoters to have actual research on the effects the implementation has had on the achievement of students. This is different from being able to point to studies that influenced the design of a method, material, or program—the more traditional test. So, why the demand for research evidence now?

The No Child Left Behind Act of 2001

Congress passed the No Child Left Behind Act (NCLB) in 2001 with full bipartisan support. This legislation might be best viewed as an intensification of federal education policy, particularly policy focused on instruction in high-poverty schools. The NCLB law was an extension and reauthorization of the Elementary and Secondary Education Act of 1966 (ESEA). The ESEA marked the first real involvement of the federal government in the instructional arena. As part of the Great Society programs instigated by then-President Lyndon Johnson, ESEA was controversial. One reason was that the U.S. Constitution gave states responsibility for education. The ESEA represented a major new federal initiative that was viewed by many as a threat to local educational control.

A key component of ESEA was Title I of that act. Title I focused on providing high-poverty schools with additional funds to support supplementary reading instruction. The more recent Reading First component of Title I was a further effort to address the needs of children enrolled in the highest poverty-stricken schools. In both Title I and Reading First schools this additional federal funding was specified as additional reading lessons, "in addition to" the reading instruction already available to children in the school. Title I funds were to be used to "supplement" the classroom reading lessons. Thus, Title I services were often designed as pullout reading lessons in which children left the classroom for an additional 30 minutes of small group reading instruction after completing their 90-minute classroom reading lessons. In many states this additional instruction was to be provided by certified reading specialists, teachers with additional graduate preparation in teaching reading to struggling readers.

However, in far too many states paraprofessionals or teachers with no graduate training in reading disabilities provided the extra lessons. In far too many schools paraprofessionals simply monitored struggling readers while they worked on some form of computer-assisted reading lessons. (This was done even though the research indicates that neither paraprofessional reading lessons nor computer-based reading lessons have accelerated reading development.) In other words, in far too many schools the design of these supplementary reading lessons contradicted what the research says about what sort of reading lessons might actually solve struggling readers' reading difficulties. That is why I noted on page 1 of this book that I was not surprised that the Reading First initiative failed to improve reading achievement (Allington, 2009b).

The design of additional reading instruction has not typically been research-based (Allington & McGill-Franzen, 1989; Vaughn & Linan-Thompson, 2003). Often, Title I and special education reading lessons replaced, in whole or in part, classroom reading lessons. The Title I legislation created the now-widespread "second system" of education (Allington, 1994b). This system is now represented by all those efforts that are not viewed as a component of the general education classroom program (remedial reading, special education, bilingual education, migrant education, gifted education, and so on). Most of these second-system educational efforts were also created by federal legislation and each had its own regulations and separate funding stream. This design, I've argued, resulted in a quite fragmented effort to design and deliver more and better reading instruction to children who struggle with learning to read (Allington, 2006).

The current situation in most schools, districts, and states is one of continued fragmentation of instructional plans for providing extra reading support. This fragmentation is best observed, perhaps, in cases of children who qualify for multiple programs. For instance, a child who is from a low-income family, is not from a home where the primary language is English, and is identified as having a learning disability would qualify for extra instructional support from at least three federal programs in most schools. But there are few schools in which a child would actually receive the full set of services and almost no schools where those services would be well coordinated with each other and with the classroom instructional program.

No Child Left Behind has changed none of this. The Reading First component of NCLB is largely an extension of Title I remedial-reading services. But NCLB brought changes that expand federal influence on the design and delivery of remedial reading instruction. The Title I legislation had long required schools, districts, and states to submit comprehensive plans for how federal funds would be used to expand reading instructional services to eligible children and adolescents. It had long required a testing program to demonstrate that federal dollars were benefiting struggling readers in high-poverty schools. The NCLB law expanded the specificity of both testing efforts and the nature of the instruction offered (Allington, 2002b).

Reading instruction in NCLB schools, at least, was to be based on "scientifically based reliable, replicable research," or SBRR. Unfortunately, little research was actually consulted when designing NCLB or in designing the reading instruction under NCLB. Instead, great hopes were placed on schools selecting commercial reading materials, materials that had a scientific base. Thus, in most states there was a push for adopting a single commercial reading program and then using that program "with fidelity." Two problems existed that the NCLB designers ignored. First, there was no research supporting the use of any of the core reading programs and none that supported the use of any supplementary reading program, except Reading Recovery. This was the message that the What Works Clearinghouse delivered when it released its report on research on reading programs. However, by the time the report was released, at least five years of mandated core reading programs use had been implemented. Second, what the research seems to suggest is that adaptation of commercial reading programs, adaptations based on student needs, produces better results than just following the reading program guidelines. But such adaptations are made only by teachers who are reasonably expert about both reading instruction and the children they are teaching (Duffy, 2004).

Thus, for at least the past decade U.S. schools have been implementing reading plans that no research supports—and doing so under the guise of "scientifically based reliable, replicable research." Congress has terminated funding for the Reading First portion of Title I funding, at least in part because the large federal study of the effects of the Reading First program indicated that no reading achievement gains occurred in Reading First schools (Gamse et al., 2009). In addition to finding no positive effects on achievement, Congress also noted the education department report from the Inspector General's office that indicated widespread corruption in the Reading First offices at the highest levels (Office of the Inspector General, 2006, 2007). The "corruption" involved recommendations for programs and assessments that had no research base, but these programs and assessments did have authors who were involved in making the decisions about what programs and assessments should be used. *Buyer beware* should have been the motto of NCLB.

Adequate Yearly Progress

Even though the earlier federal Title I legislation required accountability testing to gain federal funds, the testing plans differed substantially from state to state and district to district within states. Nonetheless, the Title I testing requirement was seen as promoting a much wider use of standardized tests, especially in high-poverty schools (Timar & Kirp, 1987). The NCLB expanded testing and reduced the variation in grade levels tested by requiring annual assessments of all children in grades 3 through 8. Also, the NCLB mandated annual assessments to determine whether various subgroups were making adequate yearly progress (AYP) in reading. Each state submitted plans for how AYP was to be met, but at the root of all plans was comparing the test scores of groups of children to the state standard.

Although earlier Title I programs also required year-to-year test score comparisons, fewer students were required to participate in the testing and a demonstration of achievement growth roughly comparable to one year's gain in the tests was the general goal. Of course, if struggling readers began the year below grade level, gaining a year in growth meant they still remained behind. The NCLB focuses on closing the achievement gap between various subgroups, and thus the goal is to accelerate reading growth such that struggling readers grow at a rate greater than one year per year. Acceleration then means that struggling readers must demonstrate achievement growth greater than the growth expected of children who read on grade level.

The NCLB requires that each state develop a schedule that ensures that all children will be reading at a targeted level by 2014. In general, the targeted level of reading proficiency is linked to each state's standards. But state standards for proficient reading vary widely. Some states have set low standards and others have set substantially higher standards. Thus, the proportion of students failing to meet AYP goals varies dramatically from state to state. An unintended impact of the NCLB law is that some states lowered their proficiency standards so that the AYP goals will be easier to meet. In addition, states have established different dates when proficiency levels must be met. So in some states, few schools fail to meet AYP standards, whereas in other states, 9 out of 10 schools already fail to achieve AYP (Ryan, 2004; Peterson & Lastra-Anadon, 2010).

Currently, the NCLB is under consideration for reauthorization by Congress. The Obama administration is working hard to get states to raise their standards in both reading and math, and so far have indicated no substantial changes in the law, including the requirement to meet adequate yearly progress goals by 2014. I have no idea when Congress will reauthorize NCLB, whether Congress will change the name of NCLB, or whether Congress will substantially alter any of the requirements of NCLB. It is clear, however, that Congress is aware that several large-scale research studies (c.f., Mathes et al., 2005, Phillips & Smith, 2010; Vellutino et al., 1996) have demonstrated that every child can be reading at grade level by the end of grade 1 and be kept on level through the end of grade 3. Thus, I expect Congress to produce a new version of NCLB that has even more rigorous standards and requirements. Time will tell.

Disaggregation of Proficiency by Subgroups

The NCLB legislation requires annual testing of reading achievement and requires that the achievement of subgroups of struggling readers be accelerated to close any existing achievement gaps between these subgroups. Thus, schools must show that the achievement gains of poor children, minority students, and pupils with disabilities are narrowing any gap between the reading proficiency of these subgroups and the larger school population.

Schools must demonstrate that with each ensuing year the achievement of all subgroups is increasing and that any gap in the achievement of the subgroups and the majority student population is narrowed and finally eliminated. To achieve this end, federal funds are used to accelerate the reading development of struggling readers. Thus, schools focus on designing interventions that accelerate the reading development of children from low-income families, for instance, such that their achievement soon equals that of middle-class students. Or schools may design an intervention to accelerate the reading development of minority students to ensure that their achievement is soon on par with nonminority students. The education of pupils with disabilities has often been the responsibility of special education programs, but NCLB now includes those children as one of the targeted subgroups. Thus, schools must now also focus on accelerating the reading development of those children as well.

This is, perhaps, one of the real shifts in the federal model. This marks the first foray by the federal education agency to track academic outcomes for pupils with disabilities (Gartner & Lipsky, 1987). Furthermore, tracking outcomes is not all that is required: In addition to the NCLB mandate that pupils with disabilities participate in the testing, it is also required that special education services produce achievement outcomes comparable to, or exceeding, those of pupils enrolled in general education. This largely represents a new conception of the role of special education instructional programs. The services now provided to special education students must accelerate achievement or risk having the school fall into the program improvement category. Of course, failure of any of the subgroups will produce that same outcome, but many students in other subgroups were already part of the federal accountability pool.

As has already been discussed, achievement gaps currently exist between each of the subgroups and the majority, middle-class population. The NCLB legislation garnered broad bipartisan political support because of its focus on eliminating such achievement gaps. I think the NCLB requirement to disaggregate achievement data by subgroups is a good idea. The 10-plus–year timeline for achieving comparable outcomes was a reasonable time period for implementing a revised design for remedial interventions that would be much more powerful than those now available in many schools. However, there are numerous problems with other aspects of No Child Left Behind—problems that may be legislated away over time—but problems nevertheless. One set of problems derives from the NCLB school improvement plans.

School Improvement under NCLB

Section 1116 of the NCLB law sets forth a number of complicated mandates that apply to schools where adequate yearly progress goals for subgroups are not being met. These mandates will be presented as they appeared in the original legislation. As already noted, these plans and mandates may be legislatively modified over time, if only because the impact will likely be widespread and in many cases quite severe. A number of state legislatures and various governors have called for substantial changes in the school improvement mandates.

The key to avoiding falling under the school improvement guidelines is to have all subgroups meet reading achievement goals; schools need to demonstrate that the federal funds they have received were allocated to interventions that accelerated reading achievement of poor, minority, English language learners, and pupils with disabilities such that the existing achievement gap is narrowed and, ultimately, eliminated. Just how much reading growth is necessary depends on how far behind struggling readers in the subgroups might be and the nature of the schedule each state has set for eliminating the gap. But it seems likely that reading growth of more than a year's gain will be needed in each subgroup to avoid the corrective actions the law mandates.

Under NCLB, each school district is required annually to review the progress of every school receiving funding from NCLB and to report to the public the results of the testing and whether the school met AYP goals. When any school fails to achieve AYP for two consecutive years, that school must develop a school improvement plan that covers a two-year period, incorporate scientifically based research to address specific problem areas that caused the failure, and adopt policies and practices for core academic subjects that have the greatest likelihood of raising student achievement to state proficiency levels.

In addition, the school improvement plan requires that not less than 10 percent of its federal funds be allocated for professional development, that extended time instructional activities (before-school, after-school, Saturday schools, summer school) be developed, and that teacher mentoring is ongoing. Finally, the district must provide all students in school improvement schools the option to transfer to another public school not identified as needing improvement. Transportation to other schools must be provided by the district and may require the use of local funds to finance it (although the NCLB legislation specifically notes that districts do not have to spend any local dollars to implement the requirements of the law). If a school in program improvement fails to achieve AYP by the end of the first year, the school must make supplementary services available to all struggling readers.

If, at the end of the second year of school improvement, the school still does not meet AYP for all subgroups, then "corrective actions" are mandated by NCLB. Possible corrective actions include (U.S. Department of Education, 2002):

- Replace the school staff relevant to the failure.
- Implement a new curriculum.
- Extend the school day or school year.
- Significantly decrease management authority in the school.
- Appoint outside experts to advise the school.
- Restructure the internal organization of the school.

If the school fails to meet AYP in the year following the corrective actions, the district must, by the beginning of the next school year, do one of the following:

- Reopen the school as a public charter.
- Replace all or most of the staff, including the principal.
- Enter into a contract with a private management company to operate the school or allow state takeover of the school.

If a school in program improvement makes AYP for two consecutive years, then it is not subject to school improvement mandates.

Public School Choice under NCLB

As soon as a school fails to achieve AYP goals, students in that school must be provided with the opportunity to leave that school and attend another school that met AYP goals. The lowest-achieving children from low-income families must be given priority in such cases. The district must pay for this transportation, which will likely leave less money to fund instructional interventions. Once a child has transferred, that child may remain in that school until the highest grade offered is completed. If, however, that child's original school achieves AYP goals and is no longer identified as needing school improvement, the district is no longer required to provide transportation to the choice school.

Although mandates on choice seem clear, there is a significant problem in some districts and even in whole states in fulfilling these mandates. In Florida, for instance, 87 percent of the schools in 2005 failed to make AYP and thus pupils in those schools had to be provided the opportunity to transfer to one of the 13 percent of the schools that met AYP. A similar situation existed in most large urban school districts. But when 9 out of 10 students attend schools needing improvement, it is impossible for sufficient space to exist at the few schools meeting the AYP goals to enroll all the students who might want to transfer.

Additionally, even if the space existed, school districts would almost necessarily have to move the teachers from the failing schools to the achieving schools just to have sufficient instructional staff. Is it likely that changing the building a teacher teaches in will automatically result in far more effective teaching by that teacher?

Supplementary Services under NCLB

Supplementary services are defined as "tutoring and other supplemental academic services" that are (U.S. Department of Education, 2002):

- in addition to the instruction provided during the school day
- of high quality, research-based, specifically designed to increase the achievement of eligible children

These supplemental services may be provided by the district, but the district must give parents a list and description of other qualified supplemental services providers, including for-profit providers (e.g., Sylvan Learning Centers, private tutors, etc.). The district must also provide transportation to and from supplemental services up to a targeted maximum amount of dollars (the formula for funding transportation is complicated and involves a percentage of the amount of federal dollars received and a percentage of the local funding).

The big shift here is that supplemental services are to be provided outside the school day in after-school, before-school, and Saturday school programs. This may ameliorate the problem of pulling children out of their classrooms during the day (which always results in loss of classroom instructional time), but it may exacerbate the problem of fragmentation of instructional support. In other words, if current programs seem fragmented, with little coordination between, for example, special education reading lessons and classroom reading lessons, then how difficult will it be to ensure a coherent instructional plan for children being served in supplemental services provided in an after-school program offered by a for-profit provider?

Other Problems with NCLB Mandates

One huge problem with the several mandated corrective actions is the almost complete lack of research support for any of the options. There exists no viable research indicating that replacing a principal, or replacing some instructional staff (let's say replacing the remedial reading or special education teachers), reliably enhances student achievement. Likewise, there is no research indicating that purchasing a new reading program reliably raises reading achievement (Berends et al., 2002; McGill-Franzen et al., 2006). Nor is there evidence that turning a school over to a management firm or to the state or that creating a charter school reliably improves achievement. No research indicates that school choice improves student reading achievement (Ravitch, 2010). It seems odd, given the emphasis on using "research-based" interventions in NCLB, that so many mandates are offered that have so little evidence of success in improving achievement.

The federal government, however, has been promoting such unsupported mandates for at least two decades now. Beginning with the Comprehensive School Reform and Development Act (CSRDA) of 1990, continuing with the Reading Excellence Act (REA) of 1998, and now with NCLB, the U.S. Department of Education, following legislative mandates of Congress, has been attempting to improve reading achievement by mandating or "incentivizing" the use of "proven" programs. The problem is that there are no "proven" programs (Allington & Nowak, 2004). At least there are no existent programs that reliably increase student achievement across multiple sites.

Berends and colleagues (2002) found that when schools adopted one of the "proven" program models touted by the federal government (e.g., Success for All, America's Choice, Roots and Wings, Comer Schools, Accelerated School, etc.), achievement did rise in some schools but there was no consistent pattern of improvement across the schools engaged in such adoptions. But this is no surprise for reading researchers familiar with more than 50 years of research on the effects of programs on student reading achievement.

In fact, in the largest national study comparing different reading programs, a study conducted 45 years ago, the authors (Bond & Dyskstra, 1967) concluded, "Future research might well center on teacher and learning situation characteristics rather than methods and materials" (p. 123). They reached this conclusion because their study indicated that all programs worked somewhere and none worked everywhere. Their arguments were similar to those made more recently by Berends and colleagues (2002), who concluded that what mattered was "local capacity"—the teachers and the workplace context in which the teachers worked. In both studies, and in others of smaller scale, programs, whether defined as commercial reading series or as systemic reform models, had small and variable impacts on student reading achievement. But in no study were any programs of any type identified that reliably raised reading achievement from site to site. None.

A second major flaw in NCLB is the heavy reliance on testing, especially standardized testing, as the basis for estimating school effectiveness and student achievement (Papay, in press). The use of standardized tests is less problematic for evaluating school improvement than for estimating individual achievement growth, assuming that the testing data are uncontaminated. But problems remain in both cases.

Group standardized achievement tests are simply not designed to provide estimates of individual reading growth. Almost any technical manual accompanying the most widely used tests clearly states this fact. Every major research and measurement organization, as well as the National Research Council, has opposed using standardized test data in making decisions about an individual student's achievement—for example, who to flunk or who to place in remedial reading classes. One major reason schools employ psychologists to assess children recommended for special education services is the recognized limitations of group achievement tests to provide reliable and accurate estimates of individual achievement. But NCLB mandates standardized testing to identify AYP attainment, to identify children for supplemental services, and so on. The achievement tests available today simply cannot provide the sort of information school districts need to make decisions about students.

Even though group achievement tests are more appropriate for estimates of school effectiveness (because the error inherent in the tests is largely ameliorated with large samples of student scores), this stance is supportable only when the achievement data are uncontaminated. Unfortunately, there are several sources of test contamination that impact the achievement data in just about every school in the nation.

Robert Linn (2000), in his presidential address at the American Educational Research Association noted, "Assessment systems that are useful monitors lose much dependability and credibility for that purpose when high stakes are attached to them" (p. 14). Because of test contamination from various sources, tests that might provide useful and reliable estimates of school effectiveness are made largely useless for that purpose. There are three common sources of test contamination that undermine the usefulness of tests for measuring AYP and for determining which schools are in need of improvement and which are not: flunking, summer reading loss, and test preparation.

Flunking   As high-stakes testing expands, so does flunking (Allington & McGill-Franzen, 1992). Although research has shown flunking to be an ineffective and expensive response to academic difficulties (Shepard & Smith, 1989), this seems not to have deterred politicians from mandating that lower-achieving children be retained in grade. Several states and large urban districts, including New York City, now require the flunking of students who fail to attain an achievement standard. But flunking is not just bad for kids—it also contaminates the accountability system. In 2003, some 30,000 third-graders were flunked in Florida. Subsequently, the fourth-grade state test scores rose. Imagine that—just removing the lowest-scoring children allows a governor to proclaim an education reform is working.

But, of course, the schools that flunked all those students were not actually doing a better job of teaching children to read, even if their fourth-grade test scores did rise. The question is what would the scores have looked like if all those flunkees had had their scores included in the fourth-grade testing results? A year later, almost half of those who flunked the previous year were again scheduled to be retained in grade because their reading achievement had not improved. So much for the benefits of being retained.

Summer Reading Loss   Poor children lose ground in reading during the summer vacation period. Cooper and colleagues (1996) conducted a meta-analysis of studies of summer setback. They found that poor children begin school in the fall about three months behind where they were when they left school for summer break. In contrast, more advantaged students actually gain a bit during the summer months, starting school a bit ahead of where they were when summer vacation began (Allington & McGill-Franzen, 2003). The accumulating effect of this summer setback means that poor children during their elementary school years may fall as much as two years behind more advantaged students, even if the instruction during the school year produced identical reading growth in both groups. In two large-scale studies it was estimated that 80 percent of the rich/poor reading achievement gap was created during the summer months, not during the school year (Alexander et al., 2007; Hayes & Grether, 1983). In other words, both economically advantaged and disadvantaged children made the same reading progress during the school year but the poor children slid backwards every summer, thus creating most of the reading achievement gap.

However, if we provide poor children with books they want to read and books they can read during the summer months, we can ameliorate summer reading setback (Allington, McGill-Franzen, Camilli et al., 2010; Kim & White, 2008). In fact, providing a dozen or so free books to primary-grade children every summer improved reading achievement as much as attending summer school did! Providing five or six books to older elementary students achieved the same result. However, hardly any schools send poor kids home with a supply of books to read over the summer months. Thus, summer reading setback potentially contaminates reading test scores because it works to lower the reading gains children enrolled in high-poverty schools make.

This is where the accountability system is contaminated, at least if the system is intended to measure how effective a school's instruction might be. In other words, schools enrolling many poor children will find it much more difficult to achieve AYP than schools with few poor children. This is true even if the high-poverty schools are as effective as the middle-class schools. Annual AYP testing assumes that any growth, or loss, can be attributed to the school. But summer setback occurs when the school is not in session. High-poverty schools will necessarily have to address students' summer reading because the evidence suggests that when children practice reading during the summer months, their reading proficiency actually improves. When children don't read during the summer months, their reading skills decline.

Test Preparation   Test preparation, if it raises scores without actually improving reading achievement, is another factor that might contaminate accountability. However, there is little evidence that the sort of test preparation that seems to pervade many schools actually increases test scores. Guthrie (2002) notes that almost all the variance in test scores is accounted for by reading ability and general knowledge of the world. Test preparation might produce a small benefit if it works to ensure that students are familiar with the test format, but too much practice on formats produces careless errors.

The best guideline for test preparation would seem to be to practice a couple of days before the test to familiarize students with the test format and to introduce, or review, general test-taking strategies. But daily periods of test preparation across the school year seems more likely to result in lower performances because most test preparation involves little, if any, teaching of useful reading strategies or development of word knowledge. Until research exists demonstrating the positive effects of test preparation on reading achievement, schools should avoid such activities except at the most modest scale.

The Future of NCLB

As the NCLB sanctions continue to be imposed, it is likely that changes in the law will come. The U.S. Department of Education has already changed some provisions relating to pupils with disabilities and with the formula for calculating AYP. The current administration has proposed extending the testing requirements into the high school years. But no matter the changes, NCLB still represents a continuation of a long-standing but failed federal policy. Missing from the NCLB is the recognition that accountability comes only with autonomy (Allington, 2002b). When required to follow a script or implement a mandated program, neither teachers nor administrators are likely to assume much responsibility for any failure that ensues. Only when federal policy shifts to providing autonomy for teachers and principals—autonomy to elect the instructional plan—will we likely see the sorts of improvement policy makers hope for. I see some hope that federal policy makers may be moving in this direction in the recent creation of the Response to Intervention initiative.

Response to Intervention

As part of the 2004 reauthorization of the Individuals with Disabilities Education Act (IDEA), Congress created a new response to intervention (RTI) initiative aimed at reducing the numbers of students identified as "pupils with disabilities." Because approximately 80 percent of all pupils with disabilities exhibited reading difficulties, the RTI initiative targeted accelerating reading development in the early grades for children who began school behind their peers. Roughly two-thirds of all kindergartners entered that grade already knowing the names of all the letters of the alphabet. Roughly one-third of entering kindergartners did not know this. Five years later, roughly two-thirds of fourth-grade students achieved the basic level of reading proficiency on the NAEP; one-third of the students fell below the basic level, or substantially behind their peers. It seems likely that those fourth-graders in the bottom one-third were the same one-third of students who entered kindergarten not knowing the alphabet.

School districts are now allowed to take the equivalent of 15 percent of their total special education expenditures and use that money to fund RTI. There is no role in the RTI regulations for special education personnel nor for school psychologists—at least not until after the intervention has been conducted and the children who failed to have their reading development accelerated are identified. At that point, then, these students become pupils with disabilities and are from that point onward served through special education resources.

However, as Johnston (in press) has noted, the RTI regulations include both a plan to provide added research-based reading instruction for struggling readers in an attempt to reduce the numbers of struggling readers and a new plan for identifying pupils with learning disabilities. In far too many school districts the emphasis has been on the latter rather than on planning powerful interventions that bring struggling readers up to grade level. One other factor for this problem might be that the majority of the books now available on RTI have been written by school psychologists with an emphasis on identifying the pupils with learning disabilities.

There are now several professional texts with an emphasis on providing high-quality reading interventions (Allington, 2009c; Howard, 2009; Johnston, 2010). Whether the RTI initiative will accomplish Congress's intended goal, reducing substantially the number of children identified as having a learning disability will depend largely on how well schools implement powerful intervention plans. But as Vellutino and Fletcher (2005) have noted, "Finally, there is now considerable evidence, from recent intervention studies, that reading difficulties in most beginning readers may not be directly caused by biologically based cognitive deficits intrinsic to the child, but may in fact be related to the opportunities provided for children learning to read" (p. 378). In other words, there simply do not seem to be any children who meet the current definition of learning disabled or dyslexic. That is because such children can have their reading development accelerated but only when they receive one-to-one expert tutoring or one-to-three very small group intensive expert reading instruction. When schools do not have kindergarten tutorial interventions, when they do not have first-grade tutorial interventions, when they do not have expert reading teachers providing these reading interventions, the result is a large number of children who become labeled as learning disabled or retained in grade or both. By and large this is not a result of having too little money to address these problems; it is more simply that most schools spend the money they have on lots of things that have never been supported by the research.

What Are Characteristics of Scientifically Based Reading Research?

When reviewing research findings to determine whether the research met the four criteria specified in federal legislation (listed in bold in the list that follows), readers may want to ask themselves questions about how well any particular study meets each of the criteria. Examples of the types of questions that could be asked about each criteria are included here.

- **Use of rigorous, systematic, and empirical methods.** Does the work have a solid theoretical or research foundation? Was it carefully designed to avoid biased findings and unwarranted claims of effectiveness? Does the research clearly delineate how the research was conducted, by whom it was conducted, and on whom it was conducted? Does it explain what procedures were followed to avoid spurious findings?

- **Adequacy of the data analyses to test the stated hypotheses and justify the general conclusions drawn.** Was the research designed to minimize alternative explanations for observed effects? Are the observed effects consistent with the overall conclusions and claims of effectiveness? Does the research present convincing documentation that the observed results were the result of the intervention? Does the research make clear what populations were studied (i.e., does it describe the participants' ages, as well as their demographic, cognitive, academic, and behavioral characteristics?), and does it describe to whom the findings can be generalized? Does the study provide a full description of the outcome measures?

- **Reliance on measurements or observational methods that provided valid data across evaluators and observers and across multiple measurements and observations.** Are the findings based on a single-investigator single-classroom study, or were similar findings observed by multiple investigators in numerous locations? What procedures were in place to minimize researcher biases? Do observed results hold up over time? Are the study interventions described in sufficient detail to allow for replication? Does the research explain how instructional fidelity was ensured and assessed?

- **Acceptance by a peer-reviewed journal or approved by a panel of independent experts through a comparably rigorous, objective, and scientific review.** Has the research been carefully reviewed by unbiased individuals who were not part of the research study? Have the findings been subjected to external scrutiny and verification? Has the study been published in a peer-reviewed research journal?

Finally, as mentioned earlier, you can now go to the What Works Clearinghouse website to find out what research says about reading programs. Each WWC entry lists the studies they reviewed along with an indication of why certain studies were rejected from consideration by the WWC reviewers. Basically, these studies all suffered at least one major deficiency that made the findings less than unbiased and less than reliable. The truth of the matter is that I, or almost anyone else, can design a "study" that shows that your favorite reading program "works." In fact, many such studies have been done, but most often those studies violated some fundamental aspect of good research design. Thus, no matter how many studies have been done, if they are poor studies they don't deserve recognition. To see a number of such studies just visit the websites of the publishers of almost any reading program. But always remember: Buyer beware.

Thinking about Research in Reading

The first guideline focuses on the *use of rigorous, systematic, and empirical methods* in the design of the study, which is not particularly surprising. After all, research has traditionally been an empirical adventure. But several potential problems are created here. Take the issue of *bias,* for instance. If a program developer closely monitors the implementation and the evaluation, is there an unintended biasing effect? In other words, would program developers pay more attention to implementation detail than an independent evaluator or the professional staff of a school district who also decided to implement the program and gauge its effects? My guess is that, yes, probably the developer would pay more attention. If so, are the effects the developer achieves reliable? That is, can they be achieved by others? Realize that the added attention the developer pays to implementation may not come from any ego- or profit-driven motive but, rather, from a clearer understanding of just how the program is supposed to work. If the program involves providing specific training to the teachers involved, can any two staff development providers actually offer identical training? And what if the teachers at your site are less experienced and have larger classes than the teachers at the developer's site? The point here is that "rigorous and systematic" methods often have to be adapted from site to site. The old saying that "a teacher is a teacher is a teacher" just isn't true any more than suggesting that classrooms and schools are all largely comparable.

The difficulty in designing rigorous, systematic research studies in real schools is typified in the armful of "adequacy" reviews that have been published (e.g., Coles, 2003; Lysynchuk et al., 1989; Pressley & Allington, 1999; Swanson et al., 2003; Troia, 1999). These reviews share a single common feature: All note how few published studies meet rigorous and systematic criteria. Swanson and Hoskyn (1998), for instance, reviewed over 900 studies of instructional interventions with children identified as learning disabled. Of these studies, only 180 met minimal criteria for rigor, and *fewer than 10 percent were rated as exhibiting high-quality research methodology.* Troia (1999) reviewed 39 studies of phonemic awareness interventions and noted that fewer than a quarter met even two-thirds of the criteria of rigorously designed research. The National Reading Panel (2000) located only 38 studies of phonics instruction that met their criteria for rigor. This same finding is why the What Works Clearinghouse has been dubbed the "Nothing Works Clearinghouse" by some educators. The truth of the matter, however, is that very few studies, if any, support the majority of decisions that principals and teachers have to make every day.

Much messiness in educational research stems from the problem of achieving purely random assignment of subjects. It would be difficult, if not impossible, to approach a school system and ask for participation in a research study that required all teachers and children to be randomly assigned to buildings across the district. But without such random assignment it is impossible to control for school, teacher, and community effects that might bias the outcome. In virtually all funded research, both teachers and children (actually their parents) must volunteer to participate. What about the teachers who don't volunteer? Are they comparable to the volunteers? In other words, does not including these teachers bias the results? Would teachers who were better teachers be more likely to volunteer? That would bias the effect of the intervention in a positive direction. Would parents of higher-achieving students be more likely to return permission slips than parents of lower-achieving students? That would also create a positive bias. Do some schools have a larger supply of better teachers? Or a larger number of low-achieving children?

In order to conduct a "true experiment," researchers must attempt to eliminate such bias in their subject sample. *Random selection* is the historical strategy for eliminating such bias. In true random assignment, every teacher or student or classroom is randomly selected from the population either to participate in the intervention or to serve as a control participant. The control participants do not receive the special treatment. But as anyone who works in schools knows all too well, getting teachers and parents to agree to random assignment to schools and classrooms is simply not feasible. Even getting schools to randomly assign students within a building has not been easy.

Think of the issue another way. If you wanted to achieve the best effects from an intervention, wouldn't selecting the interested volunteer teachers as the intervention teachers be desirable? That is just what most schools (and many researchers) do when they field test an intervention. But in a rigorous research study, such biased selection would violate this first principle. At the same time, following federal human subject protection guidelines, required for virtually all federally funded studies, means that participating teachers provide informed consent. In other words, teachers must be informed about the study and have the opportunity to decline to participate. We should not be surprised that teachers who see the proposed intervention in a more favorable light are more likely to volunteer. Thus, it seems that much research presents a best-case scenario—which is how the intervention works when teachers volunteer to try it.

Participating in an unbiased research study can create public relations problems for a school district. Consider, for instance, the sorts of parental concerns that could arise even with no random assignment of teachers. If some children are randomly selected to participate in an early reading intervention, say, and other children with similar needs are selected to be the unserved control students, parents of this latter group will undoubtedly object to this lack of services. Or if some randomly selected children receive a tutorial intervention and other similar children are assigned to work in a small group with a paraprofessional, parents can object and with reason. Also imagine how much more difficult the situation becomes when some classrooms are offering the special program while others are not. Rigorous, unbiased scientific research is an ivory tower standard that is simply very hard to accomplish in the real world of schools, teachers, and children.

The second guideline asks whether *the data analyses were adequate to test the stated hypotheses and justify the general conclusions drawn.* In an ideal world, every study would have a randomly selected group of teachers and children who received the experimental intervention and another randomly selected group of teachers and children who did not. Everything about the instruction offered would be identical, except one group would participate in the intervention and the other would not. The question is, When do we fit the intervention in if instruction is to be otherwise comparable? Would some children simply stay in school longer each day? That doesn't work because then we couldn't decide whether it was the intervention instructional design or just adding more instruction, regardless of the type, that led to any observed achievement effects.

However, participating in a special project has been observed to raise scores even if no real intervention is offered. This has been dubbed *the Hawthorne Effect.* This effect was first noticed in a manufacturing plant in Hawthorne, New Jersey, many years ago. Workers there were more productive when they were told they were being studied as part of a special project even though no actual experiment was conducted. To guard against the "added instruction" and Hawthorne effects, rigorous research design typically attempts to provide some other special intervention to the control group but an intervention thought not to have any real impact on, say, reading achievement.

So, a researcher might add a reading tutorial to the daily schedule of a group of randomly selected lower-achieving readers to assess its effects. At the same time, another group of randomly selected lower-achieving readers would receive a handwriting tutorial. In this case, the Hawthorne Effect is effectively nullified. Both groups of children receive a tutorial. But the added instruction problem still exists. One group received additional reading instruction, the other didn't. So why would anyone be surprised if the students receiving the added reading instruction had higher reading achievement at the end of the study?

To counter the added instruction problem, the researcher might offer two types of tutorials, both targeted at reading improvement. In one case the children might be tutored with an emphasis on developing decoding strategies—an Alphabetic Phonics tutorial. The other group might receive a different focus, perhaps reading fluency training with an emphasis on rereading texts until a certain fluency level has been achieved. In such cases, both the Hawthorne Effect and the added instruction problems are effectively countered, assuming that both groups of students and their tutors were randomly selected. If the children participating in one of the tutoring interventions record higher reading achievement at the end of the year (and perhaps for years to come), then with such a design it would be possible to consider that the observed effects were neither biased nor chance effects but real achievement gains attributable to differences in the effectiveness of the interventions.

But what happens if the effectiveness of the intervention is measured on a test of the ability to pronounce nonsense syllables? Does the selection of that outcome measure bias the outcome? Would significantly higher scores on a nonsense word test suggest that the decoding intervention was more effective—at fostering improved reading achievement? What if the outcome measure was a test of reading fluency? Is a test of fluency a more appropriate test of reading achievement than a test of nonsense word pronunciation? Would a test of fluency be biased toward the fluency intervention? How about a test of spelling? Or retelling of a narrative read silently? What if the decoding intervention improved nonsense word pronunciation but had no effect on fluency, and the fluency treatment produced the opposite result? Would such a finding be unexpected? Gamse and colleagues (2009) found that children in Reading First schools did do better at reading nonsense words than children in the control (non-Reading First) schools but that gain did not lead to improved reading achievement in Reading First schools. Again, given that teachers in Reading First schools spent more time on nonsense word decoding than the other teachers did, it is not surprising to me that the Reading First kids did better at reading nonsense words. But it also isn't surprising to me that better nonsense word reading did not lead to improved reading achievement. As far as I know, it never has! All of which begs the question: Is your school still teaching and testing nonsense word reading? And if so, why?

Thus, how the effects of an intervention are evaluated makes a huge difference in conclusions about effectiveness. This is an important issue because one criticism was that too much of the intervention research focused on developing decoding skills. Although there are reported effects on nonsense word pronunciation, these studies less often reported positive effects on other assessments of reading achievement (Allington & Woodside-Jiron, 1999; Cunningham et al., 1999; Gamse et al., 2009; Pressley & Allington, 1999). In other words, many phonics interventions demonstrate improved pronunciation of nonsense words but no improvement in reading achievement (e.g., reading fluency and comprehension).

There are also concerns about what sort of reading assessment was used—experimenter-developed, nonstandardized commercial batteries, or standardized commercial assessments? Swanson and Hoskyn (1998) reported that the studies they reviewed that used standardized assessments of reading routinely produced smaller gains than the studies that reported results on experimenter-developed tests and tests of subskills. In other words, it is easier to design a study that produces achievement effects, especially on experimenter-developed assessments, than a study that produces effects on standardized assessments. But that shouldn't be surprising. However, it should be a concern when considering the effects of any intervention because what we are attempting to do is to create better readers.

Another issue to consider here is the size of the effect observed. Historically, tests of statistical significance have been used to estimate the reliability of differences in achievement between groups. But a test of statistical significance only tells us that observed differences did not occur by chance, regardless of how small that difference is. So, with a large enough sample of students, even small differences in achievement can turn out to be statistically significant. But when do such differences become educationally significant?

Venezky (1998) reported on a reanalysis of the reading achievement in schools that had adopted the Success for All (SFA) program. He noted that fifth-grade students in SFA schools had average reading achievement grade levels of 3.6, whereas the students in the control schools had a 3.2 average reading level. The four-month difference in reading achievement was statistically significant, but Venezky asked whether—after six years of an intervention—such a difference was educationally significant or cost-effective. He suggested that it seemed less important that intervention results be compared statistically to control groups and more important that interventions also be evaluated against a fixed standard: How many students achieved the state standards, achieved grade-level performance, and became avid, voluntary readers?

Finally, it is important to consider the generalizability of the results. Does the population in the study represent the diversity of teachers and students found in U.S. schools? This is, of course, a standard that would be almost impossible to achieve in a single research project. Nevertheless, it is a useful question to consider. If the study was conducted in New York state, where all teachers must earn a master's degree within five years and your school is located in a state with less rigorous standards for teachers (and perhaps many teachers working with emergency credentials), can the results be generalized from one location to another? If the teachers who implemented the intervention were volunteers, can we expect the same effects from teachers who were mandated to implement an intervention? If the study was conducted in a school located in an upper-middle-class suburb, can the results be generalized to schools in any neighborhood? What if the study school had a 20:1 student–teacher ratio and your school has a 28:1 ratio? Generalizability rests, in large part, on comparability of populations—both students and teachers. Without rich information on the community, the teachers, the school context, and the students, it is difficult to judge comparability.

The third guideline asks whether the researcher *relied on measurements or observational methods that provided valid data across evaluators and observers and across multiple measurements and observations*. This could be considered a "fidelity of implementation" guideline. Did the researcher provide evidence that the intervention was actually implemented? Did observers monitor implementation? Was the effectiveness of the intervention related to quality of the implementation? Consider, for instance, California's experience: Almost simultaneously, schools in California were provided funds to (1) reduce class size in the primary grades, (2) provide primary grade teachers with staff development on teaching phonics, and (3) provide new phonics-emphasis curriculum materials. How might a researcher sort out the separate effects of these three different, but simultaneously enacted reforms?

There actually is almost no way one could attribute improved achievement to any of the three reforms without some careful observation of the staff development provided and the instruction offered before and after participation in the staff development. On the other hand, we now know that all those changes in California did not result in improved reading achievement. But it is still unclear why that is so.

In other words, to attribute achievement changes to participating in the staff development intervention, you would have to be able to document how classroom instruction changed after the staff development and then link those changes to improved student achievement. If some teachers changed their instruction substantially and others did not, then you might expect some classes to have substantial gains and others to make modest improvements, if any. In such a case, claims linking improved achievement to participation in the staff development might be reasonably made. Now, if the changes in instruction involved a greater frequency of the use of the new phonics materials, then perhaps claims could be made about their influence. But there is still the problem of sorting out the effects of the class-size reduction reform. Smaller classes produce better achievement even without professional development or new curriculum materials of whatever ilk (Achilles, 1999).

Note that in this example there is no control group per se. All teachers participated in the staff development. Judgments about the link between staff development and improved achievement are supported by linking differential implementation to differential patterns of achievement growth. Finding any such studies, however, is enormously difficult. This may be because of the expense involved in having observers in classrooms both before and after participation. It may be because policy makers rarely produce policies that are easily studied. Or it may be because policy makers seem rarely interested in evidence of the effects of their policy making (Allington, 2001). So, rather than provide funding for research, politicians just assert that their favorite policy was the basis for any improvements observed (with no evidence, scientific or otherwise, to support the assertion).

So far we have not considered the problem of ensuring that different observers actually observe and record the same teaching behaviors in the same ways. This is called *interrater reliability.* In other words, two raters watching the same lesson would rate it nearly identically on some observational scale. Similarly, we haven't discussed constructing an observational system that has been shown to focus on the key features of instruction—the features that produce the higher achievement. More often than not, research studies that include a monitoring of the fidelity of implementation fall short on these two criteria: demonstrations of interrater reliability and demonstrations of the predictive validity of the observational scale.

Now all of this seems overly technical and more than a bit nitpicky. But consider the claims of effectiveness that have been made for any number of methods, materials, and programs and then consider the evidence available to support those claims. Truth be told, it is difficult to find evidence that meets the What Works Clearinghouse criteria for any educational innovation. That shouldn't be surprising since even the highly lauded medical research—often held up as the ideal for education—has suffered through charges that much of the research available used only men as subjects; used populations that underrepresented minorities, people living in poverty, and people living in rural regions; excluded the obviously healthy in their samples; or was potentially biased because the funding for the research came from the drug company marketing the treatment. The recent flurry of contradictory medical research on the role of salt in one's diet, the utility of mammograms, the benefits of red wine, and so on, points to the difficulty that even medical science has in delivering "rigorous, reliable scientific research" that achieves consensus findings (Allington, 2004c).

Far too much educational intervention research falls short on the fidelity of implementation criteria. That is, few studies even attempt to estimate whether the intervention was effectively implemented. The cost of such a demonstration and the lack of demand for such evidence combine to create an environment whereby it is asserted that an intervention was implemented and then assertions about the effects, or the lack of them, are also made. In order to understand the effects of an intervention it is necessary to gather information on its implementation. This seems especially true in education where any number of studies have shown that rather few features of any intervention ever studied were actually implemented as imagined by the developer and few of the implemented changes survived over the longer term (Berends et al., 2002; Datnow & Castellano, 2000; McGill-Franzen, 2000).

The final guideline suggests that when papers reporting research on method, materials, and programs have gained *acceptance through publication in a peer-reviewed journal or approved by a panel of independent experts through a comparably rigorous, objective, and scientific review,* more confidence can be placed in the findings. I agree. But this is hardly a fail-proof test. Consider that the majority of the studies reviewed by Lysynchuk and colleagues (1989), Pressley and Allington (1999), Swanson and Hoskyn (1998), Troia (1999), and the National Reading Panel were published in peer-reviewed journals. Yet, typically fewer than half of the published studies reviewed met the minimum quality standards. Suffice it to say that there are many published, but less than rigorously designed, studies in educational and psychological research journals.

Part of the reason for this has been alluded to previously. It is tremendously difficult and, typically, expensive, to design and carry out well-designed educational intervention research. Given how financial support for educational research has eroded over the past 30 years, few school districts or state education agencies or publishers actually fund any research on methods, materials, or programs. That said, no one should be surprised that far too many educational research projects cut corners (and costs) in ways that impact the quality of the results—at least in terms of the confidence we can place in the reliability and generalizability of the results.

In addition, every year more educational and psychological journals and magazines appear in the marketplace. These magazines need articles to fill their pages. Thus, the past 30 years have seen a veritable explosion of lower-quality research. Relatively few journals can be considered high-quality research publications where the peers doing the review are established and recognized educational researchers. Too many educational publications exhibit precisely the opposite attitude of that exhibited by the popular media. While the popular media seems to focus almost exclusively on "bad news" stories about education, educational magazines and journals focus primarily on "good news" stories. Think about the educational magazines and journals you read. How many articles in these publications reported on the failure of a reform or an intervention?

High-Quality Educational Research Journals

There are literally a hundred or more journals and magazines that publish educational research. However, there are but a handful of journals that require rigorous peer review. While no list can be comprehensive, below are my nominees for the journals most likely to publish high-quality studies or reviews of research:

Review of Educational Research

American Educational Research Journal

Journal of Educational Research

Journal of Educational Psychology

Journal of Literacy Research

Reading Research Quarterly

Elementary School Journal

Educational Evaluation and Policy Analysis

Two plain-language books that discuss U.S. educational achievement patterns in detail are Gerald Bracey's *Setting the Record Straight* (Heinemann) and Richard Rothstein's *The Way We Were?* (The Century Foundation). Both books cover broad academic achievement patterns for K–12 and include data on various other schooling issues such as flunking, teacher accountability, minority achievement, and so on.

Summary

It is important, I believe, that educators become better informed and more critical of claims of educational effects—positive or negative. As a profession we need to become more skillful at reading the promotional claims and the research assertions for educational interventions. I think we need to become more informed consumers of methods, materials, and programs. Claims of effectiveness have increased geometrically now that "research-based" instruction sits in the spotlight. But every claim needs to be examined with a skeptic's eye while applying the general guidelines offered here.

Let me offer one example. Currently, many claims of effectiveness are being made for reading programs that include "decodable" texts (e.g., "Nan can fan the man"). The proponents suggest that it is a phonics emphasis with the accompanying use of "decodable" texts that make such programs effective. But, until recently, there has not been not a single study that systematically manipulated the use of decodable texts—texts where almost all the words are pronounceable given the letter–sound associations that have been taught—including studies examining the effectiveness of phonics programs (Allington & Woodside-Jiron, 1998). Claims about the utility of decodable texts are not supported by the research now available (Jenkins et al., 2004). But this lack of research has not inhibited proponents of a more code-emphasis—or phonics-emphasis—curriculum. Indeed, several states have now mandated the use of decodable texts and in each case assert, incorrectly, that their policies are "research-based."

Likewise, the widely distributed booklet *Put Reading First* (Armbruster et al., 2001), along with the "scientific" entrepreneurial guidelines widely used to select reading programs for use in Reading First schools (Simmons & Kame'enui, 2002), both include decodable texts as one of several non–research-based criteria for identifying "scientific" curriculum materials. The fact that your federal government has promoted both of these guides is a cause for concern. If the federal education agencies cannot reliably report what the research actually says, given enormous resources, how can teachers be expected to accomplish this feat?

All of this may lead you to think that educational research is not going to be very helpful in designing higher-quality reading instruction.

But you would be wrong. We have learned an enormous amount about the characteristics of more effective reading instruction (Allington, 2009b; Pressley, 2006; Taylor et al., 2003, 2005). To use these findings, however, you have to move beyond the current fixation on methods, materials, and programs. When we ask about which method, material, or program is most effective, we ask a question that, literally, cannot be answered by referring to the research. As noted throughout this chapter, virtually every method, material, and program has accumulated some evidence that "it works!" But the evidence is often contradicted by other evidence.

In designing more effective reading instruction, we will need to look to the research for larger issues than answers to questions about particular methods, materials, and programs. There seems a simple, but often overlooked reason for this. The search for any "one best way" to teach children is doomed to fail because it is a search for the impossible (Cunningham & Allington, 2011).

A simple principle—children differ—explains why there can be no one best method, material, or program. This simple principle has been reaffirmed so repeatedly in educational research that one would think most folks would have noticed it by now. In addition, anyone who grew up with siblings or who has more than one child of her or his own, knows from powerful experience that no two children are alike. Not even those from the same family gene pool. What, then, can you say about a classroom with 24 children from 48 sets of pooled genes?

A corollary principle—teachers differ—has been largely ignored as well, even though, again, we have lots of research evidence on the issue. In other words, no teachers are exactly the same. We've learned just how hard it is to get teachers to teach "against the grain"—to teach in ways that contradict their beliefs and understandings about teaching, learning, and reading and writing. If you want an intervention to fail, mandate its use with a school full of teachers who hate it, don't agree with it, and are not skilled (or planning to become skilled) in using it. This is what Linda Darling-Hammond (1990) has called "the power of the bottom over the top" in educational reform.

Additionally, if we are ever to create schools where all children are developing reading proficiency normally, we will need schools where every teacher believes that is possible and is committed to providing the types of individual instruction that some children need. I worry when I read a paper such as the one I recently read. That paper (Scharlach, 2008) reported that two-thirds of the teachers studied did not believe they could teach all children to read. These teachers also provided instruction that was different from the one-third of the teachers who reported they could teach everyone to read. Basically, the teachers who felt they could not teach everyone to read set lower expectations and provided less and lower-quality reading lessons when compared to the teachers who believed they could teach all kids. Interestingly, teachers who felt they couldn't teach everyone to read cited various factors to explain their response. Those factors included low motivation of some children for reading, poor parental involvement, and the presence of learning disabilities, among other factors, for why they were not successful. The teachers who felt they could

The 100/100 Goal

Imagine that we could design schools where 100 percent of the students were involved in instruction appropriate to their needs 100 percent of the day. Imagine how different the achievement patterns of struggling readers might be. I will suggest that the 100/100 goal is, perhaps, the real solution for developing schools that better serve struggling readers.

Source: National Center for Education Statistics. *National assessment of educational progress.* Retrieved from http://nces.ed.gov.

teach everyone to read offered none of these factors as excuses. So, school faculties differ not just on how many expert teachers of reading are available but also on how many teachers believe they can be successful with every child.

In any school, then, you have a horde of students who differ in innumerable ways and a cluster of teachers who also differ in a myriad of ways. Expecting any single method, material, or program to work equally well with every kid in every classroom is nonsensical.

In the remainder of this book, I will address some of the lunacy of the current reading reform movement, especially the push to standardize reading instruction. Because federal legislation has set such a visible standard for using research to re-design reading instruction, I have attempted to develop a research-based argument for how we might best use what we have learned (from research) in the redesign of reading instruction in U.S. schools.

This book focuses on the converging evidence that is available on the features of reading instruction that really matter. I leave to others to debate particular methods, materials, and programs. In this book I develop a research-based framework for rethinking reading instruction generally, and particularly the reading instruction that we offer kids who struggle while learning to read.

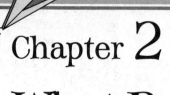

Chapter 2

What Really Matters: Kids Need to Read a Lot

Everyone has heard the proverb "Practice makes perfect." In learning to read it is true that reading practice—just reading—is a powerful contributor to the development of accurate, fluent, high-comprehension reading (Allington, 2009a).

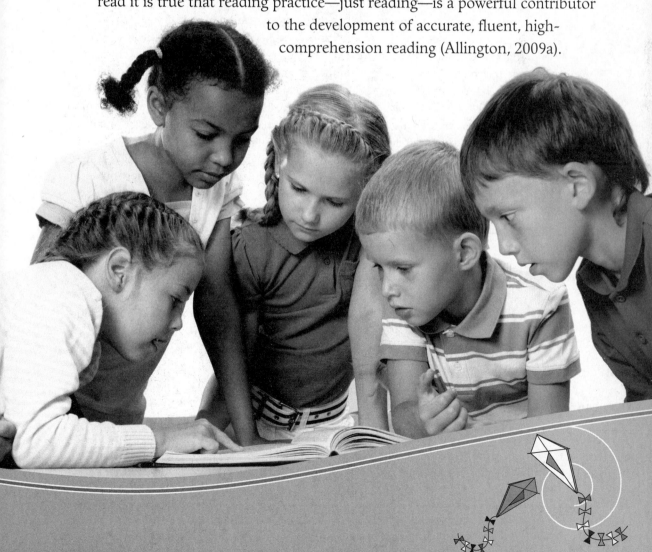

In fact, if I were required to select a single aspect of the instructional environment to change, my first choice would be creating a schedule that supported dramatically increased quantities of reading during the school day. What evidence has convinced me of the essential need for such change? Where would I start the change process? What would the school day look like if such a change were achieved?

Research on Volume of Reading

How Much Reading Is Enough Reading?

This is one of those unanswerable questions because children differ. It is also a difficult question because the answer would depend, at least in part, on what kind of readers you were satisfied with. Think of it this way: If you think most U.S. kids read well enough now, then perhaps not much more reading is needed (and given the world rankings perhaps your conclusion is right). But if you are disturbed by the fact that few U.S. students seem to read with a high level of higher-order understanding, then perhaps you would argue for more reading since the available evidence suggests that volume is linked to attaining the higher-order literacy proficiencies (Brozo et al., 2008; Cipielewski & Stanovich, 1992). Alternatively, you might argue for more reading just for the kids whose progress remains somewhat below a level you find satisfactory—those children identified as learning disabled, for instance—or maybe you are more upset by the fact that the amount of reading kids do declines as they go through school and you would redesign the middle and secondary school programs so that adolescents had the opportunity to read more in school. Finally, you might not even care so much about how students' reading stacks up on international or national assessments but be dismayed that rather few children, especially adolescents, engage in much free voluntary reading (Krashen, 2004a). In other words, you may be more concerned with reading habits than with reading achievement per se and hope that we might create instructional environments that resulted in more children, adolescents, and, ultimately, adults who were more inclined to read.

How you think about U.S. reading achievement and reading habits will influence what you perceive as an appropriate response to the question: How much reading is enough? (We will get to the question What kind of reading? a bit later in the book). There is no evidence that suggests *precisely* how much or how often children and adolescents need to read to develop high levels of reading proficiency. There are only a handful of experimental studies where increasing the quantity of reading was the primary intervention. Krashen (2004b) notes that in over 90 percent of the reading comprehension test comparisons, students who were assigned more reading or allocated more reading time in school performed as well or better than students who did not have the added reading assigned or the additional time allocated. In the nine studies that were of a year or more in duration, eight found positive achievement effects, one found no significant difference, and no studies found an achievement advantage for students in the control classes that offered less reading activity. In other words, replacing whatever went on in classrooms with added reading time was just as effective as, or more effective than, traditional instruction in enhancing reading comprehension performance.

Contrastive Studies   In contrastive studies, the volume of reading done by higher- and lower-achieving readers has been well documented. In a series of studies, I reported that differences in the volume of classroom reading were associated with elementary students' reading achievement (Allington, 1977, 1980a, 1983b, 1984a; Allington & McGill-Franzen, 1989). In these studies, the average higher-achieving students read approximately three times as much each week as their lower-achieving classmates, not including out-of-school reading. Likewise, Collins (1986) reported on first-grade instruction, noting that the higher-achieving students spent approximately 70 percent of their instructional time reading passages and discussing or responding to questions about the material they read. By way of contrast, the lower-achieving readers spent roughly half as much time on these activities (37 percent), with word identification drill, letter–sound activities, and spelling and penmanship activities occupying large blocks of lesson time. More recently, we found that the volume of reading done by students during school to be one of the important differences between children's experiences in more and less effective teachers' classrooms (Allington & Johnston, 2002; Pressley et al., 2001). Thus, contrastive studies of classroom experiences consistently indicate that lower-achieving readers simply read less during the school day than their higher-achieving peers, spending more instructional time on other activities.

There is, however, another reason for the discrepancy in the volume of reading. Lower-achieving students are more frequently reported to be reading aloud, usually to their teacher in a small group setting (Allington, 1983b; Allington & McGill-Franzen, 2010; Duke, 2000; Hiebert, 1983). Typically, when children read aloud, only one child is reading (although other children might be following the text or reading ahead). In contrast, during silent reading each reader reads. Thus, in a small group engaged in oral reading, each of the children might read only 100 words, whereas the same children in a group engaged in silent reading would each read 700 words. Since oral reading is slower and because various interruptions are more likely to occur, it may be the case that children would read more than 700 words silently given the same time period that it takes for four students to each read 100 words of text aloud in a traditional round-robin reading format.

Other contrastive studies have examined the volume of reading done by higher- and lower-achieving readers in and out of school. In a classic study conducted by Anderson and colleagues (1988), fifth-grade students kept reading logs documenting their out-of-school reading. Their findings illustrated the enormous differences in volume of reading between higher- and lower-achieving students. Table 2.1 illustrates just how large the differences in reading volume would be across a year's period of time.

Nagy and Anderson (1984) estimated that differences in the volume of in-school reading would also be substantial with some middle-grade children reading as few as 100,000 words a year, the average student reading about 1,000,000 per year, and the voracious middle-grade readers reading over 10,000,000 words per year. They argued that given the known power of wide reading in developing children's vocabulary knowledge, such differences provide powerful explanatory evidence for differences in student vocabulary growth and vocabulary size.

John Guthrie (2004) demonstrated that increasing practice is associated with increased expertise across a variety of human proficiencies. In other words, when researchers contrast the experiences of a professional basketball player and a youth basketball player, they find that the typical professional practices and plays basketball far more frequently than the typical 10-year-old playing on a youth team. World-class concert cellists, or chess players, or ballerinas practice far more than less skilled individuals. Guthrie notes that across these diverse areas, experts practiced 25 hours a week compared to the less skilled participants who practiced for only 5 hours a week—a 500 percent difference. Regarding reading, the research shows that the more proficient fourth-grade readers engage in reading at least 2½ hours a day, whereas the poorest readers read for about a half-hour a day, if that—a 500 percent difference.

Guthrie suggests that if we are attempting to accelerate struggling readers' development, a critical first step will be at least equalizing the volume of reading practice. In many cases, however, simply equaling the volume of reading done by better readers will not be sufficient; we will need to ensure that struggling readers read *more* than better readers do. Struggling fourth-graders may need as much as 3 to 5 hours a day of successful reading practice to ever hope to catch up with their more proficient peers.

TABLE 2.1 Reading Volume of Fifth-Grade Students of Different Levels of Achievement

Achievement Percentile	Minutes of Reading per Day	Words per Year
90th	40.4	2,357,000
50th	12.9	601,000
10th	1.6	51,000

Source: Adapted from Anderson, Wilson, & Fielding, 1988.

Correlational Studies   Large-scale correlational evidence for the positive effects of extensive reading on reading achievement can be found in the *1998 NAEP Reading Report Card for the Nation* (Donahue et al., 1999; also available at http://nces.ed.gov/naep). At every age level, reading more pages in school and at home each day was associated with higher reading scores. At each grade level, students who read more pages every day were more likely to achieve the proficient level of performance on the NAEP reading assessment. For instance, at twelfth grade, only 28 percent of students who reported reading five or fewer pages each day achieved the proficient level, compared to 51 percent of those students who read eleven or more pages. Although the number of pages that students reported reading each day was higher than the number reported by students on previous NAEP administrations, fewer than half of the eighth- and twelfth-graders reported reading eleven or more pages each day (though more than half of fourth-grade students read that many pages).

Foertsch (1992) examined the background factors that were most closely related to reading instruction and reading performance on the NAEP, including instructional approaches, reading experiences, home influences, and demographic characteristics. Data for these analyses were collected from a nationally representative sample of approximately 13,000 students in 1988 and 25,000 students in 1990 attending public and private schools at grades 4, 8, and 12. The major findings were (1) the amount of reading that students do in and out of school was positively related to their reading achievement; (2) despite extensive research suggesting that effective reading instruction includes moving from an emphasis on workbooks to lessons that offer more extensive reading and writing activities, many children still spent inordinate amounts of time on workbook activities (which had no positive relationship with reading achievement); and (3) students who reported home environments that fostered reading activity had higher reading achievement. The nature of these more effective reading environments seems consistent with other reports of highly effective reading instruction in its emphasis on engaging children and adolescents in a substantive volume of reading and writing on a daily basis.

Analyses of the international reading assessment outcomes also demonstrate this relationship between reading volume and reading proficiency (Brozo et al., 2008). Here, in fact, it is reported that children from low-income families who read a lot have higher reading scores than do more economically advantaged children who do less reading. In the final report, *Reading for Change*, the researchers conclude, "All the students who are highly engaged in reading achieve reading literacy scores that are significantly above the international mean, whatever their family background." In other words, reading volume is linked to reading proficiency internationally.

Correlational studies such as the national or international reports do not provide evidence of a causal link between greater quantities of reading and higher achievement. However, correlational evidence of this sort—a large-scale, nationally representative student sample, with a well-designed thoughtful literacy assessment—cannot be disregarded. These national and international reports are simply the largest and most comprehensive set of correlational data demonstrating the link between reading volume and reading achievement.

Other correlational studies have explored the relationship between extensive reading and reading proficiency in children and adults. McQuillan (1998) provides a summary of a number of such studies, including seven that examined this relationship in English-speaking children and adults. In each case they employed author and/or title recognition checklists to estimate how much reading experience varied from person to person. These studies have produced consistent findings showing positive correlations between the measures of reading activity and reading comprehension and vocabulary development.

For instance, Cipielewski and Stanovich (1992) found that individual differences in reading comprehension growth were reliably linked to differences in print exposure—volume of reading—even when decoding skills were accounted for in the analyses. McBride-Chang and colleagues (1993) also found that volume of reading was reliably correlated with reading comprehension performance in both disabled and normally achieving readers. In a study across an international sample of schools, Elley (1992) reported a strong positive relationship between teacher reports of time allocated to silent reading in their classrooms and reading comprehension proficiency of their students. The pattern of regression results in the series of studies conducted by Stanovich (2000) suggests that reading volume "does appear to be both a consequence of developed reading ability and a contributor to further growth in that ability and other verbal skills—thus they bolster the emphasis on reading experience that currently prevails in the reading education community" (p. 318).

Finally, Lewis and Samuels (2004) conducted a meta-analysis on 49 studies examining the effects of increasing reading volume of reading achievement. They report an effect size of .42, comparable to the effect size the National Reading Panel reported for phonics lessons in kindergarten and grade 1. Lewis and Samuels concluded, "No study reported significant negative results; in no instance did allowing students time for independent reading result in a decrease in reading achievement" (p. 13).

Correlational evidence is suggestive, and the available data suggest that, at the very least, more reading generally accompanies improved reading. Some would argue a stronger link: More reading produces better reading. But correlational data don't answer the "chicken and egg" problem (Does better reading lead to more reading? Or does more reading lead to better reading?). This issue is addressed by other sorts of study.

Explanatory Studies   There are several studies that illuminate the question of the link between volume and proficiency of reading. The well-proven impact of time-on-task (Fisher & Berliner, 1985) seems to account for much of the relationship between volume of reading and achievement. The research on academic learning time (ALT)—the time students spend actively engaged in academic learning tasks with high levels of success—yielded consistently positive relationships between ALT and achievement over a remarkably broad range of ages and subjects (Berliner, 1981). These research findings were found to be so commonsensical that many have trivialized this work and have seemingly ignored the potential implications for the design of reading instruction. In other words, most educators were not surprised to find that time spent in academic engagement in doable tasks was related to improved achievement; nor were many surprised that different types of tasks (e.g., worksheets, question answering, silent reading, flashcard drill, Go Fish phonics games) produced different sorts of achievement gains and had different effects on broad measures of reading proficiency (Stallings, 1980). Today, however, much of that early groundbreaking work on learning to read in classrooms seems to have been forgotten in the face of current educational reform initiatives.

For instance, with all the activity around developing educational standards, few states or school districts seem to have developed standards for volume of reading. One exception is New York state, where the English Language Arts standards require that 25 books be read every year. This extensive reading standard, as it is called, is an across-the-curriculum standard (as is the extensive writing standard of 1,000 words a month). In other words, meeting these standards is the responsibility of all curriculum areas, not just the English or Language Arts teachers.

I cannot say that I think that 25 books a year or 1,000 words of writing each month are good or bad standards in terms of adequate volume. Books vary on a number of dimensions that I think are important, and simply establishing a number of books to be read seems to have several serious limitations. Likewise, I usually prefer shorter, better-written papers to longer, badly crafted papers. Nonetheless, the New York standards have provided a clear basis for rethinking the curriculum plan in most schools, and it may be that these standards were developed because of the evidence that indicates that school and classroom contexts typically influence reading and writing volume. When a state plan calls for extensive reading and writing, such an outcome seems more likely than if no such standards are present in the state curriculum framework.

The evidence available indicates that planning for volume of reading and writing may be necessary. Keisling (1978), for instance, analyzed the uses of instructional time in four school districts and found that classrooms in some districts routinely provided more time for reading and reading instruction and that these allocations were related to reading achievement. More instructional time for reading most consistently produced greater achievement gains, especially in lower-achieving students. However, most districts were unaware that their allocations were different from those of other districts.

Allington and colleagues (1996) found substantial volume differences between classrooms in the same district and between the volume of reading children did in schools in different districts. In some schools, pupils read twice as much as pupils in other schools. These variations were linked to differences in beliefs about the importance of engaging children in actual reading.

> *We assumed that how teachers structured the learning environment would make a difference in how their students spent their time, and how students spent their time would influence the level of reading proficiency they attained at the end of the academic year. The data confirmed this expectation.*
>
> (Leinhardt, Zigmond, & Cooley, 1981, p. 357)

Other research demonstrates both the variability in reading volume from classroom to classroom and the effects that such variation has on students' reading growth. Leinhardt and colleagues (1981) studied the reading lessons offered to 105 primary-grade students identified as learning disabled. During the classroom observations, reading activity was broken into two broad categories: direct reading, in which the child was actually reading letters, words, sentences, and stories; and indirect reading in which the child was engaged in activity assumed to be related to reading that is not actually reading (e.g., copying, circling, phonics drill, questions, directions, etc.). They also coded other activities such as waiting, management, and being off-task. The observations documented that kids spent substantially more time in activities *called* reading than they did actually engaged in reading, even though 85 percent of the children were on-task and engaged in their lessons at any given point in time. The observations also indicated that there were large variations in the volume of reading between students and that these differences predicted large differences in reading development.

To better understand the relationship between direct reading and reading growth, the classroom data were analyzed using regression analysis and causal modeling. These analyses pointed to the explanatory power of direct silent reading time in predicting reading growth—neither oral reading volume nor workbook activity significantly influenced reading performance.

The observations also pointed to the importance of good teaching—modeling and demonstrating useful reading strategies. For instance, even very small increases in the amount of daily teacher demonstration produced improved reading achievement. However, their observational data indicated that most teachers offered little useful instruction. For only 1 minute a day, on average, was the teacher offering explanations or demonstrations of elements of reading, though about 14 minutes a day were spent in providing general directions about assignments. We will return to this issue in Chapter 5. Leinhardt and colleagues (1981) suggest that increasing the amount of silent reading is the most obvious strategy for improving reading achievement. They note that well over an hour each day was spent in waiting, transitions, management, and other activities that could easily be replaced by additional reading time.

Wilkinson and colleagues (1988) reanalyzed the data from the Leinhardt et al. (1981) study using a more rigorous technique for controlling the influence of initial student reading achievement. Their reanalysis substantially reduced the effect of silent reading time on achievement and suggested that oral reading time had a greater impact on achievement. They suggested that LD students in this study had comprehension difficulties that restricted the volume of silent reading for lowest achievers. Oral reading, they hypothesized, "by virtue of its requirement for an overt response, may have placed greater demands on students for participation" (p. 141). Wilkinson and his colleagues argued that the evidence of a superior effect for silent reading was not reliable, at least for the LD students in this study.

Taylor and colleagues (1990) studied the relationship between volume and reading achievement of 165 fifth- and sixth-grade general education students. The design of this study accounted for the concerns raised in the reanalysis by Wilkinson and his colleagues (1988). The students averaged 16 minutes per day of reading during their 50-minute reading period and 15 minutes of reading at home. In some classrooms, students read twice as much during the same 50-minute reading period as students in other classrooms (9.6 minutes versus 18.7 minutes). Taylor and colleagues demonstrated that the minutes of reading per day during reading period contributed significantly to individual reading achievement growth, whereas time spent on home reading did not. This relatively modest amount of reading activity during reading classes may have been the result of the reading curriculum used. Brenner and Hiebert (2010) report an analysis of the amount of reading available in different core reading programs. If the school district purchased every option, including leveled readers, decodable texts, and material available on CD-ROM format, students would be reading on average for 15 minutes daily. They note that this limited amount of reading activity is a historical fact and may be one reason that reading proficiency in the United States has not improved since 1990! Since children in American schools are now spending 90 to 120 minutes per day in instruction to foster reading achievement, the question one must ask is, What are they doing for the 75 to 105 minutes per instructional session when they are not reading? Whatever they are doing, however, for most of their reading period does not involve them actually reading.

Morrow (1992) confirmed the causal relationship between reading volume and reading achievement in her experimental study. Her intervention focused on the impact of developing classroom book centers in urban schools and restructuring the school day such that time was allocated for student use of these centers, including time to read. Guthrie and colleagues (1999) also found that reading volume predicted reading comprehension in third-, fifth-, eighth-, and tenth-grade students, even when pupil factors such as past reading achievement, prior knowledge, and motivation were controlled statistically.

A series of recent studies have also demonstrated that schools can foster reading growth during the summer months simply by providing children with books to read (Allington, McGill-Franzen et al., 2010; Kim, 2004; Kim & White, 2008; McGill-Franzen & Allington, 2008). In these studies, economically disadvantaged elementary school children were simply given books that they could read and books they wanted to read. The books were given to the children on the final day of school or mailed to them during the summer months. In each study reading gains were observed among the children who received the book—larger gains than were observed in other children who were not selected to receive books. In fact, the average effect size for providing these books for summer reading was equal to the effect size generated by attending summer school! Perhaps these studies are the best evidence we have available linking increased reading activity to improved reading achievement because the reading occurred during the summer months when the children were not participating in other school activities.

Finally, the research also provides evidence for what I consider one of the greatest failures of the federally funded Title I remedial reading and special education programs: Neither program reliably increased the volume of reading that children engaged in (Allington & McGill-Franzen, 1989; Haynes & Jenkins, 1986; O'Sullivan et al., 1990; Vaughn et al., 1998). This failure may explain the limited impact that both programs have had on accelerating the reading development of the children served (Puma et al., 1997). Simply put, children who received reading instructional support from either program often had the volume of reading reduced rather than expanded as remedial and resource room lessons focused on other activities.

At this point, then, these studies offer a number of useful guidelines while leaving some details yet to be verified. It would seem that the consistency of the evidence concerning the relationship of volume of reading and reading achievement is surely strong enough to support recommending attention to reading volume as a central feature of the design of any intervention focused on improving reading achievement.

There is substantive research evidence on the relationship between reading achievement and volume of reading. We have good evidence on the limited impact that special programs have had on the volume of reading of lower-achieving students. I will suggest that the design of any program targeting enhanced reading development in children and adolescents—or to accelerate the literacy development of lower-achieving children especially—must start by considering the issue of volume of reading.

Thinking about Volume of Reading

Where do you begin in planning an intervention designed to enhance reading development of all children, especially those children who now struggle with learning to read? Given the consistency of the evidence concerning reading volume and reading proficiency, the most useful initial discussions concern how much reading children should do during the school day.

How Much Reading Do Children Need?

The answer to this question is fluid because the necessary volume of reading seems to shift across developmental stages. In the initial stages, children cannot actually read very much—there is a limited supply of books they can manage successfully and young children read much more slowly than older, more experienced readers. There is no agreed on metric for answering this question. Studies have calculated time spent reading, words read, pages read, and books read.

All these studies have consistently shown, regardless of how volume of reading was measured, that there exists a potent relationship between volume of reading and reading achievement. Guthrie (2004) suggests that dramatic increases in reading

Andrey Armyagov/Shutterstock

volume are critically important in developing thoughtful literacy proficiencies. In addition, a variety of studies provide reliable, replicated evidence that children whose reading development lags behind their peers engage in far less reading than their higher-achieving peers. This has been found to be true even when these children participate in remedial reading or resource room programs.

It seems clear from these studies that the volume of daily in-school reading many struggling readers routinely experience is below an optimum level. So how much daily in-school reading might we plan for? I would suggest that 1½ hours of daily in-school reading would seem a minimum goal given the data provided in the various studies. This would also seem to represent a substantial increase for many kids in most schools. In addition, 90 minutes of actual reading would still leave from 4 to 5 hours each day to accomplish other instructional activities. In other

This Moncure Elementary School (VA) student checks out a book available in the school's "Books for a Buck" collection. With over 1,000 new books and another 1,000 used books, students have many choices. The books are purchased from traditional suppliers, are donated, or come from yard sales. They sell for 25 cents, 50 cents, or a dollar, depending on age and condition. The proceeds always go to purchase more books.

words, 90 minutes of daily in-school reading would leave three-quarters of the school day (in a 6-hour day) available for other instructional activities.

However, my 90-minute recommendation is for time spent *actually reading.* Many schools allocate 90 minutes to reading instruction through grade 6. But much of that allocated time is not available for actual reading as other activities typically occupy large chunks of the allocated lesson time. In observing more and less effective elementary teachers (Allington & Johnston, 2002; Pressley et al., 2000; Taylor et al., 2000b) sheer volume of reading was a distinguishing feature of the high-achievement classrooms.

Schools differ in how much time is allocated for reading and language arts instruction. Some set aside an hour and others set aside 3 hours each day. Even the various school reform models and instructional programs vary in the time recommended for reading and language arts instruction. One current high-visibility reading program suggests a 2½-hour daily reading instructional block. Another requires a daily minimum of 90 minutes of reading lessons with additional tutoring for children lagging behind. Both these programs are touted as successful "code-emphasis" programs, but many folks seem not to have noticed that substantial allocations of instructional time for reading are at the core of both programs. Both of these programs provide more opportunities for children to read than do other core reading programs (Brenner & Hiebert, 2010). These programs have been promoted as though there was some secret to success in the materials and methods they employ. However, virtually any reading intervention that reliably increases time engaged in reading should be expected to lead to achievement gains. In other words, what sometimes seems like evidence that a particular method or material produces higher achievement may actually be evidence that increasing reading volume positively affects reading achievement.

How More Effective Teachers Structure an Hour of Reading Lesson Time

The pattern of differences in reading (and writing) volume in more and less effective teachers' classrooms can be characterized by analyzing how one hour of time allocated to reading lessons might be used. In one of the schools where I observed, the more effective teacher routinely had children reading for 40 to 45 minutes of each hour allocated to reading instruction. She would spend 5 to 10 minutes preparing the children to read the material and 5 to 10 minutes engaging the children in activities following reading. While the children were reading, the teacher worked with children in small groups or individually at their seats.

In the less effective teachers' classrooms the time allocated was the same, but the time spent reading was typically quite different. These teachers often spent 15 to 20 minutes preparing children to read, and for 20 to 25 minutes after reading these teachers had the children engaged in a variety of follow-up activities, including responding to questions, completing workbook pages, reviewing the story, checking on vocabulary, and so on. Thus, in the less effective classrooms, children typically read for only 10 to 15 minutes of each hour of time allocated to reading lessons, and in some classrooms children read even less.

I observed similar disparities during social studies and science lessons, especially in the upper grades. More effective teachers simply had students reading two or three times as much material in these content areas than the less effective teachers (Allington, 2002d).

Although time spent reading (my preferred measure of volume) is important, the research does not provide clear evidence on whether one type of reading is better than another. In other words, increasing the volume of oral or silent or choral or paired reading, or almost any combination of these, has been shown to enhance achievement. It does seem reasonable that older and more experienced readers might more often read silently and beginning readers might more often read aloud, but as long as children and adolescents are reading, the type of reading seems less critical.

Restructuring School Days to Make Time for Reading

Roth and colleagues (2002) studied how time was spent in over 500 nationally representative elementary classrooms and found that one often overlooked factor was *length of the school day*. There were three clusters of elementary schools in this sample: the 6-, 6½-, and 7-hour school day. Students attending the 7-hours-a-day schools spent an average of 30 additional minutes each day on traditional academic subjects (they also had more recess, art, and music time). The students in the longer-day schools received roughly an additional *month* of instructional time each year. What was worrisome in this study was the finding that poor and minority students were those most likely to be attending schools with the shortest school day.

In our work in schools we are typically distressed by how time in many schools and many classrooms is so very inefficiently organized. For instance, the official school day—the instructional day—often begins at around 8:30 A.M. But at 8:30 A.M. in many schools, children are still on the playground or in the school cafeteria having just finished eating breakfast when the bell rings signaling the beginning of the instructional day. At the bell, students begin the process of moving to their classrooms. This often involves lining up and waiting to be released to travel down the hall to enter the classroom. In some cases, students also have to stop off at lockers or cubbies to take off boots, hang up outerwear, and drop a backpack. After they enter the classroom, their teacher takes attendance, collects lunch money, book money, excuses for absences, homework, and other such administrative details. This is followed by the Pledge of Allegiance and, normally, morning announcements on the public address system. Finally, at 8:50 A.M., the teacher cues the children to take out their books and the instructional work actually begins. In these schools, students have already sat for 20 minutes of noninstructional activity—often more time than they will spend actually reading during the remainder of the day.

In some schools this sort of organizational inefficiency occurs not only at the beginning of the day but again at lunch and at the end of the day. End-of-day routines often take another 15 to 20 minutes as yet more time is spent on lining up, packing up, and assorted other noninstructional activity than is spent on reading and writing combined. In other words, for efficient use of scheduled instructional time, teaching would continue until the very end of the official instructional day. If the instructional day ends at 3:30 P.M., then 3:30 is when kids should put down their books or journals and begin the management process of getting ready to go home. Likewise, any afternoon announcement would be made over the public address system after 3:30. But in too many schools where the instructional day ends at 3:30, the afternoon announcements and the getting-ready-to-go-home process begin at 3:15.

In many schools we can readily locate another 30 to 50 minutes every day for reading and writing activity. These are minutes that would be available if these schools were more efficiently organized. We must better organize schools to capture every minute of instructional time.

Capturing More Academic Time   A good first step in planning for improved reading achievement is reworking the organization of the school day so that teachers and children have *all* of the official instructional time for productive academic work. This may mean rethinking procedures for taking attendance and getting needed information out. Some schools take attendance at breakfast, some have bus drivers do attendance reports, and some have kids sign in when they arrive but before the school day begins. Book money, candy money, excuses for absence and all the other sorts of paperwork that waste instructional time can also be handled on a before-school basis by assigning paraprofessionals, clerks, or parent volunteers to stations where children bring the assorted paperwork. These stations can be in the breakfast area or entry area. Announcements can be posted on message boards to encourage children to apply their literacy skills.

The point here is that in most organizations it doesn't take 15 to 20 minutes to begin work, nor 10 to 15 minutes of the workday to get ready to go home. Imagine that you show up at a retail outlet that is scheduled to open at 8:30, but no one will open the doors until 8:50 because they are getting ready to work. Unfortunately, too many schools are organized this way. Even more unfortunate, in my experience, such organizational inefficiency is most common in lower-achieving schools.

To see just how instructionally efficient a school is, imagine walking the halls at the start of the school day and tallying how many children are reading or writing (or doing math or science activities) within one minute of the official start of the instructional day. If the school day begins at 8:30, the goal should be having 100 percent of the children engaged in useful academic work at 8:31. Now imagine walking the halls at the end of the official school day—how many classrooms have children working productively at 3:29 (assuming the day ends at 3:30)? If your school or classroom uses many minutes of official instructional time for noninstructional activities (listening to morning announcements over the public address system is not instruction, neither is lining up nor packing up), you have located one area to begin your efforts for expanding reading volume.

Reading Lessons with Too Little Reading   Sometimes we unintentionally create instructional plans that dramatically limit the volume of in-school reading. For instance, we routinely observe some teachers using whole-class sets of a single trade book within a three- to six-week (or more) unit. When we plan to spend six weeks on *Island of the Blue Dolphin,* we plan to limit children's reading and fill class time with other activities. Table 2.2 provides the approximate reading times for several trade books that seem popular choices for extended units. As a guide, 100 words per minute is an average silent reading rate for a second-grader and 200 words per minute is about average for a fifth-grader.

These numbers suggest that many of the teachers we have observed create plans that offer little reading volume, even in literature-based classrooms. And the situation is often exacerbated if the weekly lesson plan includes only a single literature excerpt from a core reading series. The excerpts in most reading series require no more than 10 to 15 minutes to read and if the excerpt is the primary reading material in a week-long instructional unit, students will, by design, have limited opportunities to actually read.

A key problem with commercial reading series is that they often fill up vast amounts of lesson time with activities other than actual reading. Just consider that if 90 minutes each day were allocated to reading lessons and the reading anthology excerpt takes only 15 minutes to read, then 375 minutes of lesson time each week must be filled with activities other than reading. Engagement in reading has been found to be the most powerful instructional activity for fostering reading growth. Why would publishers produce reading series with but a single excerpted feature to read during a week-long reading lesson? Perhaps it is because with longer reading selections the readers would be, literally, too heavy for children to carry; perhaps purchasing a greater volume of literature would make the readers prohibitively expensive; maybe the traditional basal reader is what most teachers want. Whatever

TABLE 2.2   Estimated Time Needed to Read the Books Listed at Different Reading Rates

Title	Approximate Total Words	200 Words per Minute	100 Words per Minute
Fox and His Friends (Marshall)	1,000	5 minutes	10 minutes
Stone Fox (Gardiner)	12,000	1 hour	2 hours
Missing May (Rylant)	24,500	2 hours	4 hours
Hatchet (Paulsen)	50,000	4 hours	8 hours

the reason, the situation today is that no core reading program contains enough reading material to develop high levels of reading proficiency in children.

In a number of the most effective classrooms I have observed, teachers used a commercial reading series only one or two days a week. For instance, in one room a superbly effective teacher quickly introduced the basal selection to the children, assigned the story to be read in pairs, called the group back together about 30 minutes later to discuss the story and return to the text for a mini-skill lesson. The students were then assigned a related page from the work text accompanying the series, which they completed, again, in pairs. This assignment was then discussed with the teacher the next morning before they began a new self-selected trade book that would be their reading for the remainder of the week.

At the end of the school day, I talked with the teacher about the pacing of the basal lesson. She said, "Dick, I just can't teach slow enough to make one of those stories last all week! I get bored and the kids get bored when we spend more than a day or so on one of the stories. If you have them in the right basal level, you don't need to teach and teach and teach all that stuff. I look through the teacher's manual and then just teach the few important things that my kids need."

It isn't just commercial reading series that offer too little reading volume. The same is true of science and social studies textbooks as well. But remember, the reading volume standards encompass all the reading children do during the school day so that enhancing the social studies curriculum with historical fiction—for example, the *Dear America* series—or the science curriculum with *Eyewitness* books adds more volume for reading and more content knowledge as well.

Interruptions during the Day   Another troublesome aspect of many school schedules is the number of interruptions that occur during the school day. There are three types of interruptions that are easily overlooked. The first has to do with interruptions of the classroom instructional day from special subject areas (e.g., music, art, physical education, computer lab, library, and so on). The second type relates to the interruptions that occur when a few children leave to attend instructional support programs (e.g., resource room, speech, physical therapy, ESL lessons, remedial reading, psychological services, etc.). A common complaint among classroom teachers is that children come and go all day long, making it difficult to plan and sustain comprehensive lessons. The third sort of interruption are those usually brief interruptions typified by public address announcements, brief queries at the classroom door from other teachers, counselors, specialists, paraprofessionals, parents, and other visitors. In some schools such interruptions commonly occur 10 or more times each day. But these brief interruptions each steal about 3 minutes of instructional time. That is the time that elapses from the point of interruption ("Jill, excuse me, but I'll need to see Jerome now") through its end and until most children in the classroom are once again engaged in academic work. Now consider that 10 such interruptions would eat up about 30 minutes of engaged instructional time—every day. This is the equivalent of 2½ hours every week, or two school days every month. Each year more than a month's worth of reading lessons is lost to these troublesome "minor" interruptions.

Creating Uninterrupted Blocks for Instruction   A good first principle in organizing a school more efficiently is to provide every classroom with at least 2½ hours of uninterrupted time—no pull-outs, no push-ins, no specials. Then ensure that other interruptions are minimized by eliminating use of the public address system during the instructional day except for true emergencies; limit who can knock on a classroom door during the instructional day; think about creating signs that say, *Teaching, Do Not Disturb,* and having them hang on classroom doorknobs. Some schools have limited student pick-up by parents to recess and lunch-hour time periods as one way to reduce interruptions. This uninterrupted block does not have to be assigned exclusively to reading and language arts instruction (but doing so has some substantial benefits, especially when a more fully integrated curriculum is in place).

Creating the 2½-hour uninterrupted blocks begins by setting that as a firm organizational guideline. In too many schools, all special teachers currently create a program that works best for them, allowing classroom teachers no control over this process. This sort of mindlessness has to end: Classroom teachers need time to teach—in fact, they need uninterrupted time to teach; kids need time to learn, read, and write—uninterrupted learning time.

There is another seldom considered aspect of reading performance that I call "reading stamina." This is the ability to maintain attention while reading longer texts or reading for longer periods of time, or both. It seems important to design instruction so that students have opportunities to read longer texts and to read for longer periods of time. As reading achievement tests have changed, the ability to sustain independent reading over longer texts and for periods of an hour or more has become an increasingly important proficiency.

Historically, reading achievement tests were constructed from a number of short passages, often only a paragraph in length, followed by several multiple-choice questions. But newer reading assessments of all types—state standards tests, commercially published tests, the NAEP reading tests—are typically constructed with fewer, but longer, passages. In some cases passages of several pages in length are used along with some shorter passages.

Analyses of student responses illustrate the reading stamina problem. Too many students seem to be able to read and respond to the shorter passages, but are less likely to demonstrate the same abilities when reading longer passages. That is, as the length of passages increases, the number of students who can demonstrate an understanding of the passage decreases. It seems that some students are unable to maintain their attention or their strategy use when confronted with longer passages. This may be a result of limited practice with extended passages, or the lack of instruction on strategy use across longer texts. As we design instruction for struggling readers, we need to make sure that we include longer texts and longer blocks of time to engage in reading on a regular basis.

If reading stamina is a problem in your school, you may want to consider implementing a progressive strategy for extended reading activity. To do this, set aside what seems to be the maximum amount of time that students can engage in independent reading, say 15 minutes each day. Then gradually increase that block of time in 5-minute increments until everyone has 30 minutes each day to read independently. Reading stamina is important, especially as reading tests include longer selections. But it isn't just on reading tests where stamina is important. All children need to acquire the ability to read for at least 30 minutes independently. However, if all we give them to read can be read in 10 minutes, they will likely never develop the stamina needed to be a proficient reader.

Rethinking the Design of Special Programs

It may be necessary to rethink special areas and support program designs. In some schools these programs now schedule fewer but longer periods of service to reduce the fragmentation of the instructional day. For instance, children receive special education services twice a week for 50 minutes rather than four times a week for 25 minutes; art and music is scheduled every other week but for a double period (80 minutes instead of 40, for instance). These longer periods for special area subjects and support services can dramatically reduce the fragmentation observed in many classrooms. This in turn makes it easier for classroom teachers to design blocks of reading and writing time and makes it more likely that instructional time lost to interruptions and transitions is minimized.

In other cases, some special area classes and support services have moved outside the official school day—instrumental music classes, remedial reading, speech, and resource services are offered before or after school for at least some kids. Reworking the work day for professional staff so that a flextime model is implemented allows schools to provide stronger and more comprehensive before- and after-school programs, while also reducing interruptions during the school day (Allington & Cunningham, 2006). In other words, classroom teachers might work with children on a traditional schedule of 8:30–3:30, whereas special area teachers and support teachers would work with children on a 10:30–5:30 schedule (or some variation of this).

One advantage of flextime is that schools can provide better services in after-school programs because, with regular school staff providing the services, there are greater opportunities

Supplemental Services

The No Child Left Behind Act includes a provision for supplemental services. The law requires that these services be provided outside the regular school day in before-school or after-school programs. Struggling readers are targeted for these programs in an effort to expand the amount of reading instructional time available.

for coordinating lessons with the classroom curriculum. In addition, core curriculum instructional time increases as some of the support instruction is moved outside the traditional day. This seems especially useful for lower-achieving children who will no longer miss some of the classroom instruction while participating in speech and language training, remedial reading, or physical therapy. Such use of flextime also allows schools to offer richer after-school programs without much added expense.

Although teachers often have little say in such matters, classroom and specialist teachers, even individually, need to begin to request the sorts of shifts discussed in this section. However, such requests seem more effective when they come from a team or a set of grade-level teachers. For instance, in one school, the fourth- and fifth-grade teachers requested a restructuring of the various special services their children received. The problem was that children seemed to be constantly coming and going and it was difficult to keep track of who had missed what. Ultimately, a new flextime schedule was created that had every fourth- and fifth-grade struggling reader participating in an after-school program four days each week. Half of the time in the after-school program was set aside for students to complete their homework or to read independently. The remaining half of the time was allocated for small group reading intervention. In this case, these fourth- and fifth-grade students had the additional instructional time needed to expand their reading activity. Perhaps not surprisingly, many of the weakest readers had their reading development accelerated and they were reading on grade level by the end of the year.

Creating Standards for Reading Volume in the Elementary Grades

Schools should develop an agreed-on standard for the expected volume of reading (and writing) that will be completed during the school day. When schools have no such standard, wide variation from classroom to classroom seems to be the norm. When creating reading volume standards, plan on including all sorts of reading. That is, reading in science, social studies, or other content areas should be counted in calculating the volume standards; guided reading, self-selected reading, partner reading, buddy reading, and every other sort of actual reading would be considered in establishing school-day reading volume. Once a professional staff agrees on such standards, it should not be surprising to find that the variation in how much students read during the school day is substantially reduced.

Along with my 90-minute volume standard for daily in-school reading, I would also set a 30- to 45-minute daily volume standard for writing. Thus, about two hours of the instructional day would be allocated to engaging students in actual reading or writing (including reading and writing in content subjects also). The reciprocal relationship between reading and writing opportunities and proficiencies has been well established (Tierney & Shanahan, 1991), particularly the links between comprehension and composing.

Volume standards could also be developed for a week rather than a day, the advantage of which is the greater flexibility available in creating lesson plans. For instance, using weekly volume standards (comparable to summing my daily standards) would allow for a full half-day allocation (150 minutes) for writing activity with time left over for shorter (10 to 15 minutes) daily writing opportunities. In some classrooms, especially at the upper grades, use of such longer blocks of time can be especially useful when students are working on thematic reports or projects, or simply taking a longer piece of writing to the publishing stage. The use of fewer, but longer, blocks of time for reading should also be considered. Imagine a fourth-grade student being able to read and entire book during a single day? This is the way an adult might read a book—in a single setting.

If one day was essentially set aside for reading opportunity and a half-day was set aside for writing activity, there would still be time for an hour of reading on three remaining days and an hour of writing on one other day and still have used only 40 percent of the instructional time for the week. If the reading and writing were sometimes related to science or social studies, we could probably expand the reading and writing blocks even more.

Longer blocks of time for reading and writing seem a more authentic instructional plan in the sense that to get truly involved in a book usually requires something more than a 10-minute block of time. Langer's work (1995) suggests that it takes a while to "get lost in a book," but getting lost in a book is the essence of skilled reading. I have helped schools organize whole-day reading and whole-day writing days—where everyone read or wrote all day long. Both students and teachers reported some amazing responses to these experiments—the most common

Whole-Day Plan

One "thinking outside the box" activity that schools might consider is Dr. Dick's Whole-Day Plan (WDP). The WDP involves scheduling just one subject a day. Thus, Monday is Social Studies Day, Tuesday is Reading Day, Wednesday is Math Day, Thursday is Writing Day, and Friday is Science Day. Kids do Science all day on Friday— that's right, *all day*—and they do the other subjects all day on the other days. This activity literally forces us to rethink the chopped-up school day, it forces us to rethink lesson planning, and creates wonderful opportunities for extended reading and writing and for research and project work and so on. It isn't the case that the WDP would necessarily continue all year—it could be run for as little as a week. But, in my experience, even a week teaching in the WDP creates an enthusiasm for the possibilities of fewer, longer curriculum blocks during the school week.

being along the lines of "It was so cool to be able to finish the whole book" or "I love being able to really work, like all day, on my report." Think of how you write when a report is due for a graduate class or how you read when you finally sit down with the latest novel from your favorite author.

I am not suggesting that every day be a "just reading" or a "writing only" day. My point is that far too much school reading and writing is marked by brief periods of reading or writing activity followed by an interruption and then a shift in activity. Our schools demand a lot of low-level, short-reading activities (e.g., a section of a social studies chapter, 10 minutes of DEAR, a few sentences on a science worksheet, and so on) and a lot of brief, shallow writing activities (e.g., 3 minutes to write in a daily journal, 5 minutes to write responses to end-of-chapter questions, 10 minutes to compose a short persuasive essay, and so on).

In the world outside of school, people read at least whole chapters and whole articles at one sitting. They write complete letters to the editor, persuasive essays, shopping lists, and reports as a single episode, not as a series of 5- to 10-minute activities; it takes time to read deeply and to write thoughtfully. But in school, "reading/writing interruptus" is too often the working model of lesson design. Such a design may be more effective in undermining real reading and writing activity than we could imagine, especially for children who don't read much outside of school.

Reading and Writing Volume in Grades 6 to 12

Given the reported decline in volume of reading and writing that begins at the middle school level (Ivey & Broaddus, 2001) and the slow growth of reading proficiency in grades 5 to 12, planning for reading and writing volume must be a K–12 concern. It seems odd that as students' reading and writing proficiency improves, schools expect less reading and less writing in and out of school.

After a period of experimentation in the 1970s and 1980s, with a larger role for trade books in content-area classes, especially in the social studies and the English language arts, most middle school and high school content classes have returned to using a single textbook as the primary curriculum source. Even literature courses often emphasize the use of an anthology of short stories and excerpts from novels and other longer works (Applebee, 1991).

The single-source—usually a textbook—curriculum plan has a number of limitations if student learning is the focus (Allington, 2002a, 2007). One primary difficulty is that the reliance on a single textbook dramatically limits the amount of reading students do in the course. The minimal reading and writing requirements of most high school courses was first driven home when I sat, as a parent, at a high school–sponsored "getting ready for college" session that featured commentary from several college students. What struck me was their assertion that one of the greatest differences between college and high school was the sheer volume of reading and writing that was expected in college compared to what had been required in high school.

As one of the college students noted, and the others vigorously agreed, "Almost any one of my professors requires more reading and writing for a single course than was required by all of my high school teachers together during my senior year." As these college students then went on to discuss courses with weekly writing assignments, with three textbooks or eight trade books as the curriculum sources, with research papers in abundance, I quickly thought back across the senior year one of our kids had just finished. Even with a couple of AP courses, there was little reading or writing expected.

Failure to keep up with college reading and writing demands seems to be a primary difficulty for even the best of our high school students, those admitted to four-year colleges. But with the very modest volume of reading and writing in high school, perhaps it is not surprising that only a little more than half of all entering college students complete a degree within six years (National Center for Higher Education Management Systems)..

But a lot more reading in grades 6 to 12 isn't just needed to better prepare students for college. When adolescents read more, they broaden and deepen their content knowledge as well. High school students who have only read their U.S. history textbooks are not likely to know much about U.S. history. In the same sense, students who have read beyond their biology textbooks know more about biology—and about thinking like a biologist—than purely textbook-bound students.

Textbooks used in grades K–12 have been described as offering a curriculum plan that is "a mile wide and an inch deep." In other words, most U.S. school textbooks are designed to foster a very limited understanding of a wide range of topics. Researchers have also demonstrated that most textbooks are "inconsiderate" texts because they are so rarely well written and are frequently written at difficulty levels two or more years above the reading level of the typical student (Allington, 2002a). Yet the use of a textbook as the sole curriculum resource now dominates middle and high school classrooms.

USA Today (September 29, 1999), in a front-page article titled *Failing Grades for Science Books,* noted that a study conducted by the Association for the Advancement of Science had concluded that "those thick, heavy science textbooks middle school students lug around are full of disconnected facts and irrelevant classroom activities." The study also reported that the texts (1) covered too many topics, (2) failed to develop any topic well, and (3) offered classroom activities that were nearly useless in fostering understanding of key concepts. The authors of the report concluded that the textbooks "neither educate nor motivate" students.

Now imagine the state of affairs for a student who enters grades 6 through 12, reading a year or two below grade level (not to mention the student who is even further behind). Although we can create a curriculum that offers students a wider range of higher-quality texts by selecting multiple texts that vary in difficulty, accomplishing this is no small feat. However, if improved student achievement—reading achievement as well as content subject achievement—is the goal, then such curriculum must be developed.

If we offer older struggling readers supplemental reading classes, we must ensure that they spend the majority of time in those classes actually reading. It is simply too common to observe high school–level remediation or special education classes where students do virtually no reading but instead fill their class period working on worksheets or test preparation activities. Given that no research supports either workbook nor test preparation activity as a way to improve reading proficiency, it troubles me enormously that so many adolescents are wasting their time. Additionally, few middle or high schools provide sufficient reading that might lead to accelerated reading development. In other words, that ninth-grade struggling reader, the one reading at the fourth-grade level, will need reading lessons two hours daily for all four years of high school in order to have a chance at catching up with his grade-level peers.

Summary

Kids need to read a lot if they are to become good readers. The evidence on this point is overwhelming. To ensure that all students read a lot, schools need to develop standards for the expected volume of reading (and writing). The cornerstone of an effective school organizational plan is allocating sufficient time for lots of reading and writing. Some of the time needed can be reclaimed from noninstructional activities. But it is important that such a plan has the support of teachers. All teachers must understand the enormous benefits that enhancing the volume of reading will provide. In such a plan there would be long blocks of uninterrupted time for reading and writing. Teachers would have access to a large collection of appropriate reading material written at differing levels of complexity such that they would be able to match texts to student reading levels. Reading and writing would be integrated across all subject areas and a curriculum that featured wide reading and writing of informational texts as well as narratives would frame the lessons and activities. The plan would encompass grades K–12, not just the elementary grades. This wouldn't necessarily cost any more than we are currently spending but we would have to spend the money we have differently.

Reading is like other human proficiencies—practice matters (Allington, 2009a). Voluntary, engaged reading, in school and out, seems most powerfully linked to high levels of proficiency. Internally motivated reading activity, then, seems to have a stronger relationship to reading growth than volume of mandated, unengaged reading (Wang & Guthrie, 2004). This reading is a form of "deliberate practice" that scholars in various fields have linked to improved proficiencies. This research finding is important in considering how we might design reading lessons that enhance students' motivation in reading as we work to expand reading volume and improve reading proficiency.

Chapter 3

Kids Need Books They Can Read

Before they leave on vacation, few adults wander down to their nearest university library looking for thick, hard books on topics they don't care about. In fact, adults, including college-educated adults, generally avoid hard reading whenever possible.

This accounts for the popularity of magazines that offer writing that is rated as high school–level difficulty. If folks liked hard reading, then magazines such as *Scientific American* or *The Economist* would outsell *Newsweek* and *People,* but they don't.

All readers generally prefer reading that is less demanding—it is only when their interest in a topic is incredibly high that most readers will tolerate hard reading. I don't think kids are very much different from adults in this regard, but adults always seem to prefer that children read difficult books rather than easy books. The evidence available has convinced me that a lot of high-success reading is absolutely critical to reading development and to the development of positive stances toward reading. So why is assigning such reading so often ignored in schools? In this chapter we will explore that question and examine the research on high-success reading and matching kids with "just right" books.

Task Difficulty, Choice, and Achievement

The issue of the difficulty of schoolwork was widely studied in the 1970s and 1980s. Researchers investigated the relationship between task difficulty and achievement gains in elementary school classrooms in an attempt to better understand effective teaching. One of the largest such studies was the Beginning Teacher Evaluation Study (BTES; Denham & Lieberman, 1980) in which three student success rates were defined: *high,* meaning students worked at tasks that were very easy; *moderate,* when students exhibited partial mastery but the tasks were somewhat easy; and *low,* for tasks that the students found hard and in which they made many errors. The researchers (Berliner, 1981) found that success rates had a substantial impact on student learning. They produced strong, consistent evidence that tasks completed with high rates of success were linked to greater learning and improved student attitudes toward the subject matter being learned, whereas tasks where students were moderately successful were less consistently related to learning, and hard tasks produced a negative impact on learning. Hard tasks also produced off-task behaviors and negative attitudes. That is, students given tasks where success was low were far more likely to cease work on the task and engage in nonacademic behavior than were students working at high success rates.

Thus, many classroom management difficulties were linked to the relative difficulty of schoolwork the students were given. The fact that success rate could be manipulated was also seen as important because it suggested that student behavior and achievement could be enhanced by redesigning lessons. When lessons were redesigned so that success was more widespread, student engagement rates improved, as did their learning.

Gambrell and colleagues (1981) found that oral reading error rates of 5 percent or greater were linked to significant increases in off-task behavior, largely replicating the findings of the BTES researchers. But Betts (1946) deserves the credit for drawing attention to the issue of success rate while reading. He studied fourth-grade students and reported that relatively low error rates seemed to produce improved learning. He established criteria for three levels of difficulty. His *independent*-level reading was marked by high word-recognition accuracy (98 percent or better), fluent reading (phrases with intonation), and strong comprehension of the material read (90 percent comprehension accuracy). Texts at this level of difficulty were viewed as appropriate for the reading children did with no assistance and little, if any, instruction from adults. His *instructional*-level criteria—for material used in guided reading lessons where the teacher provided instruction on the material and reading support—also required relatively high accuracy (95 to 97 percent), phrase reading, and good comprehension (75 percent). Betts argued that *frustration*-level reading—accuracy below 95 percent, word-by-word reading, and comprehension below 75 percent—was to be avoided because of the negative impact such experiences had on both learning and attitude.

The importance of accuracy in reading texts has been demonstrated in several other studies. Juel's (1994) longitudinal study indicated that "quality of word recognition in first grade (i.e., being able to recognize words) is more important than quantity of exposure to words . . . but once there is high quality word recognition . . . quantity of reading becomes critical" (p. 124). Ehri and colleagues (2007) studied differing intervention programs and concluded that "the reading achievement of students . . . appeared to be explained primarily by one aspect of their tutoring experience—reading texts at a high level of accuracy, between 98% and 100%" (p. 441). In this study researchers had tracked daily oral reading accuracy of struggling English language learners, something few other researchers have done. What they found largely surprised them because none of the other factors they studied explained reading growth once accuracy of text reading was taken into consideration. And it was the amount of high-success reading activity that delivered the gains. O'Connor and colleagues (2002) found that providing sixth-grade struggling readers with texts they could read accurately proved far more valuable than providing tutoring in the texts used in their classrooms. In this case the struggling readers were several years below grade level and local practice typically had reading specialists and special education teachers trying to provide tutoring such that these children could use their grade-level texts. When comparing the growth in reading proficiency, once again using texts that students could actually read with high levels of accuracy, substantially greater achievement growth was seen. Finally, Swanson and Hoskyn's (1998) meta-analysis of 180 intervention studies with students with learning disabilities identified only three factors that contributed unique variance to achievement. Control of task difficulty was one of those three factors: When students were given tasks that were difficult, achievement gains were hard to come by.

But in some schools students seem to be routinely placed in texts that are too difficult if optimum achievement is the goal. Consider that Chall and Conard (1991) found that only 1 of the 18 elementary science and social studies books they examined had readability levels at the grade level of intended use. Most of these books were one or two grade levels above the designated grade level for use, but the difficulty of four of the textbooks were three to four grade levels above the grade in which they were commonly used. As for the reading anthologies, Chall and Conard found that between 40 and 60 percent of the elementary students of average-achievement levels were working with reading texts considered appropriate, given their reading achievement on standardized tests. The rest—almost half of the average students—were using materials considered too difficult. The case was substantially worse for lower-achieving students.

A Quick Check for Appropriateness of Reading Materials

Struggling readers need appropriate, research-based reading instruction all day long. What follows is a simple scheme for quickly evaluating the intervention design's responsiveness to the needs of struggling readers. I have attempted to develop an evaluation scheme that is time efficient and yet provides important information on whether the needs of struggling readers are being met throughout the day.

To begin to evaluate how well your school's instructional plan meets one of the research-based criteria set out in this book, select 10 struggling readers from different grade levels and different classrooms. Plan to spend about 10 minutes with each student, or about a half-day of your time. You will need a stenographer's spiral-bound notepad or a pad of paper on a clipboard along with a pen or pencil for recording data.

Meet each student in his or her classroom (or if the child's instructional texts are kept in lockers, meet at his or her classroom and travel to the locker). The evaluation process consists of estimating the appropriateness of the texts each student is expected to use across the school day.

Ask each student to select one of the books in his or her desk (or locker) to read aloud to you. Have the student read quietly for just one minute while you track the reading to document reading accuracy using the procedure described on pages 80–81. Do not try to calculate accuracy percentage until later—it is important that you gather

When Chall and Conard (1991) directly assessed elementary students' comprehension of their textbooks, somewhere between one-quarter and one-half of the average-achievement elementary students achieved a satisfactory comprehension performance of their science and social studies books, whereas none of the lower-achieving students met the comprehension criteria after reading those books. All this suggests that many, many students are confronted daily by texts that are too complex for optimum learning (Allington, 2002a).

In a more recent analysis, McGill-Franzen (2009) found that the core reading programs used in many schools typically provided few if any texts that were below the targeted grade level. Even the supplementary texts, marketed as "easier" texts for struggling readers, were most often grade-level texts. She notes that struggling readers will be provided little of the sort of instruction they need if the core reading programs dominate the classroom instruction.

data on as many texts as possible in the 10-minute period. At the end of each read-aloud, you should also rate the student's reading fluency using this scale:

Good—Reads in phrases with intonation
Fair—Reads in phrases mostly; often lacks appropriate intonation
Poor—Reads mostly word-by-word

Use a separate page for each text the student reads from and try to gather accuracy data for at least six texts, especially those that are core curriculum materials. After you have gathered the accuracy and fluency rating data on multiple texts, you can use the form in Appendix A to begin to organize each student's data.

After you have completed collecting these data from each of the 10 students, you can organize those data by tallying the percentage of texts each student has that were read accurately and fluently on the form found in Appendix B. Most of the books each student has in his or her desk (or locker) should be texts that were read accurately and fluently.

If there are many texts that the students could not read accurately and fluently, then you have evidence on one factor that must be addressed if the goal is to accelerate reading development. If only the texts used in reading/language-arts classes were read accurately and fluently, you will need to consider alternative texts for other subjects. If almost none of the texts were read accurately and fluently, you have evidence on why struggling readers in your school are struggling. Such evidence represents a complete breakdown in the design of instruction for struggling readers. All students need appropriate texts all day long.

In too many schools it has become common practice to conduct whole-group lessons using a single text. This is true for reading instruction as well as science and social studies and seems to be the case in both primary and high school classrooms. The result is reduced learning for the students who have books they cannot read accurately and with comprehension.

There is another troubling trend—the use of a whole-class text even in support programs (remedial and special education classrooms). One rationale for this practice seems to be that these students need instruction on grade-level skills and content using classroom materials to build the background knowledge needed for understanding the content targeted for that grade.

I see this as a troubling practice because it flies in the face of half a century of research on supplying appropriate texts. Recent research suggests that providing struggling readers one-to-one tutoring with classroom grade-level texts produces few positive learning results. O'Connor and colleagues (2002) randomly assigned intermediate-grade struggling readers (about half were identified as learning disabled) to two types of expert tutorial support. One group was tutored using texts from the regular education classroom the students attended; the other group used texts matched to the students' reading levels. A third group of struggling students served as the control group and received no tutorial support. On average, the struggling readers were reading two or more years below grade level.

Both tutoring groups demonstrated gains compared to the control group on a variety of word reading, fluency, and comprehension measures. But the lowest-achieving readers in the tutoring group using the reading-level–matched texts performed better than the poorest readers using the classroom texts on those same measures. The struggling readers with the best reading skills made roughly comparable gains in both tutoring groups. The authors concluded that the text/reading-level match is a critical design factor if the goal is to accelerate reading development.

Thus, for 65 years the use of Betts's criteria has been recommended in an attempt to match students with texts that would optimize learning. But too often, over this same period, teachers have been mandated to place all children in the same texts, regardless of the match between the child's level of reading development and the

Historically, public schools in the United States have been built on the assumption that not every student can learn well and, hence, many students must make learning errors. . . . Accordingly, schools were designed to allow these many error-full learners to distinguish themselves from their few error-free peers. Most students rather than being given chance after chance in our public schools to demonstrate learning success, were given chance after chance to demonstrate learning mediocrity or failure. . . . If we want to produce a generation of truly learned students, then the learning student cannot experience success at only a few milestones in his/her career. Each must experience a constant stream of success [emphasis added].

(Block, 1980, pp. 98–99)

complexity of the texts in the curriculum. And when not mandated to do so, teachers often had few options, as schools supplied multiple copies of, for instance, only a single social studies text intended for use by all students. But since Betts's (1946) original study, the evidence has accumulated supporting his position (Allington, 1984a, 2002a). Having said that, let me note that I think any set of specific criteria need to be used somewhat flexibly. But flexibility is not a characteristic of the "one-size-fits-all" reforms that are appearing in school after school.

The key point here is that the research has clearly demonstrated the need for students to have instructional texts that they can read accurately, fluently, and with good comprehension if we hope to foster academic achievement. The evidence also suggests that for large numbers of students this recommendation has been routinely ignored.

Choice Is Also Important

There is accumulating research demonstrating that student choice is an important factor when it comes to reading development. Guthrie and Humenick (2004) report a meta-analysis of 22 experimental or quasi-experimental studies of reading motivation and achievement and found four classroom factors were strongly related to student reading growth. Ensuring students had easy access to interesting texts was the most influential factor; providing choices for students over what to read, who to read with, and where to read produced an effect size nearly as large as access to interesting texts; and allowing pupil collaboration during reading and writing and focusing more on student effort than outcomes both produced moderate effect sizes on achievement.

Another set of research-based characteristics of high-motivation and high-performing classrooms was developed by Pressley and colleagues (2003). Note the similarity to the findings from the meta-analysis:

- Classroom is filled with books at different levels.
- Teacher introduces new books and displays them in the classroom.
- Teacher emphasizes effort in doing work.
- Students are given choices in completion of their work.
- Teachers engage students in authentic reading and writing tasks.
- Lessons promote higher-order thinking.
- Teacher uses small groups for instruction.
- Teacher does expressive read-alouds.

Pressley and colleagues (2003) also provide a list of research-based classroom practices that undermine motivation and achievement:

- Students do not have choices; everyone does the same work.
- Teacher rarely has students working together on assignments.
- Teacher is more a lecturer than a discussion leader.
- Teacher does not model thinking process for students.
- Teacher provides extrinsic rewards (e.g., stickers, points, treats).
- Activities assigned are routine, boring, and low level.
- Teacher calls out grades; posts grades or papers with grades.

If we did a quick review of practices in your school, which list would describe the majority of classrooms? If we did the same review of the instruction offered in special programs, which list would provide the best description?

Choice is important because it seems largely related to interest and to control. In planning a unit focused on the genre of biography, it seems that more students will actually become engaged in the topic if we provide a variety of biographies for them to choose from. Similarly, in planning a unit on colonial America, providing students with a variety of texts to choose from produces higher levels of engagement with the topic and greater learning. As Hidi and Harackiewicz (2000) noted, "Investigations focusing on individual interest have shown that children as well as adults who are interested in particular activities or topics pay closer attention, persist for longer periods of time, learn more, and enjoy their involvement to a greater degree than individuals without such interest" (p. 153). They also found that giving students choices, "even when seemingly trivial and instructionally irrelevant, seems to enhance interest" (p. 154).

The research provides clear evidence of a powerful role for providing students with choices in their reading materials, choices about the assignments to be completed, and choices about who they will work with. I emphasize this research because much of what is being promoted as "scientific" reading instruction almost completely ignores most of what researchers have demonstrated are the most effective designs for promoting reading development.

One-size-fits-all reading instruction is anti-scientific. The International Reading Association's position paper "Making a Difference Means Making It Different" provides a plain-language summary of the research on effective reading instruction—instruction that meets individual needs. (You can download this statement from www.reading.org.)

Having established the research base for choice, let me now note that nothing in the research suggests that there should be no common texts or assignments. But the evidence is clear that a steady diet of one size-fits-all makes teaching harder as well as less effective (Ivey, 2010; Schraw et al., 1998). On the other hand, the evidence clearly demonstrates the powerful impact of providing students with choices much of the time. But in the end, as with all educational questions, there is likely to be no single answer to the question "How much choice?" because learners differ, as do learning situations and goals. Nonetheless, the evidence is clear that more choice enhances academic engagement and reading achievement.

Methods for Estimating Text Complexity

The most common approach for estimating the difficulty of texts has been the use of structural readability formulas. There are a variety of such formulas available, but each relies primarily on two structural measures of text difficulty: word difficulty (estimated frequency of use or word length) and sentence complexity (most often measured by sentence length). But the estimates of text difficulty from any of these procedures is just that—an estimate. All formulas have some error in measurement and all suffer from the problem. That problem is that each of the following extracts would be rated at the same level of difficulty.

John went to the store. He bought some candy.

Candy some bought he. Store the to went John.

Structural readability formulas cannot tell whether text is well written or even whether it makes sense. Similarly, these formulas cannot examine picture support, level of interest, or a student's prior knowledge about the topic being presented, and yet each of these factors has been shown to influence the difficulty of texts for students (Klare, 1984). Thus, use of any of the readability formulas provides, at best, a very crude estimate of the difficulty students might have with a text.

Some would argue that such weaknesses are good reason to avoid calculating readability estimates from the structural formulas. My view, however, is that the use of such formulas can be useful if only for providing a ballpark estimate of text difficulty, since even a ballpark estimate is better than none at all.

Several of the structural readability procedures are currently in fairly widespread use and are discussed in the following paragraphs.

The *Dale-Chall Readability Formula* (Chall & Dale, 1995) has been around for over 50 years and was updated in the 1990s. It works best on upper-elementary materials and above and provides a two-year difficulty band estimate (grades 5–6 difficulty), which nicely emphasizes the notion of an "estimated" level of difficulty. The procedure is available online (www.readabilityformulas.com) and when this process is used, one only has to type or scan samples of text and the calculations are completed automatically.

The *Flesch-Kincaid Formula* has also been available for more than 50 years and was revised in the 1970s. It is used in Microsoft Word to estimate the difficulty of documents. Again, by typing in text samples (or scanning them in) we can get an estimate, in grade level terms, of the difficulty.

The *Degrees of Reading Power* (*DRP*) procedure (Koslin et al., 1987) provides estimates of text difficulty on a unique scale that is linked directly to achievement levels on the DRP standardized reading achievement test. The developers suggest that using the scores on the DRP test and the DRP estimates of text difficulty provides a more reliable match between texts and students compared to the traditional procedure of using a standard readability formula estimate and a standardized test score to attempt to match kids and books. The support for this argument centers on the integration of the DRP measurement technique into both the formula and the test item development. The publisher, Touchstone Applied Science (www.tasaliteracy.com), also offers computer software with over 12,500 textbooks and trade books rated by difficulty, which allows the user to search for texts on particular topics within a specified difficulty range. They also provide a conversion table for converting DRP difficulty levels into grade-level equivalents (although they prefer that schools use the DRP assessment and difficulty ratings in tandem).

The *Lexile Framework* (Stenner, 1996) shares many features with the DRP in that it provides difficulty estimates on a unique scale (although, again, conversion to grade-level equivalents is possible, but not recommended). However, the procedure for estimating text difficulty is different and more similar to the procedure used in the Dale-Chall formula. The developers of the Lexile Framework provide a free tool for estimating text difficulty using the Lexile method (available at www.lexile.com) and have also negotiated agreements with some publishers of texts, trade books, and achievement tests so that they can offer services for matching kids and books in a similar fashion to the DRP developers. Currently, the Scholastic *Reading Counts* (www.readingcounts.com) system offers access to 25,000 titles rated for difficulty on several formulas (e.g., Lexile, DRP) and includes a Book Expert search option that allows you to locate books on topics within a specified difficulty range.

The *Accelerated Reader* is another widely used commercial system for matching students with books. It offers *STAR Reading,* a computer-adaptive reading test that estimates a student's reading achievement and provides lists of book titles that would be good fits with the student's level of reading development. They also publish tables that allow teachers to correlate any standardized achievement test score to book difficulty levels. Finally, the *Accelerated Reader Book Guide* (www.arbookfind .com) is designed to provide an easy search of 22,000 trade book titles.

So which method is preferred? My response is, it depends. I prefer the methods that allow teachers to estimate text difficulty in grade levels, since that metric is commonly understood (although hardly precise). But this method is time consuming if there are large numbers of books to be rated using the DRP or Lexile materials, each of which has the difficulty of thousands of books already estimated, might be a more sensible option.

The *Accelerated Reader* and the *Reading Counts!* programs provide computerized testing, a large supply of books rated for difficulty, and even a reading monitoring system (e.g., quizzes). But these can be expensive options and there is little instructional support, per se. The monitoring systems, unfortunately, seem dated and offer primarily low-level recall questions for students to answer after completing each chapter. Much of what we know about the power of high-quality comprehension strategy instruction and the potential of group discussion in fostering students' understanding is omitted from the design of these programs. But these packages might be useful in schools where teachers are largely unfamiliar with children's books, and where paraprofessionals are available to manage the program while teachers offer the expert reading instruction as well as opportunities for student discussion in lieu of responding to low-level chapter questions.

These options for estimating text difficulty, in the hope of better matching children with appropriate reading materials, all have a potential role in making it more likely that children will have access to books they can actually read and learn to read with. But, as noted earlier, all such procedures have inherent problems and the results are better considered as ballpark estimates than an estimate with any sort of scientific specificity. When teachers know their students well and are more expert about estimating the complexity of texts, they typically do not need readability estimates to find appropriate books for the children in their classrooms.

Leveling Books

The late Marie Clay, the developer of the *Reading Recovery* intervention that has demonstrated such high levels of success in accelerating the reading development of first graders in trouble (D'Agostino & Murphy, 2004; What Works Clearinghouse, 2007), deserves much credit for refocusing our attention on the importance of matching children with books at an appropriate level of complexity. In the *Reading Recovery* program a central tenet involves moving the child successfully through a sequence of increasingly difficult short books. Gradually increasing the complexity of the difficulty of school texts is not a new idea by any means. But, historically, such gradations were rather crude. There were, for instance, five levels of complexity in the traditional core reading series across first- and second-grade (preprimer, primer, first-reader, first-second-reader, and second-second-reader). *Reading Recovery* sliced this into 24 levels of complexity.

The development of these levels followed a different sort of procedure than that traditionally followed by publishers. Instead of calculating difficulty levels from structural readability formulas, Clay and her colleagues in New Zealand and the United States actually tried the books out with children. They recorded the difficulty children had and used that information to locate each book within a level of difficulty. In addition, they examined a variety of text features ignored in structural readability formulas: illustrations and their supportiveness; layout of the book; and text structures such as repetition of language, predictability of the story line, and the familiarity of the context and content.

Fountas and Pinnell (2005) have extended this line of work, with some modifications, including extending the leveling process through eighth-grade material and reducing the number of levels by about half. Their text, *Leveled Book K–8: Matching Texts to Readers for Effective Teaching* (Heinemann, www.fountasandpinnellleveled books.com) provides the difficulty levels of about 10,000 titles that have been widely used with children across grades K–8.

In addition, although many publishers now provide book levels for their titles, there is no agreed-on framework for the levels reported. Some publishers use a numbering system (e.g., levels 1, 2, 3, . . .) that looks similar to the *Reading Recovery* levels, but the similarity is typically misleading in that the two sets of numbers have no real demonstrated relationship to one another. Other publishers use an alphabetic system (e.g., levels A, B, C, . . .) that appears to be similar to the Fountas and Pinnell levels but, again, they are not equivalent.

Thus, teachers are left with a not insignificant problem: lots of texts leveled through lots of different processes. What is a teacher to do?

Leveling Your Books   In my work with teachers and their school districts, I have found that the problem of leveling books is less a problem than it seems. I have used a variation of the procedure recommended by Chall and colleagues (1996). Their book offers a "qualitative assessment" of book difficulty in which the leveling process involves the use of "benchmark texts"—texts that represent different grade levels or segments of a grade level (beginning-second-, middle-second-, and late-second-grade texts). This "how-to" work-text provides such benchmark texts, but drawing on a handful of books at any level from the Fountas and Pinnell (2005) listing seems to work just as well. Once you have the benchmark books at hand, the procedure is as follows:

1. Take the book to be leveled and skim through it, looking at the page format, type size, sentence length, topic familiarity, vocabulary familiarity, and story predictability.

2. Now look at the benchmark books and find the one that most closely approximates the difficulty of the book to be leveled. Once located, label the new book at the same level as the benchmark book. As the year progresses, ask yourself, Do kids who can read the benchmark book successfully also seem successful in the newly labeled book? If so, then let the level stand; if not, re-level the book appropriately.

When teachers work together in the book-leveling process—primary teachers in one group, intermediate-grade teachers in another—two positive benefits result. First, the levels are more reliable when several sets of eyes make the leveling judgment and there are more kids reading the books to provide more teachers with more feedback on the reliability of the leveling. Second, as teachers go through the leveling process they develop greater expertise in estimating book difficulty. As they monitor book difficulty across the year, they develop an enhanced sensitivity to the book-child matching problem.

Teach Students the Three-Finger Rule   An astonishingly simple strategy that needs to be added to every classroom is the three-finger rule. Just tell kids to read the first page or two of the book (depending on the number of words on a page; you want approximately a 100-word sample) and to hold up a finger for every word they cannot read. If they reach the point that they are holding three fingers up, the book is probably too hard and they should look for another one (unless the topic is near and dear to them). Although this is hardly scientific, it is a tried and tested classroom method. I think the key understanding being developed here is one that is important for kids to develop—some books are just too hard. I would point out that there are books adults find too hard—tax manuals, for instance, which they pay someone else to read and figure things out for them. But learning that selecting appropriate books is important is a necessary understanding in itself.

Observe Students Reading to Better Match Them with Books   In the end, no matter what procedure is used to attempt to put more appropriate books into the hands of students, it comes down to each kid and each book. Every procedure discussed thus far provides an *estimate* of the fit between a kid and a book, and estimates are always just estimates. They help us find books that seem good choices given a child's level of development, but estimates are not always good enough.

Once a child has a book in his or her hands, we can observe whether the book seems to "fit" the child. There are both far observations and near observations that can help us determine the fit of the book.

Far Observations   Look around the classroom during a silent reading period. Are there children whose bodies, faces, or even fingers provide signs of frustration? Are there kids who seem to be "wandering"—mentally or physically—when they should be reading? Do some kids have the book close to their face, brow furrowed, and finger-stabbing at the words? Do some kids turn the page much less frequently than others—or at all? If this is a grade 3–6 classroom, can you hear subvocalizing? Do you observe much lip movement and finger following of the text?

All of this could be considered possible indicators that children are reading only with difficulty. But be cautious because almost any of these indicators can also represent something else going badly that day. Frustration-level reading activity is, well, frustrating, and you can often observe that frustration from afar and well before it breaks through the surface and produces a discipline event.

Near Observations   Now move next to those children who seem to be experiencing difficulty. They will frequently be subvocalizing and you need only to sit there to hear the difficulty they are having. At other times you might want to have them read quietly to you; ask them to read aloud a passage they just completed as you arrived (especially if they seem to be struggling—if they still struggle after having already read it, they are in a text that is truly too hard). As they read to you, you need to be taking notes.

Record the accuracy of the word recognition. The simplest procedure for this is simply a modification of the "running records" strategy developed by Clay (1993) and verified as a reliable indicator of reading growth by Fawson and colleagues (2006). In a spiral notebook, write the page number of the book at the top of the page (and maybe the book title). As the child reads, simply jot a check mark for every word correctly pronounced and an *X* for each word mispronounced. Put checks and *X*'s in rows that match the text being read. That is, every time the child reads a new line, drop down and begin a new row of checks and *X*'s. Also note the fluency level: *Good, Fair, Poor.* After a few pages, thank the child and move away and calculate the overall accuracy (number of words read correctly divided by total

A Completed Accuracy Record

Ideally, children would be reading with a high level of accuracy (97+ percent correct words) and at least a *fair* level of fluency. Such are the typical characteristics of readers reading appropriate level books that allow children and adolescents to develop and polish useful reading strategies.

Text Child Read Aloud	Teacher's Record
tried Minny was ~~tired~~ of walking.	✓ ✓ ✗ ✓ ✓
She just wanted to sit down and rest.	✓ ✓ ✓ ✓ ✓ ✓ ✓ ✓
But, there were so many people at the fair	✓ ✓ ✓ ✓ ✓ ✓ ✓ ✓ ✓
that there seemed to be no place to sit.	✓ ✓ ✓ ✓ ✓ ✓ ✓ ✓ ✓

30/31 words are read accurately = 98-plus accuracy.

words in the passage) and fluency levels (see p. 71) and write them at the bottom of the page and circle them. Note also whether this was a first reading or a repeated reading of the text.

These procedures are not meant to be a formal diagnosis; their purpose is primarily to assess the appropriateness of the text the student is reading in an up-close manner. The process should be completed quickly because the goal is to produce a better estimate of the text's appropriateness than is provided by the readability estimates or the book's estimated level. Remember, we want children to have consistently successful experiences with the texts they read. Regular monitoring of the difficulty, or lack thereof, that students experience when reading is a necessary component of effective instruction.

When you are new to this procedure for monitoring students' oral reading accuracy, using a tape recorder will allow you to check on your record for each student's reading. Once you become more skilled, the tape recorder will no longer be needed.

If doing this sort of instructionally useful assessment is wholly new to you, you may want to consider obtaining Peter Johnston's book, *Running Records* (2000, www.stenhouse.com). The book is accompanied by audiotaped recordings of children reading for use as practice before attempting to assess children in your classroom and takes you beyond the initial recording of student performance to a deeper examination of just what the patterns of errors might mean for instruction.

Recall Summary

Finding out how well the text is understood is also important. The most direct method for such an assessment is to ask the child to retell what has been read. Just listen at first and perhaps prompt with, "Can you tell me more?" Teachers can make quite good judgments about a child's understanding of a text using this simple, time-honored method of evaluating understanding. Because continuing to read makes little sense if there is no understanding, every near observation should entail some assessment of how well the material is being understood. After the retelling, complete a recall summary similar to the sample provided here by placing a check next to each text element included in the summary.

For Narratives:

Key characters? _____

Setting? _____

Story line? _____

Story ending? _____

For Informational Texts:

Key topic? _____

Major facts? _____

Link to prior knowledge? _____

Enhancing Access to Appropriate Books

Certain kinds of classroom environments make teaching not only easier but more productive. One key feature is a large supply of books across a range of difficulty levels—a range at least as wide as the range of reading achievement levels of the students who come to that room every day. The classrooms of our exemplary teachers (Allington & Johnston, 2002; Pressley et al., 2000) invariably had a much larger supply of books than were found in the typical classrooms of the school they worked in. In our earlier work (Allington et al., 1996; Guice et al., 1996; Johnston et al., 1998) we had noted the following:

- Higher-achieving schools had more books in classroom library collections than were found in lower-achieving schools.
- Schools in wealthier neighborhoods had classrooms with larger book collections than were found in schools in poorer neighborhoods.
- Classrooms with a larger supply of books had kids who read more frequently.
- Classrooms with a larger supply of books usually had more kids reading books they could read successfully.

These findings replicated those from other studies (e.g., Dickinson & Smith, 1994; Knapp, 1995; Morrow, 1992; Robinson et al., 1996; Smith et al., 1997),

In this school the custodian installed plastic rain gutters below the chalk trays so that many books could be displayed with the covers showing.

demonstrating the potential of easy access to a wide range of books of appropriate complexity on children's reading opportunities and, ultimately, on achievement.

The classrooms that were best able to put appropriate books into kids' hands (and into their desks) had hundreds of titles available in the classroom collection. These titles represented a substantial range of difficulty as well as a range of genres. In other words, these hundreds of books were not, typically, class sets of a few titles (25 copies of 10 children's books). Although there were, in some rooms, class sets of particular titles, we more often found smaller sets, say 5 copies, of some titles with the quantity of books accounted for primarily by single copies of many, many books. If I were required to establish guidelines for quantity, I would recommend at least 500 different books in every classroom, with those split about evenly between narratives and informational books and about equally between books that are on or near grade-level difficulty and books that are below grade level.

As with all criteria, no specific quantity can serve all classrooms equally well. For instance, beginning readers can, and should, read multiple books every day. In the exemplary first-grade classrooms we studied, it was common for children to read 10 or more titles every day (counting rereading of books). Thus, 500 titles do not go as far in first grade as they do in a fifth-grade classroom where children might be expected to read a title a week. But by fifth grade, there is often both a wider range of achievement and a wider array of books than might be included in a first grade collection. (I should also note that many of the exemplary teachers we studied had classroom collections in the 1,500 book titles range.)

Two other factors influence the numbers of books needed in a classroom collection: Ease of access to books in the school library and the availability of supplies of books for use in the classroom.

Ease of Access to Books in the School Library

School libraries vary enormously in the size and adequacy of their collections; the availability, supportiveness, and expertise of the library staff; and the actual access children have to the library and its books (Krashen, 2004; McQuillan, 1998). But adequately stocked and staffed school libraries are essential, even when classroom collections number into the hundreds of books. School libraries will always have resources that are unavailable in the classroom (or at least well-stocked school libraries will) and will have a deeper and broader collection of texts (and other information resources) than can be supplied to any given classroom. Unfortunately, school library resources are directly linked to community wealth. That is, a consistent finding in study after study is that schools that enroll many children from low-income families have half as many books available as do schools in wealthier communities (Guice et al., 1996; Krashen, 2004a; McQuillan, 1998; Neuman & Celano, 2001).

Some of this discrepancy is related to inequities in education funding patterns (Kozol, 1991), but some is also the result of local decisions on how funds will be spent. For instance, schools in lower-income communities have smaller school and

School Libraries Stacked with Outdated Volumes

"Man has not landed on the moon. The Soviet Union still exists. African Americans are negroes. Proper ladies wear hats and never compete with men. Penicillin is a new discovery. Welcome to the world of the public school library and The Book Shelves Time Forgot." Thus read the headline and introduction in an article that appeared in the *Boston Globe* (January 18, 2000). The article noted that the typical Boston public school elementary library contained 1,000 to 2,000 volumes, but with half or more of those books woefully outdated. The article didn't note that such a collection is 10,000 or more books short of the American Library Association's standard for a small elementary school. Unfortunately, the Boston school libraries reflect what seems to be a common deficiency in urban schools—far too few books, many of which are racist, sexist, and outdated. The most outrageously inappropriate book mentioned in the *Globe* article was one titled "A Young Woman's Guide to Business" that contained a cartoon illustration of a young woman being chased around a desk by an older male.

classroom libraries but employ far more paraprofessionals than schools in wealthier communities. Personally, if I were working in a high-poverty school and had to choose between spending $15,000 each year on more books for classrooms and libraries or on one more paraprofessional for the building, I would opt for the books—especially given the research on the positive impact of book access and the negative or, at best, neutral, evidence on the effects of paraprofessionals on children's reading achievement (Gerber et al., 2001). Children from lower-income homes especially need rich and extensive collections of books in the school library and in their classrooms, if only because these are the children least likely to have a supply of books at home (Neuman & Celano, 2001).

But for libraries to be truly useful, their books and staff must be available on an "as-needed" basis as recommended by the American Library Association (1998) in its publication, *Information Power: Building Partnerships for Learning*. This publication also recommends before- and after-school access to the library, especially in schools where many children have few books or other information resources at home. Two primary roles of the library media specialist are (1) linking library resources to the core curriculum for teachers and students and (2) helping students find just the right book to satisfy their current curiosity or literacy needs. Paraprofessionals or student volunteers can check out books for children, they can re-shelve books that have been returned, they can stamp new books and enter them into the cataloging database. Librarians should be free to act on their expertise, not saddled with clerking duties.

Too many school libraries have been underfunded so that collections are undersized and the facility is understaffed. In these schools, children typically have very restricted access to library collections, perhaps visiting only once a week, and are restricted to a single book exchange (Guice et al., 1996). As McQuillan (1998) so powerfully demonstrates, library adequacy is among the better predictors of reading achievement, with a correlation of .85 between library adequacy and NAEP reading achievement scores. In other words, you could quite accurately rank each state's NAEP scores just by knowing their ranking on school library quality. States where schools have larger school library collections (Connecticut, New York, Delaware) have reading scores superior to states where school library collections are smaller (California, Louisiana, Mississippi).

School Book Rooms   A more recent development for enhancing children's access to appropriate books is the "school book room" (Fountas & Pinnell, 2005). Such rooms house supplies of books that teachers may check out for use in their

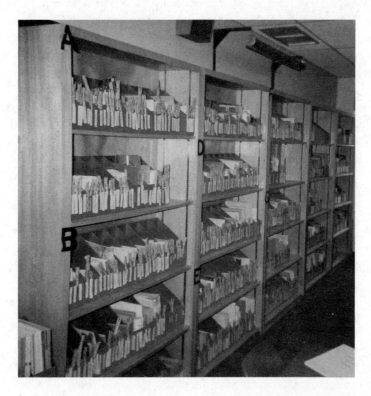

This is one of the six aisles of copies of circulating instructional texts in a Texas school's book room.

classroom. I have encountered several schemes for school book rooms but the basic idea is always the same—providing a larger library-like supply of books for classroom use. This design provides a wider access at lower expense than traditional plans that purchase multiple copies of identical books for each classroom.

In the basic school book room, you would likely find multiple copies of leveled books (Fountas & Pinnell, 2005; Mace, 1997), which are stored in magazine sleeves or specially designed little book boxes or bins and arranged on shelves by difficulty level. Typically, 10 to 15 copies of a single title are stored in each box or bin and teachers check out sets of books, often limited to no more than 5 copies of any given book at a time, meaning that several teachers can have access to copies of the same titles simultaneously. Of course, when starting a school book room, you need to decide whether to begin by ordering 5 copies of three different books or 15 copies of a single book. I always vote for the former and then add more copies of high-demand titles over time.

A fully stocked school book room would have a collection of books that spanned the grades in the school. In addition, in some school book rooms there are also available bins of books organized by genre, author, or topic. These bins are typically multilevel (except perhaps in the case of single author bins) and linked to science, social studies, and language arts curriculum goals. For instance, a school book room in Texas contained bins of books on the Alamo, biographies of famous Texans, Native American histories in the Southwest, the Rio Grande, and so on. Teachers could check out any of these bins to support social studies lessons and to provide additional social studies reading materials at various levels of difficulty.

In a California school book room there were bins of books organized by genre—following the district English Language Arts curriculum plan. Thus, fifth-grade teachers who were working to develop an understanding of the genre of biography could check out the biography bins and have available another 30 to 40 biographies for students to select from as they read the required 3 or 4 biographies for the unit.

In Wisconsin a school book room had bins of books for author studies, again so that students would have opportunities to read multiple books by the selected authors. Thus, there were bins filled with books by Donald Crews, Cynthia Rylant, Mildred Taylor, Russell Freedman, and many other authors. When teachers decided to focus on the work, the style, or the themes of a single author, they could draw from over 30 bins of books. Each author bin typically contained one or two copies of multiple titles by that author.

The school book room is a wonderful innovation, but it does take collaborative planning and a sense of sharing. In planning purchases, schools need to take the long view and not attempt to stock the book room all at once. A five-year plan seems appropriate for bringing the book room up to speed, but every subsequent annual budget should have some money allocated to book room purchasing (there is always wear and tear and always good new texts available).

Books at Home and School

One study (Smith et al., 1997) recorded the number of children's books available in homes and classrooms located in schools in three different communities. Their findings point to the enormous inequity in access to books that exists in the United States.

	Books at Home	In Classroom Library
Middle income	199.0	392
Lower income	2.6	54
Lowest income	0.4	47

Once the school book room has been stocked, especially initially, there have to be guidelines for how much material any one teacher can have checked out at any given time and guidelines on how long materials are to be kept before they are returned to the book room shelves (or how long another teacher must wait for them to be returned). One system that works is for teachers to put a snap clothespin (with their name on it) on the book sleeve they have selected books from, or on the shelf where the book bin they are using was stored. This alerts other teachers about who has what and allows for informal negotiations about usage.

Remember that everyone cannot have the biography bin out at the same time (nor the Iroquois bin or the Arnold Lobel bin). Thus, some collaborative planning is needed ahead of time. Everyone can still teach the biography unit, but everyone cannot teach it the same month and use a single biography bin.

The cost savings can be substantial if teachers can agree to work within a school book room plan. For instance, if biography is a fourth-grade curriculum goal and a school has five fourth-grade teachers, then developing a single bin of 40 biographies costs the same as giving each teacher 8 copies of the same biography or 1 copy of 8 biographies. In neither case will any teacher have anything but a very minimal collection of biographies. On the other hand, to provide each teacher with 40 biographies of their own would cost five times as much. If each biography, in paperback, could be purchased for an average cost of $5, then the single bin costs about $200, whereas it would cost $1,000 to put the same 40 titles in every classroom. Although 40 biographies may not be a sufficient number to actually satisfy the reading needs of a diverse class of fourth-graders, such a collection has a chance of putting at least some appropriate biographies in every child's hands (and desk), and there are still other biographies available from the school library collection.

A New Zealand Perspective

The author of the following extract is a program coordinator with *The Learning Network,* a national school reform and teacher development effort sponsored by Richard C. Owen publishers. In this short piece she describes some of the surprises she encountered after she arrived from New Zealand and first began working in U.S. elementary schools.

> *Teachers who had a set of books referred to them as "my books" because they had been allocated the money to purchase them [or had purchased the books themselves]. One New York teacher who had changed to a lower grade level had no books in her room when she arrived. She was expected to buy them herself or scrounge from other teachers who were reluctant to part with any of theirs. . . . In New Zealand the school takes full responsibility for the purchase of instructional texts.*
>
> (Mace, 1997, p. 276)

Some school book rooms also have bins containing 20 to 30-plus copies, or class sets, of selected titles—a few titles that all children will be expected to read. Because the research on the importance of both matching kids with appropriate books and on the power of providing students with choices in selecting books, I am not a big fan of class sets—or of curriculum plans that insist on all children reading the same book. Nonetheless, the school book room is useful when such plans are in use. As in the biography unit example, schools can purchase a single class set that rotates among teachers. This system works as long as everyone does not plan to teach with the same class set during the same one- or two-week period. Such a scheme means buying fewer class sets, which should make additional funds available for better stocking of classroom collections and school book rooms with multiple titles.

If creating a school book room is not likely to occur in your school, there is another option to consider that will expand student access to books. I suggest a strategy that Pat Cunningham and I proposed in our book *Classrooms That Work* (Cunningham & Allington, 2011), which involves getting together with other teachers at your grade level and sorting all the books each of you has into a number of book bins. (We usually recommend the use of the plastic milk crate–type file containers that are readily available at office supply and general merchandise stores.) You might want to organize the books into bins that relate to curriculum units or to specific series or to broad themes. These bins then rotate every two weeks. If you and your colleagues manage to create several bins for each classroom, not all of the bins will have to be moved at every rotation—perhaps only one or two bins are rotated each cycle. But this system of rotating bins produces, typically, at least twice as many choices for students over the year and often allows even greater opportunities for students to locate the book that is just right for them.

Teachers should expect to have a sufficient supply of books available in their classrooms to teach the children they are assigned. In other words, if a fifth-grade class has some lower-achieving students, perhaps reading at a beginning-third-grade level, then it would seem the basic responsibility of the school to ensure that the classroom book and curriculum materials collections were stocked with an ample array of third-grade-level, or below, texts linked to core curriculum standards for fifth-grade students.

It has long puzzled me why the adequacy of school libraries and classroom book collections are not a key topic in teacher labor agreement negotiations. Similarly, I have frequently wondered why the appropriateness of the curriculum materials isn't more often a negotiable item. I assert that research points to the importance of easy access to appropriate texts as being at least as important as the number of minutes of planning time allocated, class size, and length of the school day—all issues regularly negotiated in teacher contracts.

Magazines?

Adults spend substantially more time reading magazines and newspapers than books. But magazines are not often found in classrooms even though there are, perhaps, a hundred or so magazines published for children and adolescents. Stoll (1997) provides a comprehensive listing (and ordering information) of magazine titles. In an ideal world, schools might supply every child with one or more magazine subscriptions of their choice in order to level the playing field.

Currently, children from wealthier homes are far more likely to have one or more magazines delivered to their homes each month. And the NAEP survey indicated that the only group of fourth-graders who achieved reading performances above the national average were those who indicated that they regularly read story books, informational books, *and magazines* (Foertsch, 1992). Many schools have library subscriptions to a variety of magazines (although, again, schools in low-income neighborhoods have far fewer subscriptions than do wealthier schools) but often these magazines are not allowed to leave the library.

A rich classroom magazine supply should become a staple in elementary school classrooms. *Ranger Rick, National Geographic Kids, Cobblestone,* and *Sports Illustrated for Kids* are but a few of the popular children's magazines that I would recommend for every intermediate-grade classroom. These magazines should become part and parcel of the reading material that children have access to during self-selected reading periods and to take home for weekend reading activity.

Magazines for Children and Adolescents (That You May Never Have Heard Of)

Ages 6–11	Ages 8–14	Ages 14 and up
American Girl	Calliope	Blue Jean
Barbie	Cracked	Cicada
Black Belt for Kids	Earthsavers	Dramatics
Chickadee	Hip	ESPN Magazine
Click	Koala Club	GamePro
Dolphin Log	Metrokids	J-14
Kid City	Muse	Karate/Kung Fu
Nickelodeon	Otterwise	Science World
Owl	Racing for Kids	Slap
Skipping Stones	Soccer Jr.	Teen
Spider	Sports Illustrated for Kids	Teen Newsweek
Stone Soup	Teen Beat	Teen People
Zoobooks		YM

Information on each of the magazines can be found in Stoll's (1997) compilation *Magazines for Kids and Teens.*

One school I visited recently placed magazine racks in every toilet stall. Talk about authentic reading! The goal was simply to entice kids to pick up reading materials and take a look. If students seemed to take a while in the restroom, it was usually because they had found a magazine story of interest.

I believe schools should work toward the goal of making one or two magazine subscriptions available to every student. In other words, each student would be offered a choice of several magazines they could regularly receive, free of charge. The magazines might even be delivered to the students' homes. This seems especially important for students in grades 6 through 12. Yes, such an initiative would cost between $25 and $35 per student—but that is a miniscule portion of the $9,000 average per-pupil expenditure in the United States.

We are currently studying whether giving middle school students from low-income rural families two free magazine subscriptions during their middle school years improves their reading proficiency (Allington & Gabriel, 2009). The preliminary results look positive but the full results won't be known for another year. What we have learned, however, is that *GamePro* and *J-14* were the most commonly selected magazines by boys and girls, respectively. Neither of these magazines is available in any of the libraries in the schools these kids attend. In fact, almost none of the top 10 magazines are available in their school libraries. We also learned that at least some of the students with reading problems had little difficulty reading and understanding articles that had readability levels two and three grade levels above their current reading levels. It seems that if you are a "gamer" and a struggling reader, you don't struggle nearly as much, if at all, when reading *GamePro* when compared to reading your school supplied social studies text. This even though these two texts are comparable readability levels. Whether the key issue here is prior knowledge, interest, choice, or even format is less interesting than that these boys can read grade level texts of one sort but not the other.

Series Books, Junk Reading

There is another often under-appreciated genre of reading material that we need to consider when rethinking children's access to books they can read accurately, fluently, and with understanding. These are the often maligned series books. Without getting too technical, I have defined *series books* as those books that either (1) have continuing characters (e.g., *Arthur, Junie B. Jones, Diary of a Wimpy Kid, Harry Potter*) or (2) are predictable in plot and story line even though the characters change (*Goosebumps, Animorphs, Choose Your Own Adventure*). Some series books are viewed as having more literary merit and some sell by the millions regardless of their literary merit. But as a group, series books have been largely shunned by the commercial anthologies, the literary awards committees, and local curriculum developers. This seems a shame since so many adult avid readers recall those first series books that hooked them into reading.

Egoff (1972) captured what seems to me to be a prevailing sentiment among many educators: "Perhaps mediocre books do no harm in the sense of actual damage. But they do harm in the sense of deprivation—the subtraction of opportunity to know and experience the best" (p. 10). Her argument is that since time is a finite variable, time spent reading "mediocre" books, and she does not limit mediocrity to series books (in her view only 2½ percent of all published children's books are of excellent literary quality), limits the time available to read quality literature. Although I believe I understand her concern, I simply do not agree with the argument.

In fact, I would argue that it may be the time spent reading series books, and even other mediocre books, that creates the skill and interest necessary to read the better-quality books. I do think that adults, including teachers, have an obligation to help children find quality books to read but we must also, and perhaps first, help children find out why to read and how to read.

Here is my hypothesis about series books and their potential role in reading development, especially in the transitional years (grades 2 through 6). I think series books are enjoyable because the characters are a bit flat, the plots a bit too predictable, and the settings too familiar. These, of course, are the sorts of criticisms leveled at series books by those promoting the reading of quality books. But imagine how difficult it must be for some children, maybe many children, to understand the larger skills of plot development, character development, perspective taking, and so on, when we feed them a steady diet of (1) excerpted materials in basal reader series or (2) high-quality children's books, representing a variety of genres, authors, literary styles, plot structures, and characters.

I will suggest that reading a half-dozen *Boxcar Children* books, *Encyclopedia Brown* books, *Polk Street School* books, or even *The Baby-Sitters Club* books may actually make acquiring these higher-order literacy skills easier. After a couple of books, the central characters become familiar, even predictable. It is easier to predict how D.W., Arthur's little sister, will respond after having read three *Arthur* books, which means that you have read a lot about D.W. and her relationship with her brother. Likewise, after a couple of *Polk Street School* books, Richard Best, the "beast" in Mrs. Rooney's room, becomes a familiar presence. Suddenly it is easier to think about who in your classroom reminds you of D.W. or Richard and to tell (or write) why. After a half-dozen *Arthur* books it becomes even easier to answer the question: What would D.W. do?

Of course, series books also simplify the reading act by reducing the word recognition load, particularly proper nouns (e.g., characters, locations). Unlike the traditional reading anthology that primarily provides excerpts from books, thus offering a plethora of new names and places, series books offer a comfortably familiar

Popular Series Books for the Transition Years

Greg Brooks and I have surveyed approximately 1,000 teachers in 10 states. Below are the series that these teachers most frequently report their students love.

Primary Grades	Intermediate Grades
Arthur	*Goosebumps*
Frog and Toad	*The Baby-Sitters Club*
Clifford	*Boxcar Children*
Cam Jansen	*Animorphs*
Henry and Mudge	*American Girl*
Junie B. Jones	*Harry Potter*
Captain Underpants	*Lemony Snicket*

vocabulary. But series books also offer a commonality in text structure—or author's style. All of this seems to work to make the books more readable as each one is completed (McGill-Franzen, 1993; McGill-Franzen & Botzakis, 2009).

So let's add series books to our classrooms; let's promote series books by reading them aloud once in a while; let's have kids share their favorite series. We can even help organize student "clubs" promoting particular series across classrooms and even across grade levels. Some series books seem to have a substantial reach—*The Baby-Sitters Club, Star Wars, Dear America, Harry Potter,* and *Goosebumps* books, for instance, are popular from around the end of third grade well into middle school. Teachers should celebrate series books even if they don't include them in the official curriculum.

There is a concern that we must attend to, however. As in so many other aspects of schools, children who come from wealthier families are those most likely to have read series books. This is because paperback book sales are largely a middle-class phenomenon and according to a study conducted by the American Booksellers Association, 70 percent of juvenile books are purchased by families with incomes above $50,000.

It is the grocery stores in middle-class neighborhoods that allocate shelf space to books, and for kids' books that shelf space is almost always for series books (Neuman & Celano, 2001). It is the mall bookstores that offer series books galore—the middle-class mall. It is in middle-class schools that the mail-order book clubs thrive (Strickland & Walmsley, 1993). As teachers in lower-income schools find few orders coming in, they often stop distributing the order flyers, for it becomes too emotionally draining to hear children continuing to imagine which books they *would* order if they had any money to order a book.

Putting Books in Their Bedrooms   Although I think we must first be concerned with children's access to books at school, I also think we must become more concerned about ensuring children's access to appropriate books outside of school. There are several possibilities to consider. First, schools might participate in an inexpensive book distribution program, which focuses on providing all children with books, typically at no charge to the child or family.

The Reading Is Fundamental (RIF) program was designed to put no-cost books into the hands of children from low-income families. In many respects, RIF has been incredibly successful, but RIF reaches so few poor children and provides those it reaches with so few books that it seems, at best, a drop in the ocean of needs. The RIF program currently funds few new projects because much of the available funding is already allocated to existing initiatives. But there is a stupendous need for a broader, wider RIF-like program. Another option for inexpensive books is the Reading Recycling Project (www.colorcodedbooks.org/lef/ReadingRecycling.htm). This nonprofit organization distributes new and used books free of charge (recipients pay shipping and handling). No specific titles can be ordered but the application form asks for information on the kids that will be receiving the books. .

All children deserve books of their own; all children deserve bedroom libraries where they have at least a handful of books of their own. We are a wealthy nation and we can afford to provide all children with a few books of their own. Finding funding for such a venture may not be as difficult as you think as potential donors seem to understand the importance of books of one's own. For instance, the Moncure Elementary School in Stafford, Virginia, operates a "Book for a Buck" program two mornings a week. Students can purchase used books and some new books for 25 cents, 50 cents, or a dollar in a store staffed by students. The used-book titles primarily come from donations that are solicited community-wide and from books purchased at garage sales with the small profits made.

Schools make choices about how available funds will be spent. What if schools spent as much money on providing children with books of their own as they now spend providing children with workbooks of their own (phonics workbooks, spelling workbooks, math workbooks, reading workbooks, penmanship workbooks, test prep workbooks, etc.)? In at least one school district putting books in students' hands is seen as important.

In the Sweet Home Public Schools (NY), all students, K–12, were provided with a $25.00 gift certificate worth $33.00 toward the purchase of books at participating bookstores (with the arranged discount). The assistant superintendent who championed the project said, "We spend thousands of dollars per pupil in this district. If I cannot convince the taxpayers that this small allocation per child is a worthy investment, I shouldn't be an assistant superintendent."

Building and Displaying the Classroom Collections

You will need a general plan to redesign your school program based on the reliable, scientific research that shows the critical importance of providing kids with easy access to books they can read accurately, fluently, and with understanding. You know you will need to begin the process of thinking about what sorts of books will be ordered for the classroom collections in the initial year. You know you need to develop a plan for ordering books within certain ranges of complexity and develop a school-wide procedure for identifying the difficulty of the books ordered. You also need to plan for the school book room, which will need shelving and storage boxes and bins and a schoolwide procedure for sharing the books across the year and throughout the school.

But there is one more concern that needs attention. Where do you put all the books in the classroom? How do you make the books accessible and visible to children? Well, the worst plan is to put the books on shelves with their spines facing out. This makes the books less accessible simply because you have to work so hard to find a book you might want to read.

Two broad approaches have demonstrated value for enhancing children's access to the book collections. First, create classroom displays and change them frequently. These might be author displays or genre displays or topic displays. I might walk into a fourth-grade classroom in New York State and see a collection of two dozen or more books on the Hudson River, a theme in social studies, displayed on top of a book shelf at eyeball height. Some of the books are from the school library, a couple are from the classroom collection, but most are from the Hudson River book bin kept in the school book room. On a flat wire rack there is a display of fables, for the current language arts focus, with their covers visible; on a small

This Illinois teacher has organized this section of her classroom library into bins of books representing both types of books and favorite series books.

Juriah Mosin/Shutterstock

This young man seems entranced by this book and it is just such entrancement that creates children who become life-long readers.

table there is a display of books by Jean George who will be featured next month in language arts in an author study. The children can select any of her books to read now to begin to develop a familiarity with her style, her craft, her works, but many more of her titles will be added to the display in a few weeks.

On the teacher's desk is a small stack of books that she will "bless" today (Gambrell & Marinak, 1997). These blessings are blessedly brief, just a few seconds each: The teacher holds up the book and mentions the title and offers a few words of information or response to the book and then moves on to another. She may mention that the book offers information on a topic they will be studying or was written by an author they know; or she may simply say something like, "If you like scary books/funny books/sports stories this book may be for you." For some books she may read just a bit of it, others may have the illustrations exhibited. The goal here is to offer children a quick introduction—something to entice them to read these books. So each day, each teacher selects 5 to 10 books from the milieu to feature. This helps ensure that children notice the range of books available, it works to entice the child who would not search the collection very long for a book to read, or at least wouldn't when he began the school year.

Summary

Kids not only need to read a lot but they also need many books they can read accurately, fluently, and with comprehension right at their fingertips. They also need access to books that entice them to read. Schools can foster wider reading by creating school and classroom collections that provide a rich and wide array of appropriate books and magazines and by providing time every day for children to actually sit and read. They can make it easy for children to take books home for the evening or weekend by worrying less about losing books to children and more about losing children to illiteracy.

The emphasis must first be on ensuring abundant reading opportunities during the school day. We also need to create school literacy programs and environments that entice children and adolescents to take our books home to read on their own time.

I must admit that when I walk into a lower-achieving school and see a library with few books and student access restricted to a single weekly visit and I see classrooms with few books and no book displays, I am dismayed. When I see remedial rooms and special education rooms filled with workbooks and with computers that offer electronic workbooks, I cringe. When I see little time allocated for just reading but find a mandate that parents read with their children every evening, I get angry over such "blame the victim" policies.

In these situations I wonder just how the folks who run this school got so far off track. How is it that in such schools there is money for paraprofessionals in every classroom, for a home–school coordinator, for an assistant principal, for a social worker, for a gifted coordinator, for an in-school suspension supervisor, and so on, but no damn money for books?

Reading Ladders

Teri Lesesne (2010) uses the term "reading ladders" to describe just how we might move adolescents from reading simpler to reading more complex literary texts. The bottom rung of the ladder is a text that every student in the class can read and will read without much prodding. The later texts become progressively more complex until, at the top of the ladder, we find the much admired but complex texts that so many English teachers adore. Below is one example of reading ladder; Lesesne's book has many more. Remember the less complicated texts are at the bottom of the ladder.

The Boy Who Dared. Bartoletti, 2008.
The Boy in the Striped Pajamas. Boyne, 2006.
Bridge to Terabithia. Paterson, 2007.
Walk Two Moons. Creech, 1994.
Olive's Ocean. Henkes, 2003.
The Savage. Almond, 2008.

In many schools there is money to purchase test preparation books for every student, even though the research suggests little, if any, benefit for test preparation activity (Guthrie, 2002). In fact, test preparation beyond a couple of short sessions to familiarize students with the test format often seems to have more negative effects on achievement than positive. This happens because test performance is largely determined by two factors: reading ability and general world knowledge. Few test preparation packages offer much in the way of explicit reading instruction and even fewer provide opportunities to expand a student's knowledge of the world or of core curriculum knowledge (e.g., science or social studies).

Schools spend substantial funds on workbooks and photocopying of work-sheets, but research suggests that such expenditures are not connected to improved achievement. In one high-poverty Alabama school I visited, teachers were given no workbooks, no test preparation materials, and only two reams of paper for photo-copying. Any additional photocopying had to be paid for by the teacher. The princi-pal asked me, "Why would I provide all those things [workbooks, test preparation, photocopying] when research does not support their use? Why would I make teachers pay out of their own pockets for the books they need to teach the students that are assigned them? Instead, I take the money that many schools allocate to things we know don't improve achievement and allocate that money to teachers for purchasing the books they need to teach every child well." If only all principals had such a clear view of what really matters.

All too frequently I enter schools where I find it hard to imagine that any but the most determined child will ever learn to read, given the mindless decisions the adults have made about spending the money available. Two decades of research on effective classroom and schools documents that schools without rich supplies of engaging, accessible, appropriate books are not schools that are likely to teach many children to read at all, much less develop thoughtful, eager, engaged readers.

Chapter 4

Kids Need to Learn to Read Fluently

Several observable behaviors accompany difficult reading. One of the most obvious is a slowing of reading rate, which is often accompanied by finger pointing, even in adults. Phrasing and intonation also frequently break down, and rereading a passage or a segment of a passage is another signal.

Rereading occurs when we recognize that our reading seems to have gone off track and the text is not making sense to us. If we routinely monitored signs of anxiety or stress, we would find that hard reading, particularly reading that is not making sense, increases bodily signs of anxiety, a physiological signal of frustration (Johnston, 1985). The difficulty we experience may come from a lack of familiarity with the topic being presented, which may lead to difficulty with word pronunciation as well as the ability to understand the word meanings, and may stem from poorly organized information (think of the directions accompanying your income tax forms or a software program). When our motivation is high, we will typically persist with difficult reading (Wigfield, 1997), but when motivation and interest are low, we often simply terminate the reading activity—sometimes with obvious symptoms of frustration.

A key point to understand is that everyone encounters texts that present difficulties. And everyone responds to difficult texts in predictable ways. Beginning readers seem almost necessarily to move through this word-by-word, finger-pointing stage (Biemiller, 1970; Weber, 1970) before moving on to a more fluent reading style. But some children's reading continues to routinely exhibit these signals (e.g., finger pointing, word-by-word reading, lack of self-monitoring, anxiety, and so on) even when the topic is familiar and word pronunciation and familiarity pose no particular problems. These children often have a historical pattern of slower development of reading proficiencies and are often those served by any of the several instructional support programs (remedial reading, resource room). The primary focus of this chapter is on fostering more fluent reading in these struggling readers.

Understanding the Importance of Reading Fluently

There has been much research on the role of reading accuracy in reading development (see Allington, 1984b), but far less work has examined the development of reading fluency. Fluency, in beginning reading, has historically been measured primarily by recording oral reading rate. The *Gray Standardized Oral Reading Paragraphs* began this tradition in 1915 by providing reading rate criteria to determine the adequacy of an oral reading performance. More recently, schools have been using various assessment products that have minimum reading rate goals, usually named something like *words correct per minute*. In many respects, reading rate is a general measurement of fluency in that word-by-word reading is always slower than reading in phrases. Reading without rereading is always faster than reading with rereading necessitated by difficulties in making sense out of the material being read.

Gathering Useful Reading Rate and Fluency Information

The notion of using oral reading speed as one factor in making instructional decisions has a long history. The usefulness of reading rate and fluency measures is determined by two primary factors: who collects the information and the curriculum relatedness of the measures. In other words, it is possible to gather rate and fluency data that are useless in improving instruction. For rate and fluency data to be useful, they need to be gathered regularly from texts that are used in the classroom. This was the idea behind the original informal reading inventory, the running record system, and curriculum-based assessment (words correct per minute).

Over time, commercial publishers have marketed a variety of products that provide information on children's reading rate and fluency. A primary problem with all of these products is that they provide only indirect information for making instructional decisions. Some provide virtually no useful information for instructional planning. Assessment data that fail to inform instruction are largely useless for teachers.

For instance, rate of reading for isolated word lists has been shown to be relatively useless for estimating students' text reading and comprehension (Jenkins et al., 2003). The same is true with reading rates for pseudo-words (Cunningham et al., 1999). If these assessments included only items drawn from the curriculum used in the classroom (sight words from the reading series, pseudo-words created from phonic elements taught), they might have some limited value, but most commercial systems are designed to be curriculum-free so that sales are not limited to schools using one specific curriculum material. These systems are even less useful for instructional planning when they are administered by someone other than the classroom teacher when working with the students.

It isn't just fast reading that is the issue here, however. Although fluent reading is faster, there are other features to consider as well. Clay and Imlach (1971) conducted the classic study on the development of reading fluency by examining the reading behaviors of 100 beginning readers. They noted that those early readers making the greatest progress not only read faster and more accurately but also with better phrasing and intonation. Whereas the lowest-progress readers read aloud in one- and two-word segments, the highest-progress readers read in five- to seven-word phrases. Of course, reading in phrases produced faster reading as well. The high-progress readers also spontaneously self-corrected four and five times as many of their word pronunciation errors as did the lower-progress readers. Thus, these two characteristics, phrase reading with appropriate intonation and spontaneous self-correction of many misread words, were clearly associated with those children making better progress in learning to read. However, because it is so difficult to study such subtle linguistic features of reading, most other researchers interested in the development of fluency have focused on reading rate, an easily measured factor, rather than on measures of juncture, prosody, intonation, and stress.

Reading rate research shows a steady increase in the numbers of words read per minute (wpm)—the most common rate measure—as children progress through school, with larger increases evident in the elementary years than in the middle and high school years (Rasinski, 2000). Reading rate is related to reading volume because children with slower rates simply read fewer words than faster readers in the same amount of time. At the intermediate grades, for instance, one child may finish *Stone Fox* in a little more than an hour (reading at around 200 wpm), but it may take a slower-reading child almost three hours (at 75 wpm).

In any high school, some students read 100 wpm and others read 300 wpm. Thus, some students will spend three hours reading the same homework assignments that other students complete in an hour. Slower reading means that some

Reading Rates

Harris and Sipay (1990) present a summary of information on reading rates established on several standardized reading rate measures. This chart was developed from those data.

General range of adequate reading rates by grade levels:

Grade	WPM	Grade	WPM
1	60–90	6	195–220
2	85–120	7	215–245
3	115–140	8	235–270
4	140–170	9	250–270
5	170–195	12	250–300

Reading rate guidelines must be applied with caution because a number of factors will influence rate. For instance, although oral reading is slower than silent reading, the reading rates for younger children are typically established from oral reading activity, whereas the rates for older children are established from silent reading activity. Younger children may exhibit little difference in oral and silent reading rates, but for older students that gap should be quite substantial.

students will read far less, even when given the same amount of time as others. As was noted in Chapter 2, volume of reading matters in reading development.

But we cannot get too carried away with a focus on reading rate. I do think the development of reading fluency and rate amongst students needs to be monitored and when children deviate enormously and regularly from general adequacy standards we need to explore the issue further. What I worry most about is the possibility that we literally teach some children slow reading and that slow reading becomes a habit.

LaBerge and Samuels (1974) linked the concept of "automaticity" to the development of proficient reading. At its simplest, *automaticity* refers to the ability to engage and coordinate a number of complex subskills and strategies with little cognitive effort. For instance, as children develop as readers, a growing number of words are recognized with little effort—that is, without much, if any, conscious attention to the word structure. This is not quite the same as "sight word" reading because some of the words are decoded quickly using larger word patterns instead of a process of letter-by-letter analysis (Share & Stanovich, 1995). Reading fluently requires automatic information processing.

Why Do Some Readers Have Fluency Problems?

Some children read with little fluency because they have been given reading material that is simply too difficult for them. In these cases, readers make a number of oral reading errors that would not be observed had they been given texts they could read with 99 percent accuracy as suggested in Chapter 3. Difficult texts create word-by-word reading, many hesitations while reading, sounding out and attempting a word, and so on—all factors that result in a slower rate of reading. On the other hand, some children seem to be able to read with a high degree of accuracy yet still do not read fluently—that is, with phrasing and intonation. Word-by-word reading limits their rate of reading and, in many cases, has a negative impact on comprehension. Although this developmental lag is not well understood (Allington, 1983a; Kuhn & Stahl, 2003), several hypotheses seeking to explain it have been advanced.

One suggests that some children come to school having had relatively few books read to them and that these limited experiences may negatively impact the development of reading fluency. However, studies that provide struggling readers with a fluent reader model (through tape recordings or teacher read-aloud models) offer only mixed support for this explanation. Dowhower (1987) and Rasinski (1990) compared assisted repeated reading (teacher providing a model of fluent reading) with unassisted repeated reading (students simply reread passages with no model) on second- and third-grade students. Both reported that similar results were produced by either technique, although Dowhower suggested some improvements in intonation and prosody for the assisted group. Overall, however, both techniques did improve students' general reading rate, accuracy, and

Why Do Older Readers Struggle?

Four studies (Buly & Valencia, 2002; Dennis, 2008; Leach et al., 2003; Pinnell et al., 1995) report detailed breakdowns of the reasons older struggling readers (age 10 and older) struggle with reading. The findings of these studies suggest why the National Reading Panel (2000, p. 2–133) found that "systematic phonics instruction failed to exert a significant impact on the reading performance of low-achieving readers in second through sixth grade."

In each of these four studies, decoding problems were evident in some of the older readers, but more often these older struggling readers had other issues that accounted for their reading difficulties. In one study, only 1 of 10 older poor readers had true decoding difficulties. Another group could decode in isolation but did not transfer these skills to text reading—they could pronounce words on isolation tasks but exhibited substantial problems with oral reading accuracy. About 1 in 5 readers exhibited adequate, but slow, deliberate decoding processes combined with adequate comprehension. That same pattern was observed in another study in which 1 in 5 struggling readers exhibited decoding problems but no comprehension problems. In both studies, about 40 percent of the poor readers decoded adequately but exhibited comprehension problems.

Another group of older struggling readers seemed able to decode and comprehend but read very slowly, which produced lower scores on timed reading tests. This problem was also evident in the third study where the older struggling readers read text aloud with 94 percent accuracy but at only a 65 word-per-minute rate. By contrast, the older achieving readers read with 97 percent accuracy but at a rate of 162 words per minute.

These studies illustrate the limitations of one-size-fits-all intervention designs. This research also points to the need for diagnostic studies of older poor readers prior to beginning an intervention. Some older poor readers do need decoding instruction, but that instruction needs to be informed by analyses of just what sort of decoding problem exists. These studies suggest that a few older readers (fewer than 10 percent) may need basic decoding lessons, others need lessons on transfer of existing decoding skills to the larger act of text reading, and some simply need to develop more automatic application of existing decoding skills while reading. The same sorts of variation exist with those older poor readers who exhibit comprehension difficulties and so effective intervention designs must vary based on reader needs. And never forget that these older struggling readers have read millions fewer words than their better reading peers.

comprehension. It may be that there are some children who benefit more than others from the modeling of fluent reading. On the one hand, in the studies available, results are reported for a group as a whole and the groups of children, on average, did not benefit much from having the model available. On the other hand, no study reported any negative effects of providing a fluent reader model and there is modest evidence of a small positive effect.

These studies represent but two of the more comprehensive studies examining the impact of repeated reading on reading fluency and comprehension. Other studies have demonstrated that repeated reading is more effective than listening to stories repeatedly, than practicing rapid word recognition of passage words on word lists or flashcards, and providing students with indications of where phrase boundaries are located in the text they are asked to read (e.g., Dahl, 1977; Herman, 1985; O'Shea et al., 1985; Rashotte & Torgeson, 1985). The available evidence provides reliable, scientific evidence of the positive impact of repeated readings on a variety of reading tasks and outcome measures. These studies also indicate that engaging children in repeated readings of a text is particularly effective in fostering more fluent reading in children who are struggling to develop proficient reading strategies (Kuhn & Stahl, 2003; Samuels, 2002).

An alternative hypothesis as to why some children can read texts reasonably accurately but with little fluency is that word-by-word reading may be a learned adaptive response to a specific type of instructional setting (Allington, 1980b). Children read word-by-word when they have learned to rely primarily on an external monitor (the teacher, aide, or other students) when reading aloud. Research has demonstrated that teachers are more likely to have lower-achieving readers read aloud than better readers (Allington, 1983a; Chinn et al., 1993; Collins, 1986) during traditional round-robin reading activities in which each child reads a short passage in turn. During this activity, teachers are far more likely to interrupt the lower-achieving readers than the higher-achieving readers, regardless of the quality of errors, and to interrupt poor readers more quickly and to have the interruption focus on sounding words out (Allington, 1980b; Chinn et al., 1993; Hoffman et al., 1984). Furthermore, some teachers allow other children to interrupt struggling readers but discourage such interruptions when better readers read aloud (Eder & Felmlee, 1984).

Thus, struggling readers are

- more likely to be reading material that is difficult for them,
- more likely to be asked to read aloud,
- more likely to be interrupted when they miscall a word,
- more likely to be interrupted more quickly,
- more likely to pause and wait for a teacher to prompt them, and
- more likely to be told to sound out a word when interrupted.

Better readers are

- more likely to be reading material of appropriate difficulty,
- more likely to be asked to read silently,
- more likely to be expected to self-monitor and self-correct,
- more likely to be interrupted only after a wait period or at the end of a sentence, and
- more likely to be asked to reread or to cross-check when interrupted.

In the face of such different reading lessons, it isn't surprising that struggling readers begin to read hesitantly. I describe the word-by-word behavior as a learned "checking the traffic" response. When struggling readers grow used to a steady stream of rapid, external interruptions, they begin to read with an anticipation of interruptions—word-by-word. At the extreme you can hear children pausing after each word while awaiting the teacher's confirmation of a correct pronunciation. On some of the audiotapes of struggling readers reading aloud (to an aide, their class-

Lots of practice, including repeated readings of favorite texts, is important in the development of fluency.

Andrew Lundquist/Shutterstock

room teacher, or resource teacher) there is even an audible "Um-huh" from the teacher after every word is pronounced by the struggling readers. In some severe cases, the struggling reader actually looks up from the text to check with the teacher after every word is read.

However, this is a trained behavior, not an indication of anything else in particular. Some have thought that word-by-word reading suggests an inadequate sight vocabulary or limited decoding proficiency. But there have been a number of studies indicating that struggling older readers, those who read word-by-word, when compared to reading-level matched younger readers often know more sight words and have more phonics skills than those younger better readers. The difference is that the younger better readers read more fluently and with superior self-monitoring (Allington, 1984b). Other studies have shown that training struggling readers to recognize individual words faster had little positive effect on reading fluency or overall reading achievement (Dahl, 1977). What does seem effective is providing struggling readers with lots of opportunities to develop self-monitoring skills and strategies (Kuhn & Stahl, 2003; Samuels, 2002) and providing repeated reading with limited, if any, interruptions while the child reads.

A final hypothesis on why some children don't develop adequate fluency or rate of reading is quite simple: They have had limited reading practice in appropriately leveled materials. Kuhn and her colleagues (2006) provided the clearest test of this hypothesis when they compared repeated reading interventions with wide reading interventions. The question they hoped to answer was whether repeated reading worked because it provided struggling readers with greater opportunities to read. They had one group of children repeat readings of the same story each week. The wide reading struggling readers read at least three texts each week and engaged in only a minimal amount of repeated readings. The researchers found that the wide reading treatment produced reading fluency growth faster and, additionally, produced gains in vocabulary development and comprehension that were not observed in the repeated readings students.

At this point I am willing to put my money on the wide reading intervention design. Like Kuhn and colleagues, I'd do repeated readings on Mondays and then on Tuesday through Friday I would have the children engaged in extensive high-success reading (99 percent accuracy, in phrases, with understanding). I think the primary benefit of repeated readings may be that it works to break down the word-by-word reading that too many struggling readers have learned as a result of too much teacher interruption. Thus, I would devote one day each week, at least initially, to repeated readings of one text. This could be done as choral reading or in paired practice. The goal is to get everyone reading the text accurately and fluently.

However, the widespread evidence that struggling readers are often placed in texts that are too hard (given the level of support available) and the commonness of fluency problems in these students suggests that we must work to foster fluent reading. I do know from my clinical experiences that providing children access to appropriately leveled texts and a non-interruptive reading environment typically produces profound changes in reading fluency and self-monitoring. We will discuss how to design such lessons in the following section.

Interventions to Develop Fluency in Struggling Readers

A number of intervention strategies have been studied that have demonstrated effectiveness in developing fluency and, concurrently, fostering comprehension (Kuhn et al., 2010). In this section, the most successful strategies are reviewed in three clusters: tutorial approaches, small group approaches, and an approach that requires whole-class instructional redesign.

Tutorial Approaches

Some studies have used tutorial interventions to foster improved reading fluency (and the accompanying growth in rate, comprehension, and volume of reading). Tutorial approaches could be offered in the classroom or in a resource room and could be delivered by the classroom teacher, a specialist teacher, a trained paraprofessional or adult volunteer, or even an older student in a peer tutoring plan. There are few studies that actually compare the potentially differing effects that might occur based on who delivers the instructional support. Virtually all of those studies that have been conducted report a facilitative impact on fluency, regardless of who leads the tutorial intervention. Nonetheless, I will suggest that the more expert the tutor, the greater the likelihood of progress in the greatest number of struggling readers. Thus, whenever possible, tutorial support should be offered primarily by teachers—ideally, by expert teachers (Ehri et al., 2007; Wasik, 1998).

The very first step I recommend is a schoolwide training effort, including anyone who might be listening to struggling readers read aloud—even if no fluency tutorial, per se, is planned. The training would simply focus on a set of procedures for responding when readers produce a mispronunciation or simply stop while reading aloud. The training is intended to heighten awareness of interruptive responses and the potential that such interruptive responding has on the development of readers who rely on an external source to monitor their reading.

Paired Reading Peer Tutors   In this system, children are provided a *Preview-Pause-Prompt-Praise (PPPP)* strategy. This paired-reading peer-tutoring technique has been well researched and popularized by Keith Topping (1987; Topping & Ehly, 1998), who has evaluated this procedure in a number of sites in Great Britain. These evaluations and a number of others (e.g., Shany & Biemiller, 1995) point to the positive effects this strategy has on developing fluency and general reading achievement. The basic procedure is: *Preview,* when the tutor simply engages the child in a very brief discussion of the title and cover art focusing on the question, "What do you think this story is about?" The tutor and the tutee then begin reading aloud together until the tutee wishes to read alone, at which point he or she taps the table or desk, and the tutor allows him or her to continue without support.

However, if the tutee stumbles or misreads the text, the tutor will *Pause*, and count to three silently or wait until the tutee reaches the end of the sentence. This technique provides the reader with an opportunity to self-correct, work through the decoding of the word, reread the sentence, or use other powerful strategies associated with good readers.

If, after the pause, the reader has not self-corrected, not figured out the word, or not yet responded, the tutor will *Prompt* helpfully and strategically. Now this can be the complicated part. A usual first prompt is, "Let's read that again." If the misreading is not corrected or if the tutee still fails to pronounce the word, the tutor then provides the pronunciation and begins to read along with the tutee again.

If the tutee self-corrects or figures out the word, the tutor offers *Praise* for the reading strategy used and then begins to read with the tutee until the tutee again taps on the table. After reading, the tutor offers praise for the use of good reading strategies and then simply requests that the tutee, "Tell me your favorite part of the story." Following this response, the tutor can also share a favorite part of the text.

This rather simple strategy can be profitably used by virtually anyone who listens to children read. Assisted reading helps smooth out choppy word-by-word reading while simultaneously supporting better self-monitoring and improved accuracy.

Because progress toward fluent reading might be hampered if the PPPP strategy is implemented only occasionally, I recommend that parents and paraprofessionals, as well as teachers and peers, be trained to use a similar strategy when they listen to children read aloud. It seems important, if the goal is eliminating the reliance on an external monitor, that virtually all reading aloud that a student might do would support the development of self-monitoring and fluent reading.

Rereading to Meet a Standard

One feature of repeated reading that does seem important is having struggling readers read to meet a predetermined standard of rate and fluency. Kuhn and Stahl (2003) and Therrien (2003) both found that having students read a passage until they had reached a standard produced better results than simply requiring them to engage in a specified number of re-readings. The reading rate and fluency standards presented on pages 70–71 and 102 would be one starting point for setting such standards within a classroom. But remember that the most appropriate standard would seem to be the one for the reading level of the individual student (not the standard for the child's current grade placement). Furthermore, each reader needs to begin with books the child is able to read with good accuracy, not with texts he or she reads slowly and with little fluency. In the following section, I present two teacher-tested, research-based strategies for organizing rate and fluency practice around rereading to meet a preset standard.

Tape, Check, Chart   Another individual procedure for increasing reading rate and fluency is the use of audiotape recordings—in this case by having students audiotape their own reading. Begin by giving the students a four-color pen, and then have them turn on the tape recorder and begin to read aloud from a self- or teacher-selected text. After the first reading, the students replay the tape while following along with the text (a photocopy of the text works best). As they listen, students attempt to mark all their mispronunciations in black ink (simply by placing a small check above all mispronounced words). Once they have done this, they will reread the text once more recording the reading; again they listen to the tape and mark all mispronunciations on the same copy of the text, this time with red ink (or blue or green). Finally, they read the text a third time and again listen and mark the misreads in a different color ink. Students can tally and chart the number of mispronunciations made on each reading. Typically, each rereading produces fewer misread words and each reread sounds better—more fluent. The error-marking procedure makes this progress readily visible to the reader.

Tape, Time, Chart   A similar strategy has the student read a text aloud several times, using a simple stopwatch (trying to record time from a classroom clock does not work very well) to record how long it takes to complete the passage (in seconds, usually). These times can then be charted and students can observe their own progress. Typically, each rereading will take less time to complete.

But remember that proficient reading is different from fast reading. Certainly, fluency practice and monitoring reading rate are useful techniques, but the goal isn't just to attain faster, more fluent oral reading. The goal is improved comprehension of the material read and perhaps an improved confidence that reading can be an *improved* and an *enjoyable* personal experience. Following repeated failure, some children benefit greatly from the simple signs of progress, such as fewer misread words or increased speed, that come from repeated readings (or assisted reading).

Older Kids, Baby Books   One problem that is frequently encountered, particularly in the upper grades, is that some struggling readers need really easy texts to practice on, but that easy books are stigmatized. In other words, sixth-graders reading at a second-grade level don't want to be caught dead with a copy of a *Junie B. Jones* book in their possession. It is not hard to understand their reluctance to stick a beginning reader book in their back pocket.

But what if they are using that *Junie B. Jones* book in a peer tutoring arrangement with a third-grade struggling reader? The focus now becomes one of reading the book so they can help their tutee. This is frequently just the sort of arrangement that allows older elementary (and middle school and even high school) students to work with easy texts without feeling wholly inadequate.

Small Group Approaches

Several studies have examined the impact of small group interventions on the development of reading fluency and comprehension. These can be offered in the classroom or in special programs.

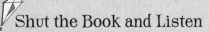

Shut the Book and Listen

One technique that will eliminate interruptions when children are reading is to have everyone but the reader close the book and simply listen to the passage being read. (The teacher and students might keep their finger in the book to mark the page for easy location after the reader completes the segment.) This technique focuses other group members' attention on how the reading sounds, as well as on whether the reading makes sense. When it does not make sense, which usually can be determined only when the reader reaches the end of a sentence, the listeners can simply prompt the reader to reread the passage.

Choral Reading   An age-old technique is choral reading, or having all the students in a group read aloud together. The choral reading activity is usually led by the teacher and typically occurs after the teacher has read the text aloud with the students following along, or after the students have read the story silently. This activity does not require the whole story to be read aloud and it is typical for just segments to be practiced this way. Teachers may select particular segments for different reasons: They might select a passage that is central to understanding the plot, one that includes dialogue (if helping readers better read dialogue aloud is the goal), or perhaps a segment where tone and voice seem important (a scary segment that deserves to be read in a whisper, for instance). The key feature in this type of activity is the fluent reading that is practiced.

I mention this because choral word-by-word reading serves no useful purpose as far as I can tell.

Teacher Models Initial Pages   Smith (1979) provided evidence that when a teacher begins the reading of a text (a basal story in this case), with students following along in their own texts, the students read the remainder of the story with greater fluency and fewer misread words. This may occur because, as the teacher reads the first two or three pages aloud, unique words are pronounced for the students, especially character and location names, or because the fluent reading model provides a good sense of the story line as well as a model of fluency.

Echo Reading   In echo reading the teacher typically reads a paragraph or a page (in easier texts) aloud and then has the students chorally reread that segment. The teacher provides the fluent model, reading in phrases and with appropriate intonation. The benefit of this method is that it introduces new words and gives the readers a sense of the story, as well as a fluent model to emulate.

Whole-Class Instructional Redesign

In most of the reported research, the use of tutorial or small group approaches to improve reading fluency has been studied. In these studies, the focus was on improving the fluency and comprehension of struggling readers in particular. However, there may be times when a focus on improving reading fluency might be considered useful as a whole-class intervention. The most convincing evidence on the power of a whole-class approach that uses repeated readings to foster improved reading achievement comes from a study of fluency-oriented reading lessons reported by Stahl and Heubach (2005).

Fluency-Oriented Reading Instruction

Stahl and Heubach's (2005) study was a two-year project conducted in the second-grade classrooms of three elementary schools, all with diverse student populations. The intervention had three major components. First, basal reader lessons were redesigned with an emphasis on repeated readings and partner reading to improve fluency. Although fluency was emphasized, the lessons were comprehension oriented because a focus on comprehension seems to enhance fluency and vice versa. Thus, the teacher discussed the story using a story map framework after first reading the story aloud to the students. The story was then echo read with either the whole group or with small groups of students. Next came partner reading with pairs sharing the rereading of the story. This was followed by a third rereading that was sometimes made into a performance activity with, for example, different students reading different characters' roles.

Second, students had home reading assignments that involved rereading the basal story to a parent or other adult one or two days a week. In this way students would read and reread each basal story approximately five times to at least three different audiences (teacher, peer, and parent).

Third, students engaged in a daily self-selected reading activity in which a 15- to 30-minute block of time was set aside to allow children to read books from their classroom or school libraries, to reread previous basal stories or little books that have been used instructionally, or to read books brought from home. In addition, self-selected reading was encouraged throughout the day as a "sponge" activity when children had finished other assigned work.

Over the two years of the intervention, all but two of the children who had entered second grade reading on the primer level or higher were reading on or above grade level at the end of the year. Yearly gains averaged 1.8 grade equivalents, or almost twice the expected gain and more than twice the historical gains of second-graders in these schools. Half the students who entered second grade unable to read even primer-level materials were reading on grade level by the end of the first year. The largest gains in achievement were made by students who entered second grade reading below grade level.

One final comment about this study must be made. The intervention was implemented within the constraints of district mandated basal reader instruction, including, in some sites, mandated whole-class lessons from a single basal. The interesting thing about the findings was that the repeated reading and comprehension support seemed to help make the basal texts more appropriate, in the sense of difficulty, for the lower-achieving readers. Stahl and Heubach (2005) comment that on the initial reading of a basal story the lower achieving children's accuracy often fell below the instructional level standards. With the support provided by the several rereadings and comprehension emphasis, however, their accuracy improved with each rereading.

Obviously, many students made substantial gains even though the texts would seem to have been more difficult than is usually recommended. However, the level of support provided, as well as the opportunity for repeated readings, seems to have allowed these more difficult texts to be used profitably. Nonetheless, it seems possible that the use of texts of a more appropriate level of difficulty might have benefited those lowest readers who made the less impressive progress during the intervention period.

Shared Book Experience

Researchers have also redesigned classroom lessons with a focus on repeated readings and found positive effects. For instance, Reutzel, Hollingsworth, and Eldredge (1994) have compared the shared book experience (SBE) with the oral recitation lesson in second-grade classrooms in two schools. The same researchers (Eldredge, Reutzel, & Hollingsworth, 1996) compared the effects of 10 minutes of daily SBE to 10 minutes of round-robin reading practice on second-grade readers' fluency, accuracy, vocabulary acquisition, and comprehension. In both studies, the SBE produced statistically superior impacts on all measures of reading proficiency. In fact, the results demonstrated a substantial positive impact for SBE, especially on the reading performances of average and struggling readers.

Although the SBE was adapted for the reading lessons offered in many basal anthologies, some evidence suggests that many teachers continued to use variations of the more traditional directed reading activity and many continued using round-robin reading practice (Hoffman et al., 1998). This seems an unfortunate turn of events (as is the return of some publishers to the traditional directed reading model) given the consistently positive evidence demonstrating the greater success of the SBE in developing reading fluency and comprehension. The shared book experience can be implemented with many different reading materials, although most of the current research has been done using predictable and patterned language texts or authentic children's literature.

In the preceding studies noted, the SBE was implemented following the general guidelines provided by Holdaway (1979). The teacher takes a big book version of the text to be read and places it in a position where all children in the group can readily view the print (usually from their seats on the floor in a designated group reading area). The teacher then

- leads a discussion of the title, cover art, and the illustrations,
- invites students to predict the story line,
- reads the text aloud dramatically,
- leads the response to the story, with discussion and perhaps a retelling, after which,
- the text is read and reread several times.

On subsequent rereadings the teacher often highlights word structure (letter-sounds, onset-rhyme patterns, inflections, syllables) and language patterns (repetition, rhyme, unique words) by covering words (or word parts) with sticky notes and asking students to predict and confirm. Often children reread the story in pairs or chorally read the story aloud with their teacher.

In the shared book experience it is the teacher who largely decides just what features of the text to focus on in rereadings. In other words, the teacher responds to students, selecting text elements based on student needs as observed in their responses during and after reading. Although the basal lessons often provided a focus based on an analysis of the text being read, the designers could not reliably predict just which text features might need attention in different groups of children. Thus, the successful use of SBE requires that the teacher pay more attention to student responses and then adapt lessons based more on student responses than on the suggestions found in the teacher's guide that might accompany a reading series.

Rigorous scientific research went into these experiments with SBE interventions and the results demonstrated positive effects on the development of reading proficiency. After four months, students in the shared book experience classrooms had better word analysis performance, better comprehension of materials read, and an improved level of fluency. The repeated readings of the texts as a group and the word study in the context of the stories read, along with the discussion of the stories and the focus on text features, fostered the improved performances that were seen.

Repeated Readings for Interpretation   Francine Stayter and I (1991) described one middle school classroom where repeated readings were used to help foster higher-order comprehension. In this classroom, students reread materials, often aloud, attempting to become fluent and experimenting with different intonation and stress. Of particular importance was an attempt to read dialogue with accuracy and intonation. In other words, how did the character utter that line? Sarcastically? Spitefully? Apologetically? Students told us how the repeated readings often opened their eyes to alternative interpretations of the text and that they "saw" new things about characters as they reread and became more familiar and comfortable with the text and the character's voice.

Rereading for Performance

In some respects what we observed is akin to what seems to happen in Readers' Theater, Be the Character, and in the Oprah activities. In each case, readers must attempt to take on the actual voice of the characters as well as attitude, stance, and personality. In each case multiple readings of the text, or segments of the text, are necessary. In the classes where these techniques are regularly used, some restructuring is necessary, if only the elimination of some more traditional follow-up activities (question answering, worksheet completion, journal writing), in order to provide time to rehearse and perform. Although it is normally upper-grade teachers who have undertaken such redesign of their lessons, younger readers can also benefit from these activities (Martinez, Roser, & Strecker, 1999; Millin & Rinehart, 1999).

Readers' Theater

There are two basic approaches to Readers' Theater. The first is the use of commercially prepared materials, usually scripts developed from scenes in children's books. Basal reader anthologies frequently contain at least one script that can be performed as a play.

However, I prefer a second approach—the development of short scripts from the books and stories that children are reading. My preference for the self-developed approach stems from the fact that I believe (no reliable scientific research here) that having students involved in the selection and preparation of a script has its own value. First, students are more engaged because they must locate a segment that is of interest to them or that they believe portrays an important aspect of the story or book they have been reading. This, in itself, involves higher-order engagement with a story. Second, having students develop the script focuses attention on just how authors embed dialogue in stories and books. This is another useful learning experience and would seem potentially productive for improving the use of dialogue in the students' own compositions.

Commercially available scripts may be useful in helping students understand the basic format of scripting, since it seems unlikely that most students will be familiar with just how scripts are structured. But after a short experience with a commercial script, I suggest the use of teacher- and student-developed scripts. Begin with a jointly developed script that draws on a book or story that is familiar to students. In developing the script with students, use an easy book with few characters

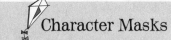

Character Masks

One idea I recently observed was the use of paper plates stapled to Popsicle sticks as character masks during a performance. The students had simply drawn faces that they felt represented the character on the paper plates and then stapled on the sticks as handles. As they performed, they held the paper plates up in front of their faces. This technique seemed to alleviate the anxiety that some students had about performing in front of others. The ease of construction and the eagerness of the students to create and use the masks sold me on the use of such masks.

for the model; *Frog and Toad* (Lobel) and *Three Up a Tree* (Marshall) are two suitable texts that come to mind. Read the story aloud and then select a scene with a few lines of dialogue to script. Model the format and produce the script on large sheets of chart paper. The scene should not be too long as a few lines for each character is usually sufficient.

After the scene is scripted on the chart paper, give the students a few minutes to read through the script several times. You might then do a choral reading of the script, modeling changing voices for different characters. Ask for volunteers to read different parts and have the students pair up (in the case of *Frog and Toad* or triple up for *Three Up a Tree*) to practice performing the script. Finally, have different sets of students perform their rendition for everyone.

With this preparation, students should now be allowed to simply plow ahead on their own and experiment with script development from stories or books of their choice. Students might work individually, in pairs, or in teams to develop scripts, practice, and, ultimately, perform their scripts for others.

Be the Character This is typically a solo performance, although I have seen duets. In Be the Character, a child assumes the role of a character she or he has selected from the story or book and prepares a short performance, often a solo dialogue developed from the book. Sometimes the child might even create a simple costume to carry the portrayal a step further.

In one San Diego fourth-grade classroom, for instance, I watched as a young man transformed himself into Augustus Gloop from *Charlie and the Chocolate Factory,* including dressing in a large blue windbreaker supplemented by a couple of pillows. He had written a brief script from the novel that simply began, "I am Augustus Gloop . . ." and he then summarized his various dilemmas in a two-minute performance. The performance was quite convincing, even though I understood not a word since this was a dual language classroom and this young man was reading the novel in its Spanish translation and delivered his performance accordingly.

Being on Oprah This activity can be organized in several ways, but the basic feature is the same: Children take on the role of a book character who is appearing on a talk show. In other words, they step into the role of one of the characters in the story or book they have read. The teacher often plays the role of the talk-show host by announcing the guest and beginning the dialogue with a general prompt such as, "So tell me a little bit about yourself." Although similar in intent to Readers' Theater, the organization of this activity is different in that students do not act out a scene but instead assume a role and respond extemporaneously as if they were the character.

I have seen individual character representations in which one student assumed the role of the key character while the teacher and other students (or a small group of students who have read the same text) engaged the character in a discussion of his or her role, actions, and feelings during one or more episodes. In other classrooms, a number of students assume the roles of different characters while the teacher and the remaining students query them about their roles and responses.

For instance, in one New York City fourth-grade classroom, half a dozen children assumed the roles of key characters in *Charlotte's Web* (White). They were seated facing the class and the remaining children posed questions to the performers. These were based on queries that every member of the class had written in their journals as they read the book. In this classroom, the students easily took on the voice and personality of the characters they were portraying—some acted a bit

Commercial Audiotapes of Texts

You may have noticed that I've not recommended the use of commercial audiotape recordings of texts. The reason is that there are so few such tapes where the reading is done slowly enough for struggling readers to actually follow along. Now this may seem an odd complaint, given the emphasis in this chapter on developing fluency and improving reading rate. However, professional readers simply read too fast and struggling readers cannot keep up. This first occurred to me when I observed struggling readers in listening centers just looking at the pictures as they listened to book tapes. A little investigative work soon located the problem—no matter how they tried, even with bell tones signaling when to turn the page, the kids couldn't keep up with the professional reader.

It may not be surprising, then, that little evidence indicates that such tapes enhance fluency or reading achievement. The commercial audiotapes allow children to hear stories they cannot read, but they don't seem reliable in fostering fluency or achievement. However, you might want to have students make book tapes for other, perhaps younger, students to listen to. This is one strategy for making rereading a purposeful activity, as the student will practice reading a text in order to sound good on the tape.

snooty, others a bit shy. In another California fifth-grade classroom, three students took on the roles of key characters in *Island of Blue Dolphins* (O'Dell). The young man playing the role of the dog even growled as he responded to queries from the teacher/hostess and the remaining students/audience!

The Puppet Show   The use of puppet shows also provides an alternative performance activity to foster fluency and interpretation. Students create simple puppets, sock puppets, string puppets, stick puppets, and so on, and from behind a screen introduce a character through the puppet. In one classroom, students created puppets representing the historical characters whose biographies they had read. Each prepared a three-minute performance taking the role of their character and presenting a first-person narrative that they had composed.

Summary

Fluent reading is an important milestone in reading development. Some students struggle mightily and slowly improve their reading scores but never seem to achieve fluency. These struggling readers frequently lag behind their peers and are often children who read only when we request them to. In other words, they rarely engage in voluntary reading, perhaps because word-by-word reading just does not provide any personal fulfillment. Perhaps they have had only the rare opportunity to read texts of an appropriate level of complexity and so comprehension has rarely been strong. Given the demonstrated links between fluency and comprehension, it isn't particularly surprising that many word-by-word readers choose not to read much. When reading generates little or no comprehension, why would anyone continue to read except to comply with a teacher (or parent) request? But children who do not read voluntarily stand little chance of ever engaging in enough reading to become proficient readers.

The good news is that there are a substantial number of rigorously designed research studies demonstrating (1) that fluency can be developed, most readily through a variety of techniques that involve expanding the reading of texts; and (2) that fostering fluency has reliable positive impacts on comprehension performance. Thus, when fluency is an instructional goal, and it should be for struggling readers, we have a wealth of research to guide our instructional planning. Central to virtually all research demonstrating improved fluency has been expanding the amount of reading that struggling readers do. Expanding the amount of reading children do and focusing our instruction on developing each reader's self-monitoring proficiency fosters the development of a basic strategy that all readers must acquire, but there are other important proficiencies for which fluent reading seems necessary.

For instance, fluency is important in the development of higher-order literacy proficiencies. This is because engaging in these sorts of thinking about texts, ideas, characters, and themes would seem to require substantial mental activity space. Such demonstrations of higher-order literacy are more likely if the material was read accurately, fluently, and with reasonable recall of text content. In such situations, the reader would have the basic building blocks of thoughtful literacy, but when a reader struggles with word-by-word reading, having difficulty reading the sentences in phrases, it isn't surprising that little in the way of higher-order literacy is evident. So much cognitive effort was deployed at the word and sentence level that little remained for thinking about the ideas, emotions, and images found in the text. Working to develop fluent reading is important for fostering more thoughtful literacy performances.

Finally, one largely unanswered question is whether the observed effects on fluency were simply the result of engaging in a lot more reading activity. As Kuhn and Stahl (2003) note, few of the repeated reading studies controlled for reading volume. Furthermore, in one study that did have the control group engage in extended independent reading while the experimental group engaged in repeated reading for the same amount of time, the researchers found comparable gains in both groups (Rashotte & Torgeson, 1985). In a series of studies that compared wide independent reading with repeated reading (Kuhn, 2005; Kuhn et al., 2006), both groups made similar gains in fluency and word reading, but only the wide reading group improved in comprehension. I will suggest that repeated reading and other fluency-supportive activities can be useful, but should be considered largely short-term interventions with the goal of moving the struggling reader quickly to extended independent reading activities. In other words, once you get the instructional environment well-designed you should expect that fostering fluent reading would be a task that took a few weeks, not all year long. But if we fail to get the instructional environment just right, we may find that students still have not become fluent readers after months of work. So, work on fostering fluency by ensuring that struggling readers have books they can read accurately, engage them in a little repeated reading, and guarantee that you have expanded the amount of high-success reading activity they do every day.

What I mean is that the latest assessments of reading proficiency typically include extended response items that often require students to (1) actually think about what they have just read and (2) explain or describe this thinking. Being asked to think about the text you've just read is different from being asked to recall the text you've just read. And it is quite different from being asked to simply copy information from that text into a blank on a worksheet or to match information in the text with answer stems on a multiple-choice test. But even on these low-level tasks it is becoming increasingly clear that interventions focused on developing word reading skills actually do little to improve understanding while one is reading. As Cutting and Scarborough (2006) note, "Although demonstrating that instruction to strengthen children's bottom-up skills [decoding] is extremely valuable, these studies also indicate that mastering bottom-up skills will not automatically yield gains in reading comprehension, presumably because other necessary components of successful comprehension have not been developed through such interventions" (p. 279). Thus, much of the instructional activity that has dominated interventions for struggling readers has missed the mark (if the mark is improved reading comprehension, especially understanding of complex and longer texts).

The reason for these new state standards and assessments is clear: State test performances are almost wholly unrelated to NAEP reading scores. Consider that no state pegs proficient reading at a level that approximates the NAEP proficient level. However, 19 states set their proficient reading level at a level comparable to the NAEP basic level, much below the proficient level. The remaining 31 states label students as "proficient" readers even though their performances are below the NAEP basic level (Fiester, 2010). We can argue whether the NAEP levels are too high or state levels too low but in the end we simply have too many students who cannot perform literacy tasks beyond the lowest levels on either state or NAEP scales. Fostering the development of more complex understandings of texts is going to be the primary role of all teachers and especially intervention teachers.

These new thoughtful literacy standards and assessments are attempting to move closer to measurement of the proficiencies that seem to mark a person as literate. Consider how, in the world outside of school, we judge a person's literateness. Let's say you and I both read the same news story about the direction in which the stock market is going. When completed, do we then quiz each other, or create a multiple-choice test to be answered after reading the article? No, we talk. Actually we converse. Each of us makes judgments about the other's understanding based on the conversation. I might even ask you about a word or phrase used in the article, but usually only if I know that you are more expert about the stock market than I am. In other words, I don't ask questions to *test you* but to *help me.* If you are more expert, you will usually answer my question. You don't tell me to guess or to go back and read the article again. Even if you aren't more expert, you will try to help. In such cases, we will try together to make some sense. We will hypothesize and weigh the evidence and draw on our combined experiences as readers, as well as

Chapter 5

Students Need to Develop Thoughtful Literacy

The new national standards for proficient reading have targeted a more thoughtful literacy than has traditionally been expected of school reading programs.

our combined experiences with the stock market. If the issue seems personally important enough to one or both of us, we will likely try to find someone else who can help. If it is not deemed personally important, we will jointly shrug our shoulders, shake our heads, and curse financial writers for their failure to write in plain English.

But the conversation could turn in a different direction. If we are both reasonably knowledgeable, we may converse about the adequacy/accuracy of the article. If, for instance, the author cautions about a possibly impending market decline, we might debate whether the predictions and advice offered seem accurate. We might judge whether the cautionary advice is supported by the data in the article *and* by our own individual prior knowledge and experiences. We would not necessarily be surprised to find that we disagree wholly with each other on whether we believe that the author has accurately predicted the market's behavior. Alternatively, we could agree on the prediction but not on the value of the recommendations. One of us might accept the advice while the other rejects it, even though we both agreed that the prediction the author made was likely to be accurate.

We might also revisit this conversation at some later date, perhaps after the market prediction was fulfilled. We would again converse and even return to what the article *said*. We might even conclude that one of us had acted more appropriately on the prediction.

My point here is that our conversations about texts we've read are much more sophisticated than the usual "recitation script" (Tharp & Gallimore, 1989) found after reading in school settings. Outside of school we normally converse about what we have read. But in schools, children have typically recited, in the sense that the emphasis has been on just the facts, what they've read. Furthermore, these are often trivial facts because school questions are typically "known-answer" questions, so-called because the person asking the question already knows the answer. Known-answer questions have dominated school reading lessons, at least since researchers began classroom observations (Cuban, 1993). But known-answer questions are largely unique to school and are rarely used in out-of-school conversations. Outside of school, known-answer questions are associated with interrogation, not with conversation.

Imagine that you are talking with a friend and you ask a known-answer question. You might ask for the location of the nearest hardware store, even though you already know the answer. Your friend replies correctly, and you give her a sticker and say, "Good job, you've got your thinking cap on." Would your friend be pleased with your reply and the sticker? Or would she be confused, wondering whether you've gone mad, or whether you were just acting like a teacher?

Now imagine that your friend has been reading the same newspaper that you read earlier today. You sit down and construct a set of known-answer questions based on what you remember from the news story (or better yet, you go back through the article to find sticklers that you think your friend probably won't remember). As soon as your friend finishes reading, you begin the quiz: "What was the name of the INS official quoted in the front-page story? What model aircraft experienced problems last night at that airport in Arkansas? Which tobacco company did the lawyer quoted in the Great American Smoke Out article represent? What was the job title of the Pakistani official quoted in the article on nuclear proliferation?" Your friend will probably not be an eager participant in this activity.

We do not quiz friends on the newspaper articles they've read, nor the books they've read. However, we do *discuss* articles and books. We engage in *conversations* about the texts, typically focusing on the ideas in the texts—the gist of the article or book. We also offer our responses, reactions, and evaluations of the ideas and information offered.

Often we discuss the perspective of the writer of the text. In other words, we look for bias. In such instances we consider the status of the author; in news reports we consider the status of the informants who are quoted. If we know that the author or informant is linked to particular political or advocacy groups (e.g., Democratic party, Christian Coalition, Greenpeace), it makes a difference in how we view the information and ideas offered; if we know the age, gender, ethnicity, or religion of the author or informant, it may affect how we weigh the information; if we know the informant is likely to profit financially (or professionally) if her advice is accepted, we may take this into account. In other words, we constantly monitor an author's or informant's perspective as we imagine it.

When we discuss books that we've read outside of school, we focus on our response to the book. We actively promote some texts ("You have to read this . . ." or "This was a wonderful book . . ."), pan others ("Don't waste your time . . ."), and we talk comparatively about what we are reading ("I liked her other books better . . ." or "This book is better than . . ."). When our conversational partner has also read the book, we may focus, positively or negatively, on certain aspects of it ("Wasn't his description of the savageness of the poverty in Dublin chilling?" "What did you think of her depiction of teachers?"). Often our judgments about the adequacy of an author's portrayal of people, events, or situations draw heavily upon our own experiences.

When you consider the richness of the dialogue about texts that occurs outside of school, the typical patterns of school talk about texts seem shallow and barren. Outside school we rely on the richness of a person's conversation about texts to judge how well they understood it and their literateness; in school we typically rely on the flat recitation of events or information to make that same judgment. Outside of school settings we engage in conversations about the adequacy of texts and authors to inform, engage, and entertain us; in school we engage in interrogations around what was in the text. Reading lessons must change and begin to foster the sorts of thinking about texts that is commonly accepted as literate behavior outside of school.

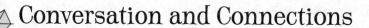

Conversation and Connections

I hope this discussion helps make the enormous differences between school interactions around texts and normal out-of-school interactions a bit clearer. My main
point is that school literacy interactions have often been very different from real-
world literacy interactions. It is this difference that has led to the development of
new standards and assessments of reading proficiency. One key difference is that
outside of school we make a variety of text-to-self, text-to-text, and text-to-world
connections when we converse about shared texts (Keene & Zimmerman, 1997).
Let me try to develop each of these connections a bit more thoroughly.

Making Connections

Text-to-self connections occur when, after reading the financial news article, we say
things like, "I'm worried. I need the money I have invested for tuition" or "I lost a
bunch of money the last time the market fell, so I am worried it might happen
again." After reading a novel in which a divorce figures centrally, we might say, "I
felt the same way" or "My sister's divorce was not nearly so unpleasant." In other
words, as we read we make connections between personal experiences and the
text—even with informational texts. When we talk about what we've read, the
text-to-self connections just naturally appear.

Text-to-text connections occur when we discuss other texts in relation to the
text just read. For instance, as part of the financial article discussion, we might al-
lude to other texts we've read on the topic. We might say, "There was a *Wall Street
Journal* article on this topic that offered a clearer explanation" or "There was a
Money magazine article this month that used the same data but came to a different
conclusion," and then add a text-to-self connection such as, "I'm going to play it
safe and move my money out of the stock market." When reading a novel we might
also make a text-to-text connection. "This book just reminded me so much of
Sue Grafton's work" or "This character is so similar to Officer Jim Chee in the
Hillerman books."

Finally, in text-to-world connections we link what we've read to what we already know about the world. This world knowledge may have come from daily observations, reading, listening, watching television, travel, and so on. Most often, our
world knowledge is an amalgamation of the information and experiences we've accumulated over time. We may know, for instance, that palm trees grow only in mild
climates. We may or may not know why. How we know this is typically hard to dis-
cern precisely. We may have noticed palm trees when we visited mild climates, we
may have seen palm trees in movies or TV shows set in mild climates, we may have
read illustrated books where palm trees appeared in the pictures when the setting

was in a mild climate. Of course, if we have lived in Minnesota or Vermont or Finland we have also noticed that no palm trees grew in these environments. But few of us have ever taken a course on palm trees, or even read a book about palm trees. Nonetheless, when we pick up a magazine with a photo of a location that includes a palm tree we infer the mild climate. When we read about "sitting under the palms on the beach" we infer a particular geographic setting—a geographical band where the story might take place. In other words, we make text-to-world connections to help us puzzle through life and literacy.

Similarly, we would be skeptical, to put it mildly, of a history text that had General George Washington arriving at Valley Forge in a Range Rover, or that depicted President John F. Kennedy as a devout Southern Baptist, or as a conservative Republican. Rarely could we pinpoint the exact source of our world knowledge in these instances. In other words, I "just know" Kennedy was Catholic and Democrat. I could tell you how to verify this information but I could not tell just how I came to know this—at least not by identifying the specific sources that provided me with that information. Nonetheless, as I read I cannot suppress my world knowledge. It is always back there, fostering a constant comparison of what I'm reading to what I know.

When literate people talk about the texts they've read outside of school, their talk is laced with connections they have made. It is these connections that drive the conversation.

Demonstrations of thoughtful literacy seem to require that the reader be able to talk in certain ways that go beyond simply making connections, though. Literate talk about texts also involves summarizing, synthesizing, analyzing, and evaluating the ideas in the text.

Summarizing
We are constantly called on to summarize texts outside of school. If I ask you, "Did you read the article about phonics in today's paper?" you may respond, "No, what did it say?" Typically what you want to know is the gist of the article, if it was positive or negative. If negative (or positive), what evidence or examples were presented? What else you want to know will depend a lot on other factors, such as your occupation (first-grade teachers might be more interested than stock brokers, for instance) or your experiences (you have a child enrolled in a school where that approach dominates). Regardless, you most often do not expect a full recounting of all of the details. If the topic is of great personal interest you may find the paper or magazine and read the piece yourself.

Now summarizing is actually a bit more complicated than this. When you summarize, you may also include references to your own experiences (text-to-self) or other things that you have read (text-to-text). In fact, your experiences and your familiarity with the topic have an enormous impact on your summary (Gaskins, 1996). In other words, you might begin summarizing an article on flunking by saying, "It's another one of those teacher-bashing articles that the *Post* is famous for."

Someone else, with different experiences, might begin by saying, "The *Post* hit the nail on the head again about teachers and that social promotion nonsense." In fact, one of the skills we develop as listeners and readers is the ability to analyze a speaker's perspective or stance on an issue. Summarizing is rarely a "Just the facts" retelling in real-world exchanges outside school.

Analyzing

When we read a text outside school we typically engage in various forms of analysis. For instance, we evaluate plot lines in novels—too outrageous, believable, imagined. We analyze the assertions in an informational text—accurate, supported, reasonable. Often, again, these analyses are connected to other experiences. We make text-to-world comparisons when we reject the premise that the hero could survive for four months with no food and water, or that he survived on coconuts in the Arctic. We engage in text-to-text connections when we note the similarity of a plot line to that of one in another book, or when we notice that the newspaper article on wealth omits data we recently read in *Time* about the rising numbers of children living in poverty. We reject an author's claim that nicotine is not addictive with a text-to-self analysis based on our own experiences with smoking and quitting—or attempting to. In fact, often our analyses involve both summary and synthesis.

Synthesizing

Synthesizing is the combining of multiple sources of information in a coherent fashion; it requires that we have summarized the key elements of what we've previously read. And synthesis typically requires some analysis. For instance, synthesis typically requires that we make judgments about the relative accuracy of information in various sources. We might analyze information on the importance of children's preschool experiences across a number of texts looking for data that supported or undermined the assertions made in an article that made light of such experiences in predicting school success. But many of these analyses would be rooted in text-to-self, text-to-text, and text-to-world comparisons. Ultimately, though, we have to try to pull all the information judged relevant together into the coherent whole we call synthesis. In doing this we go beyond just providing a summary of summaries.

Evaluating

Finally, we also routinely offer our evaluation of the texts we've read. As we talk with a colleague about an article on school vouchers, we may characterize the piece as "malicious," "right-wing," "scary," or even "rambling." When we read novels, we evaluate them on engagingness, pace, length, and, maybe, on literary qualities.

Suffice it to say, outside of school we talk about the things we've read in complex and varied ways. Interestingly, some kids talk that way about the texts they've read also—outside of school. But too often in school, talk about the texts that have been read reflects few of the dimensions of complexity found in the out-of-school talk about texts. The in-school talk frequently seems unlikely to foster much thoughtful literacy of the sort that literate adults demonstrate every day. At the same time, the new standards and the new assessments all point to developing a more thoughtful literacy in all students.

Although these sorts of conversations and connections are rare in classrooms, they seem even more unlikely to occur in the settings where struggling readers work. Research on the instruction provided poor readers portrays a very unliterate environment: There is little actual reading, especially silent reading; there are few connections to the core curriculum themes and topics; there is little focus on comprehension, generally, and almost no reports of motivated readers working in collaborative teams and engaging in both problem-solving and literate conversation. Why would instructional settings for struggling readers look so unliterate?

I think it is time for us to begin rethinking the nature of this thing we've called comprehension. I think it is time we reorganized school lessons so that thoughtful literacy proficiencies are developed in all students, especially the struggling readers.

Isn't Thoughtful Literacy Just a Buzzword for Comprehension?

The school tasks we have traditionally labeled as comprehension tasks have largely focused on remembering, a very narrow slice of what is needed for understanding what we read. The two types of tasks—remembering and understanding tasks—are linked at some level. If you couldn't remember anything about a text that you'd read, then it would be impossible to demonstrate any sort of understanding, or to engage in any intelligent conversation about that text. At the same time, perhaps you can remember that a newspaper article reported that the Dow-Jones Industrial Average (DJIA) fell by 150 points, but you have no real sense of what that might mean, nor any understanding of how the DJIA is calculated, nor what companies comprise the DJIA, nor even whether the drop has any impact on your retirement investments. We could memorize the companies that are included in the DJIA and still be no closer to understanding the information in the article.

Likewise, we might remember characters, setting, and the basic plot of a moral tale without understanding the moral message; we might remember facts about the Battle of Gettysburg or the process of photosynthesis and yet have no real understanding of the importance of either; or we might remember the words to the Pledge of Allegiance with no understanding of what they mean. But a thoughtfully literate conversation about any of these topics would involve a demonstration of various sorts of understanding. Quizzing each other on the details of the Battle of Gettysburg would be an unlikely out-of-school activity (except on *Jeopardy!*).

Discussing and sharing information, experiences, and understandings about the horror of Gettysburg and its strategic role in the War of Northern Aggression would not only be a more typical event but also a more obviously thoughtful one. (Note to all readers who have spent their lives living above the Mason-Dixon Line: What some folks call the Civil War is, or was, called the War of Northern Aggression by others, usually those who live(d) below the Mason-Dixon Line.)

My point is that in school we have too often confused remembering with understanding. We have focused on recitation of texts, not thoughtful consideration and discussion of texts. The situation for struggling readers is often even more depressing. There are times that I think our emphasis on remembering actually impedes children's understanding and the development of thoughtful literacy proficiencies. Think back to the example of the news story questions posed earlier in this chapter.

It is entirely possible for us to understand a story without remembering all of the details. We may not remember the official title of a person who is quoted, but that will not necessarily detract from understanding what he or she said. We may not be able to recall Officer Jim Chee's name, but we can describe him in detail, including information about his heritage, occupation, marital status, personality, and so on. In other words, we could discuss him as a character—likable, dogged, spiritual, and so on—without being able to remember his name.

Now when we begin to discuss such things, we are entering the arena called *thoughtful literacy.* In other words, we are going beyond remembering, and through the discussion we demonstrate our thinking about Officer Chee, or about airline safety, or the stock market. In demonstrating our thinking we demonstrate our understanding.

To me, then, thoughtful literacy represents something different from the narrow, remembering-focused tasks that have dominated school comprehension lessons. Thoughtful literacy goes beyond the ability to read, remember, and recite on demand. Generally speaking, U.S. students are better able to demonstrate proficiency on those sorts of tasks than on thoughtful literacy tasks (Brown, 1991; Donahue et al., 1999). But if we focus children's attention almost exclusively on remembering after reading, I worry that they will confuse recall with understanding. And if we fail to provide students with models and demonstrations of thoughtful literacy and lessons on how to develop those proficiencies, I fear that we will continue to develop students who don't even know that thoughtful literacy is the reason for reading (Wilhelm, 1997).

School and Thoughtful Literacy

Much of my research career has been devoted to simple demonstrations of the commonsense notion that children are most likely to learn what they are taught. In other words, if we observe the nature of the work that children and adolescents do during the school day, we can predict what sorts of skills, attitudes, habits, and knowledge they will be most likely to acquire (Bruer, 1994; Doyle, 1983; Goodlad, 1983; Guthrie & Humenick, 2004). If school comprehension tasks are primarily remembering tasks, then we should expect that students will get better at remembering. They are more likely to develop skills and habits that foster remembering in environments that emphasize remembering.

If few school tasks require students to think, to demonstrate that they actually understand what they have read, then it is unlikely that most will demonstrate the sorts of thinking and understanding that seem central to thoughtful literacy and attainment of the new literacy standards. When students have few opportunities to summarize, analyze, synthesize, and discuss what they've read, we should not be surprised that they demonstrate little proficiency with such tasks. When they have not only few such opportunities but have also experienced little instruction focused on fostering thoughtful literacy, we should expect that rather few students will develop thoughtful literacy.

The research on the nature of school tasks suggests the reason that few U.S. students seem thoughtfully literate. In study after study (Allington et al., 1996; Dahl & Freppon, 1995; Elmore et al., 1996; Goodlad, 1983; Hoffman et al., 1998; Johnston et al., 1998; Knapp, 1995; Pressley et al., 2000; Taylor et al., 2003; Wong et al., 2003) researchers report that in the typical classroom the assigned tasks overwhelmingly emphasize copying, remembering, and reciting, with few tasks assigned that engage students in discussions about what they've read.

But we have evidence that opportunities to engage in discussion are related to improved achievement (Applebee et al., 2003; Nystrand, 2006; Taylor et al., 2003). In these studies, discussion-based instruction was more effective at each grade level and for students from every achievement group and ethnic group. But lower-achieving classes had discussions less frequently and of much shorter duration than students in higher-achieving classes. However, more frequent and longer discussions in lower-achieving classes produced higher achievement. Still, it is difficult to know the full impact that discussion-based lessons might have on lower-achieving student performance because they were less common in lower-achieving classrooms. These findings indicate that interventions for struggling readers that provide far greater opportunities to engage in literate discussion are a necessary component of effective intervention designs.

However, the situation for struggling readers seems dire. Researchers have consistently reported that lower-achieving readers spent little of their school day on comprehension tasks of any sort. Struggling readers simply read less often in their classrooms, which limited the availability of comprehension tasks. Instead, for these students the lesson focus was often on words, letters, and sounds (Allington, 1983b; Collins, 1986; Hiebert, 1983; Vaughn & Linan-Thompson, 2003; Ysseldyke et al., 1984). It is tough to do much comprehension work with phonics worksheets or drill or with flashcards or contractions dittoes. Worse, the same patterns were found in studies that examined the nature of the lessons offered these students in their re-medial reading and learning disabilities classes (Allington & McGill-Franzen, 1989; Jenkins et al., 1988; Johnston & Allington, 1991; McGill-Franzen & Allington, 1990; Thurlow et al., 1984; Vaughn et al., 1998; Zigmond et al., 1980).

The demonstrated failures of the skills-emphasis instructional programs—in general, remedial, and special education programs—to foster improved reading generally and improved comprehension especially (Carter, 1984; Gamse et al., 2009; Glass, 1983; Knapp, 1995; Leinhart & Pallay, 1982; Venezky, 1998) has stimulated substantial interest in rethinking the nature of reading instruction. Curriculum fo-cused on promoting more thoughtful lessons produced not only better compre-hension achievement but also equal or better skills achievement than the curricu-lum that emphasized mastery of isolated skills (Borman et al., 2003; Dole et al., 1996; Guthrie et al., 2004; Knapp, 1995; Pressley, 2002; Purcell-Gates et al., 1995).

Thus, the skills-mastery curriculum has generated much experimentation in U.S. classrooms and stimulated a wealth of classroom-based studies, including the large-scale federal study of the Reading First initiative of NCLB (Gamse et al., 2009). That study demonstrated no positive effects of the Reading First initiative on reading achievement and led to the demise of further funding for the initiative. Perhaps this means federal programs in the future will finally move away from skills-emphasis designs and initiate a new era of research and program funding focused on fostering thoughtful literacy. Only time will tell.

The Effects of Thoughtful Literacy Instruction

Researchers have used a variety of methods in studying thoughtful literacy, in part because different research teams had different research questions. Some were inter-ested in studying how aspects of thoughtful literacy instruction emerged in class-rooms (Allington et al., 1996; Allington & Johnston, 2002; Applebee et al., 2003; Duffy, 1993; Elmore et al., 1996; Johnston et al., 1998; Nystrand, 2006; Scharer, 1992; Taylor et al., 2000b). In these studies it was commonly reported that creating thoughtful classrooms was often difficult. Thoughtful literacy lessons seem to re-quire a different organization of instructional time and a different sort of curricu-lum design than those found in most schools. Thoughtful literacy lessons needed larger blocks of uninterrupted time than many schools made available to classroom teachers. Discussion and collaborative work came off easier when tables, rather than desks, were available. It required different materials—single copies of multiple texts rather than multiple copies of single texts. But most of all, thoughtful literacy lessons required teachers to think about teaching and learning differently; it required teachers to take professional risks and teach differently. Organizational support was also necessary for the teacher learning, experimenting, and the risk taking that was required (Taylor et al., 2005).

Others studied the effects of introducing aspects of such instruction into classroom lessons on student achievement (Anderson & Roit, 1993; Beck et al., 1997; Block, 1993; Dole et al., 1996; Duffy et al., 1986; Guthrie et al., 2000; Nystrand, 2006; Palincsar & Brown, 1984; Pressley et al., 1992; Taylor et al., 2003). The common finding was unsurprising in retrospect: More thoughtful lessons produced more thoughtful readers. This enhanced thoughtfulness was demonstrated on standardized tests of comprehension (typically not very sensitive to thoughtful literacy), through student writing, and on experimenter-devised assessments of problem-solving and text processing.

And others investigated outcomes beyond those assessed on standardized tests. For example, Turner (1995) reported that students in classrooms that emphasized thoughtful literacy work were more skilled in peer collaboration, took more personal responsibility for their work, and demonstrated higher levels of engagement in academic work. Knapp (1995) reported that students enrolled in thoughtful literacy classrooms were better at problem solving, informational text comprehension, and writing. Dahl and Freppon (1995) noted persistence when confronted with difficulty was more common among students in thoughtful literacy environments, whereas students in the skills-emphasis classrooms demonstrated greater passivity. Pressley and Woloshyn (1995) reported not only improved test scores for the experimental comprehension groups but also enhanced content knowledge acquired as a result of their application of thoughtful literacy strategies when reading from textbooks. Hoffman and colleagues (1998) found that student motivation, independence, and persistence were reported by teachers as among the more common outcomes in their study of a shift to more thoughtful curriculum materials and tasks. Nystrand (2006) noted that enhancing opportunities for students to engage in literate conversations after reading produced reading improvement on both basic skill assessments as well as assessments of understanding. Donahue and colleagues (1999) reported on the NAEP survey data that demonstrated that students who were more often asked to explain, discuss, or write about the texts they had read were also more likely to demonstrate the higher-order, thoughtful literacy proficiencies than were students who had fewer such opportunities.

Thoughtful Literacy and Exemplary Teachers

Thoughtful literacy lessons were also characteristic of the classroom instruction offered by exemplary teachers (Allington & Johnston, 2002; Brandt, 1986; Nystrand et al., 1997; Pressley et al., 2000; Ruddell et al., 1990; Taylor et al., 2000b; Taylor et al., 2003). In these studies exemplary teachers routinely produced superior achievement on standardized tests and the other evidence gathered indicates their students not only read and write more but also read and write differently from students in more typical classrooms. In these classrooms, teachers and students were more likely to make connections across texts and across conversations. The talk was more often of a problem-solving nature. In addition, the students in the exemplary teacher classrooms were more likely to be engaged in peer conversations about texts they had read. Thus, the quality and quantity of classroom talk also differed between traditional and exemplary classrooms (Johnston, 2004).

Summary

Thoughtful literacy can be fostered, but the classrooms most successful in developing such proficiencies look different from traditional classrooms. Nonetheless, if we want students to develop the thinking around reading and writing activity that marks thoughtful literacy, classroom instruction will necessarily change.

Research on Effective Comprehension Instruction

There have been several major reviews of the research on the development of enhanced comprehension skills and strategies. However, much of this research has focused on how to help students perform traditional classroom comprehension tasks more adeptly—that is, how to help students prepare more effectively for recitation tasks, primarily. But since recitation tasks seem to be a mainstay of schooling, and have been a core school activity for centuries, we must also consider what we have learned about how to foster improved recitation performance.

The comprehensive reviews provided by Almasi and colleagues (2005), Dole and colleagues (1996), Kamil (2004), Pressley (2002), Guthrie (2004), Mastroprieri and Scruggs (1997), Pearson and Fielding (1991), and Rosenshine and Meister (1994) converge on several conclusions. First, and most important, they point to strong evidence that reading comprehension performance, measured in a variety of ways, can be significantly improved with effective teaching. This is an important point because some folks have assumed, incorrectly, that reading comprehension was largely related to that thing we call intelligence. In other words, some people think that reading comprehension "just happens" if the reader pronounced the words correctly.

In our review of research on comprehension with struggling readers (Allington & McGill-Franzen, 2009) we noted that little actual research on reading comprehension has been conducted with struggling readers. The research that is available often focuses on remembering rather than understanding or thoughtful literacy. In far too many cases the nature of the comprehension difficulties experienced by struggling readers are related to supposed weaknesses of the readers rather than weaknesses in the instruction they have been provided. The 30-year skills-emphasis focus of interventions for struggling readers has largely escaped notice by those conducting intervention studies. But as I wrote earlier, children are more likely to learn what they are taught than what they are not taught.

Nonetheless, what the reviews of the research demonstrate is that reading comprehension, even recitation, involves active thinking. This thinking can be improved when students are provided explicit demonstrations of the comprehension strategies that literate people use when they read—in this case, when they read school texts for school tasks.

A second conclusion from the research was that teachers could learn to provide effective instruction in comprehension strategy development, but this required moving away from traditional notions of how to foster comprehension and away from heavy reliance on the teacher guides that accompanied the textbooks that were frequently used in classrooms. In other words, most "lessons" offered in the teacher guides in reading, social studies, and science texts were designed more *to assess* student recitation proficiency than *to improve* that proficiency. The lessons focused more on immediate recall of the information than on the development of transferable strategies that promoted independent use of effective thinking while reading. The teacher guides were chock-full of activities but most would provide the teacher only with information on who was able to recall information from the story being read.

As Dewitz and colleagues (2009) recently noted, "The large numbers of skills and strategies taught in the core programs means all get superficial treatment, often demanding one skill a week" (p. 120). This is in contrast to research studies where often a single strategy is the focus of several weeks of instruction or more. The authors note that the reading comprehension found in core reading programs reflects little of what we know about effective reading comprehension development. They write, "Fidelity to a flawed program is not a virtue" (p. 122).

For instance, teacher guides were filled with questions to ask students—questions for oral interrogation, written end-of-chapter questions, worksheets and graphic organizers to be completed, and so on (McGill-Franzen et al., 2005). In fact, one recent analysis reported that the number of "mindless, useless activities" was staggering. Crossword puzzles, hidden word searches, and vocabulary definition tasks all frequently accompanied the steady stream of low-level questions offered for students to answer. But all these tasks simply assessed whether or not students could adequately respond. Rarely was there any instructional component unless individual discovery learning was counted as instruction.

It wasn't just the teacher guides that accompany textbooks that reflected this lack of instruction; some of the most popularly used materials and activities offered no instructional component either. For instance, the *Barnell-Loft* materials (find the Main Idea, Levels A, B, C . . .) provides nothing but activities that assess student strategy use. I call these "assign and assess" materials because no instruction is provided. Unfortunately, the textbook teacher guides and many popular comprehension curriculum materials rely on the student acquiring useful strategies through self-discovery. But many students seem not to discover these strategies without teacher demonstration.

A third conclusion from the research was that strategy learning took time. The most successful interventions developed strategy use through longer-term instruction and repeated application activity. Whereas the traditional "main idea" lesson in a teacher guide, for instance, might last one day or, in some cases, one week, effective strategy teaching often offered 10 weeks to one year of focused instruction and application of main idea comprehension strategies. Whereas the teacher guide lesson focused on a definition (A main idea is an important idea), the effective strategy instruction focused on the thinking that students needed to apply while reading. (Summarizing involves two key strategies: selecting important ideas and deleting trivial, redundant, and unrelated ideas.)

Unfortunately, the lesson design in teacher guides moved quickly from definition to assessment and most of the suggested activities were assessments as opposed to instructional activities (questions about main idea, worksheets requiring identification of main idea, graphic organizers to be completed, etc.). On the other hand, the effective comprehension strategy lessons immersed students in teacher demonstrations of the thinking, the strategy-in-use, and the application of the strategy repeatedly across a number of different texts. After the longer-term focus on effective strategy use, substantial improvements in comprehension were typically demonstrated. The greatest improvements were often found among the lower-achieving students.

A fourth conclusion from the research was that there were only a handful of strategies that seemed apparently central to improved school comprehension performance. (Six research-based strategies are provided in Figure 5.1.) Remember, though, that these were the strategies that (1) demonstrated value in multiple research studies and (2) improved performance on traditional school comprehension tasks. In other words, some of the strategies may be of more use when lower-level comprehension—recitation, for instance—is the goal, than when higher-order comprehension, thoughtful literacy, is the desired result. But also remember that thoughtful literacy requires at least some recall of the text, though not necessarily the ability to recite all of the details. In my view, the research summaries provide enormously useful guidelines for initiating instruction that leads to the development of thoughtful literacy. At the same time, I feel the research studies summarized in these reviews typically emphasized improved recitation, a necessary, perhaps, but still low-level indication of understanding of texts read.

FIGURE 5.1 Useful Research-Based Comprehension Strategies

Activating prior knowledge. It is important that students develop the habit of reflecting on what they already know about a text or the topic of a text before they begin reading. In classroom practice, activating prior knowledge is often linked to developing predictions about the text content before reading.

Summarizing. This is perhaps the most common and most necessary strategy. It requires that the student provide a general recitation of the key content. Literate people summarize informational texts routinely in their conversations. They summarize weather reports, news articles, stock market information, and editorials. In each case, they select certain features and delete or ignore other features of the texts read.

Story grammar lessons. The use of a story grammar framework (setting, characters, problem, attempts at problem resolution, and resolution) is one of the most commonly researched instructional techniques. The goal of story grammar lessons is helping students develop adequate summaries of narrative texts. *Adequate* is defined largely as a recitation of the key elements of the story—the story grammar elements listed previously.

Imagery. Two broad types of imagery strategies have been studied. First, fostering an internal visual image of aspects of the setting, characters, and events offered in a text. The lessons were designed to help students create a visual image of what a character looked like (tall, blond, agile, 20-something) or of a setting (a prairie sod house or the floor plan of the heroine's apartment). The second sort of imagery strategies were helping students manufacture a distinct mnemonic image to facilitate recall (imagining your friend Dan on an inner tube floating by Budapest ("Dan-in-tube") to remember Danube as the name of the river).

Question generating. This research had students develop questions about the text as they read. There have been a number of twists on this technique ranging from developing "teacherly" questions (What question might your teacher ask about the information in this paragraph?), to author-purpose questions (What was the author trying to convince you to believe?), to text adequacy questions (What else should the author have explained if he wanted you to understand this chapter?).

Thinking aloud. These studies sometimes focused on having the teacher "think aloud" as a technique for demonstrating the thinking strategies good readers use (After reading a particular sentence aloud to students the teacher might say, "As I read this sentence I thought to myself, this doesn't make any sense because . . . ") and at other times on the effect of having students think aloud as they read. A key aspect of this technique seems to be the intent to promote in students the sort of internal dialogue that good readers use as they read. That is, as you read this text you think to yourself about what you are reading. You make connections to other things you've read and to your own experiences as a reader and as a student and, perhaps, as a teacher. (Perhaps right now you are thinking, "Yeah, I agree with Allington on that. I do think to myself as I read." Or "Is he crazy? I don't 'think to myself,' I just try to remember what he writes for the test.") However, use of the think-aloud techniques was often linked to developing other strategies (The teacher says, "When I read a story I pay attention to the setting . . .").

Finally, Almasi and colleagues (2005) found that a rigorous review of qualitative research on comprehension suggested that the National Reading Panel (2000) report that emphasized the need for improved comprehension strategy instruction was on the mark. But the qualitative studies suggested another complexity that was less emphasized in the experimental work reviewed by the NRP. Successful comprehension strategy instruction involved teaching students "bundles" of strategies rather than treating the strategies as isolated skills. In other words, comprehension tasks such as summarizing involve a number of strategies and might include imagery, activating background knowledge, paraphrasing, topic importance assignment, deletion of redundant information, and so on. The qualitative studies suggest that attempting to teach "a strategy" and then another and another is likely to be less successful than an approach that focuses on strategy integration.

Summary

The research on comprehension strategy teaching provides powerful evidence that most struggling readers (and many not-so-struggling readers) benefit enormously when we can construct lessons that help make the comprehension processes visible. Many students only develop the strategies they need with much instructional support. Few reading intervention programs address comprehension and many focus instead on developing decoding proficiencies. Unfortunately, perhaps, fewer than 10 percent of struggling readers have decoding problems. Put another way, struggling readers know more about decoding than they know about successful comprehension. More work on decoding doesn't address the basic problem many struggling readers exhibit: weakness in understanding what they read. Traditional "assign and assess" lessons (read the chapter and answer the questions at the end) offer little useful assistance for these students. Instead of "assign and assess" lessons, these students need demonstrations of effective strategy use and lots of opportunities to apply the demonstrated strategy over time.

Vocabulary Knowledge Is Important for Thoughtful Literacy

Knowing lots of words and their meanings is an important component of thoughtful literacy. Wide, independent reading has been shown to be the most critical factor in acquiring new word meanings, as Stanovich and colleagues (1996) have demonstrated the importance of reading volume, or the lack of it. They concluded, "Inadequate exposure to print prevents children from building important knowledge structures such as vocabulary, metalinguistic knowledge, and general world knowledge. These knowledge sources are necessary for efficient reading comprehension at the more advanced levels" (p. 29). So expanding volume of reading, as suggested in the previous chapters, is a good first step to increasing knowledge of word meanings.

But we can accelerate vocabulary growth by focusing attention on words while students are reading and by teaching some words directly. In this section I describe several instructional strategies for both situations. I would recommend *Bringing Words to Life* (www.guilford.com) by Isabel Beck, Margaret McKeown, and Linda Kucan (2002) and Cunningham's *What Really Matters in Vocabulary* (www.pearsonhighered.com/educator) for an in-depth plan for developing vocabulary.

Focusing Attention on Words

Although wide reading is important, it has been estimated that the meanings of only 10 to 15 of every 100 new words encountered will be learned from exposure in context (Nagy et al., 1987). This is the case because authors often assume readers will know the meanings of the words they write and so provide little contextual support for determining their meaning. In addition, too many students have not developed useful strategies for figuring out the meaning of an unknown word they encounter while reading, which often seems the result of having had little instruction on such strategies.

Beers (2003) provides four types of clues that readers might use to figure out the meaning of an unknown word. She begins by looking at the definition clue. Authors often introduce a new word and then define it. For example, an author might write, "Cowboys often wore chaps, leather trousers without a seat, over their pants to protect their legs from thorns." But not all students know how to use such definitional clues. Some simply think that cowboys wore something called chaps and also wore leather trousers without a seat. This, Beers notes, gives them a very different meaning for riding bareback.

Authors also provide restatements of information, typically using a more common vocabulary. For instance, "The soldiers *looked haggard* after the long march from Fredericksburg. General Hooker decided that these soldiers were *too tired* to begin an assault that day."

Another strategy authors use is to provide a contrasting, but more common, word to help explain the new word: "General Lee was *fastidious* about his personal appearance, but General Grant was something of a *slob*." Here, students need to notice the *but*, a signal for the contrast. Even if they don't know exactly what fastidious means, they should understand that it is the opposite of being a slob.

Finally, authors provide gist clues to help with unknown words. Readers have to use the sense of the passage and their prior knowledge to figure out new word meanings. For example, "They had marched on dirt roads for three days straight with the sun, the hot July sun, beating down on them. Each man was carrying not only his weapons but supplies as well. This 60 pounds of extra weight made the marching even more difficult. And this *arduous* journey was not yet over. Two more days of marching was needed to arrive at Ford's Crossing and there was no sign that the heat was going away." Here, the reader has to put together a variety of pieces of information—the heat of the summer sun, the dirt roads, the weight of the baggage each carried, and the length of the march—in order to infer the meaning of arduous.

Showing students how to use each of these strategies is an important first step. You might begin by modeling each of these while reading aloud. Model the thinking you use (or would use if you didn't know the meaning). Then, model that thinking again with words in the texts the students are reading. After you have modeled the thinking on a number of occasions, you begin to see if the students have begun to engage those thinking strategies when they read. In this case, you don't simply ask, "Keisha, what does the word *arduous* mean?" Instead, you ask, "Keisha, can you tell us whether you were able to figure out what the word *arduous* means? Can you tell us what sort of thinking you were doing to understand that unusual word?"

In many of the exemplary teacher classrooms we studied (Allington, 2002c), we observed lots of attention being paid to developing word meanings. Some teachers helped students become "word detectives" by having them keep track of new words that they came across in their reading, usually in a notebook, on a 3" x 5" card, or on a chart posted on the wall of the classroom. The point was to celebrate new words, weird words, long words, rare words, and so on. A few minutes each day was spent having some students recount their experiences with a new word and how they came to understand its meaning. Some teachers focused more on well-turned phrases students found in their reading, especially phrases that included a new meaning for a known word or an unknown word.

Others created targeted vocabulary lists of words from the texts that students were reading and had them rate their knowledge of the word before and after they read the complete text. The rating systems were simple, often taking the form of "never heard of it," "heard of it but can't use it in a sentence," "know what it means and I think I could use it in a sentence," and "I know what it means, really." These teachers might take a few minutes after reading to have students compare their ratings and discuss whether the author was helpful in figuring out what the word meant.

Expanding knowledge of word meanings is important, and calling attention to words and to the strategies skilled readers use to figure out unknown words they encounter is a critical beginning. Ensuring all students are engaged readers, reading voluntarily in and out of school is critical for vocabulary development. But all readers, and especially struggling readers, typically benefit from a more structured vocabulary program as well.

Teaching Word Meanings Directly

Before we begin, let me note that research suggests that a reasonable target for direct vocabulary instruction might be 10 words per week. That results in about 400 new words being taught each year. But it is estimated that students learn between 3,000 and 4,000 new words each year, with the typical student knowing some 25,000 words by the end of elementary school and 50,000 words by the completion of high school (Graves & Watts-Taffe, 2002). It is obvious from the statistics that most of the words learned are never taught directly; they are learned through multiple exposures while reading extensively.

So if you decide to teach word meanings directly, how do you decide which words to teach? Beck and colleagues (2002) suggest that because there seem to be about 8,000 words that might be considered generally familiar to most elementary school students (e.g., *bed, run, dark, water, laugh,* and *principal*), we don't usually have to worry about teaching their meaning. This doesn't mean that most children can read all these words, but that they understand what the word means.

Then there is a second cluster of about the same number of words that appear with sufficient frequency that they could be targeted for direct teaching (e.g., *perform, required, absurd, errand, shifting,* and *fury*). These words will be encountered in a variety of texts and in adult conversation. Selecting these words for study involves first noting the appearance of these rarer words in a text, asking whether the author provides lots of support for determining the word meanings, and finally deciding just how important the word is to understanding the particular text.

Let's take an example from Patricia Beatty's historical novel *Turn Homeward, Hannalee.* I've underlined the words that I think might be problematic for my granddaughters, who are fifth- and sixth-graders.

> There was a wagon and a team of horses waiting for the woman who had talked to me at the ferry crossing, but she didn't offer me a ride. I didn't need one anyway. Camelton was right on the river. It wasn't a big town, but it was neat and tidy. It was filled with wood houses and shops, and wagons and buggies went up and down the streets. The folks walked fast. . . .

Because this historical novel is set in the Civil War era, I've underlined a couple of words that I'm sure the girls know but that here have different meanings than their more familiar usage (*wagon, team,* and *shops*). I wouldn't spend much time on most of those words. But I would want to pay attention to their understanding of the words if only because assigning the most common meaning to *team,* for instance, might create some confusion.

Notice that I didn't underline the name of the town, because it is largely irrelevant to the story and it is one of those words a person is likely never to see or hear again. If I were to consider teaching any of these words, I think I would pull words related to transportation of the era from the text and teach those (*ferry, buggies,* and *wagon*).

I've selected these words because the story is a historically based fictionalized account of a young white southern millworker, who at age 12 is convicted of treason and sent, along with all the other young women working in the mill, North to become indentured servants for Union families who have lost a son in the war. We follow Hannalee on her journey North and then follow her return home to Georgia after escaping from a farm in Indiana.

Selecting words from the whole book would result in a list like this: *ferry, buggy, wagon, steamboat, horseback, mule,* and *locomotive.* I might also include related words such as *depot, dock,* and *railcar.* Perhaps the simplest way to develop an understanding of transportation terms would be an illustrated book on transportation, or perhaps an illustrated book portraying the Civil War era. Students could read and review the illustrations to develop a deeper understanding of the various terms. I might ask them to arrange the transportation words in order of speed of travel and then discuss their ordering with them.

Now all of this is done for facilitating their understanding of the text as well as developing or extending word meanings. One point that seems critical to understanding this novel is the distance Hannalee traveled between Georgia and Indiana and back, as well as an understanding of just how arduous that travel was and how long it took.

There are other clusters of words in the novel that I would also identify to teach more directly. Words related to farming and millwork, or to the Civil War, for instance. But remember that we should try to teach only 10 words per week. Teaching words in related clusters makes it easier for students to remember them. In *Hannalee,* many of the words I selected are concrete words, which are easier to learn than less easily portrayed words (*dismal, vulgar, coarse,* and *traitors*).

The teaching episodes should be brief and to the point. Any middle-schooler reading *Hannalee* will encounter numerous new words and will have to use the strategies developed for figuring out the meaning of most of them. We cannot teach every word and should not spend too much instructional time focused on the direct teaching of words. But several 10-minute direct vocabulary lessons every week, along with a consistent focus on developing students' abilities to work out word meanings when they encounter new words, will be instructional time well spent.

Biemiller (2010) likewise describes a vocabulary development project with first- and second-grade students. In this project the students were taught one or two unfamiliar words before a story or book was read to them. Then as the book was being read, the teacher would stop briefly when encountering an unfamiliar word and reread the sentence with that word and then offer a short explanation of what the word meant. The teacher then continued reading the book. After the reading of the book was completed the teacher would quickly review the unfamiliar words taught that day along with the explanation of what the word meant. Later the teacher would take each unfamiliar word that had been taught, and place it in a new sentence for the students to read along with a discussion of what the word meant. They found that the meanings of roughly 40 percent of the words taught were recalled six weeks later.

What both of these instances show is that direct instruction of new word meanings has a payoff in that students recall the meanings of many of the words taught. Perhaps it seems that recall of the meaning of fewer than half the words taught may seem like the lessons were a failure. However, at the end of a school year each of these students now knows hundreds of new words they might never have learned without these lessons.

How Not to Develop Vocabulary

A number of years ago (Allington, 1987) I wrote about a boy called Jeremy. He was a middle school remedial reader in one of our observational studies. Jeremy went to remediation every day for 30 minutes. Because someone had noticed his reading achievement test vocabulary score was low, Jeremy spent each and every period working on what we called electronic worksheets. He sat in front of a computer that presented him with a sentence with a word underlined, and had to select the definition of that word from four offered choices. The computer software indicated if he was wrong, in which case he was to reread the sentence and make another choice.

On good days, Jeremy read 30 or more sentences and chose a definition, and acquired the meaning of not a single word. In most cases, the only time he selected the correct answer was when he already knew the word. This is not surprising because the sentences provided few clues about the word meaning and, even when the sentence contained a clue, Jeremy did not know useful strategies for using it.

At the same time, Jeremy encountered lots of words in his school books every day that he didn't know, but which rarely, if ever, appeared on the computer screen. What Jeremy really needed was instruction in using the clues in texts to figure out unknown words. He also needed instruction that focused on some of the important unknown words in his school books.

Unfortunately, vocabulary "instruction" of the sort Jeremy received is all too common. There are variations: Sometimes the vocabulary sentences are in a vocabulary workbook; other times the vocabulary words are simply listed on the board and Jeremy is supposed to look the words up and then copy the definitions of those words from the glossary or dictionary. There seems to be no less effective strategy for developing word meanings than these sorts of activities. Jeremy would learn more words just by reading. And he would learn even more words if he were taught how to derive word meanings in the texts he reads.

Thoughtful literacy is an underemphasized but important goal for designing reading lessons for all students. However, thoughtful literacy requires readers to have an adequate and expanding vocabulary. Poor readers often exhibit huge vocabulary deficits because they read infrequently and, when they do read, they have no useful strategies for puzzling out unknown words. We can address both problems by designing instruction that reflects what the research has to say about fostering vocabulary growth. Central to that growth is wide reading of high success texts if only because most readers develop approximately 80 percent of their new vocabulary from extensive reading.

Crafting Opportunities That Enhance Students' Comprehension and Understanding

The research points to the power of particular types of instructional environments in fostering the development of thoughtful literacy, especially in struggling readers. In this section I will sketch some of the powerful instructional activities that I believe should be available in every classroom. These are the instructional lessons that benefit struggling readers. Actually, all readers benefit, but in study after study, it is the least successful readers who benefited the most from useful strategy instruction.

There are two broad emphases discussed: Promoting comprehension in traditional school tasks and promoting thoughtful literacy. This is my arbitrary division and not one that is absolutely essential. Nonetheless, I think the evidence available suggests that lessons that foster improved recitation and lessons that foster thoughtful literacy, although sharing some commonalities, differ in substantive ways. It seems to me that the most effective instruction offers both types of lessons.

Comprehension in Traditional School Tasks

Perhaps the very first proficiency we expect children to develop (or arrive with it already developed in first grade) is summarization. At first this may be expected only after students have listened to a story read aloud to them. "What was the story about?" is the sort of query that signals the expectation that a heard or read story will be summarized. In the past three decades there has been much research on the successful use of story maps as an instructional strategy (Pearson & Dole, 1987; Pressley et al., 1990). However, much of this research was conducted using older children and using a graphic organizer. Simply put, summarizing a story for school typically has meant recalling specific story elements: setting (long ago and far away), key characters (a prince and a maiden), problem confronted (the prince is under a spell), attempts at problem resolution (the maiden kisses the sleeping prince), and resolution (they lived happily ever after). These elements were often outlined in a graphic on which children were expected to fill in the details. Instruction of the specific elements, usually with the teacher walking the children through a story and providing a model of how one would identify each element, was typically suggested. The research indicated that such lessons fostered story-summarizing proficiencies.

In one of the exemplary classrooms I have been privileged to observe, I saw a first-grade teacher use the same general format to introduce her students to the story summary process. But in this case, the teacher began the instruction during the first weeks of school—before the children could read or write much. Thus, she began with a read-aloud of *Stellaluna*. After reading that text aloud several times over several days, she gathered the students at the story carpet and told them:

> Today we are going to learn how to tell someone else what a book is all about. In school there are certain things people expect to hear when they ask you, "What was the book about?" What people expect in school is that you will tell them where the story took place, who was in the story, what the problem was, and how the problem was solved. We are going to use the book, *Stellaluna,* that I've been reading to you.

The teacher then began reading *Stellaluna* aloud again, stopping after a couple of pages. Now she noted, "Well, we know that Stellaluna is one important character in the book. So who are the other characters in this story? Who else is important in this story?" The students responded with names of the characters. She then asked, "Let's look at the pictures again from the beginning. Where does this story take place?" Students offered several answers including, "In the trees . . . In a forest . . . In the woods." "In a forest," replied the teacher, "I like that one. We'll have to remember that the story takes place in a forest with lots of trees." The teacher continued reading. After a while she again stopped and asked the students, "Stellaluna has lost her mother. I think that is the problem in this story. Do all of you agree? Would it be a problem if you lost your mother and didn't know where to find her?" Children chimed in with various sorts of assenting comments. The reading aloud then continued to the end of the book. At this point the teacher said, "Goodness, I am glad that Stellaluna solved the problem and found her mother. How about you?"

Next, the teacher again reviewed the story summary points. She then assigned one story element to the children who sat at each of the four tables in the room. One table-group drew a picture of the important characters and copied their names from the book, another drew a picture of the forest and labeled it, another was assigned to illustrate Stellaluna without her mother and to label the illustration, and the final group drew a picture of Stellaluna and her mother reunited at the end of the story. The children proceeded quickly to the tasks. The teacher moved about

This quilt-sized pictorial story map for the book Stellaluna *was a critical component in developing students' understandings of just how a "school retelling" is expected to go.*

from table to table, offering advice (usually on the labeling) and at times having students return to the text to locate the words they wanted to use.

After a few minutes, the teacher regathered the group at the story carpet and asked one person from each table to bring the group's illustration to the front of the room. She then directed the students' attention to a large piece of butcher block paper she had taped to the wall next to the story carpet area. In the center was a photocopy of the book jacket for *Stellaluna.* Now she called on a different child from each group to display and explain the group's illustration and to read the caption written by the group. The teacher taped these up on the butcher paper poster: character illustration in the upper left, setting in the upper right, problem in the lower left, resolution in the lower right. And she read the book again, this time pointing to the captioned illustrations as she read the relevant sections.

Finally (though only about 20 minutes had passed since she began the first read-aloud of the day), she reminded the students that in school people expect that we will tell about a book in a certain way. She said, "I am going to use the chart we just made to help me remember how to tell someone what the book, *Stellaluna,* is all about. So, I would begin by saying that this is a story (pointing to the illustration of key characters) about a bat named Stellaluna, her mother, an owl, and some birds. Then I would say that the story (pointing to the illustration of the forest) takes place in a forest. I would explain that the problem was that Stellaluna lost her mother (pointing to that illustration) but that with the help of the owl and the birds, she found her mother (pointing to that illustration) and was very happy again. Now let's all use the chart to tell about the book."

At this point the teacher pointed to each illustration in sequence and prompted by saying, "This is a story about . . . . It takes place in a . . . . The problem was . . . . But in the end . . . ." Throughout this sequence, the children chimed in with the relevant information. On completion, the teacher congratulated the students and promised they would return to the chart again.

Over the next few days, the teacher reread *Stellaluna* several times and used the chart as a story summary prompt or scaffold. With each rereading and retelling she offered less advice and expected the students to provide more of the information. The following week, she read another book (*Make Way for Ducklings*) and with the children developed another chart. Again she reread and they retold the story using the chart as their prompt or scaffolding. A third book was presented in the same manner. On the fourth book, the teacher read it aloud but had individual children create their own story chart on a large piece of manila art paper. Again, the placement of the story elements remained the same, starting in the upper left and ending at the lower right.

As she began this new activity, she again walked the children through the story and the elements before they were expected to write or draw. Six weeks after this activity had begun, students were creating charts largely by themselves. The teacher moved from child to child and asked them to tell her what the book was all about. Mimicking the teacher's hand movements, the students pointed to each captioned illustration as they retold the story. After about 10 weeks, the teacher had the students create the charts in their journals. By mid-year she had students creating story charts in their journals for books they had read independently—books they especially liked and wanted to remember. By the end of the year, students were sketching story charts as a precursor to writing journal summaries of books they read.

I have taken a bit of time to develop this activity because it illustrates several essential aspects of effective strategy instruction. First, the teacher provided enormous support initially. Second, she created collaborative activities and activities where children had to verbalize their thinking. Third, she provided a sustained engagement with the summarizing activity. Fourth, she gradually moved students to greater and greater independence in using the strategy. Finally, by year's end all students could produce written story summaries of the books they had read and books that were read to them.

This classroom was populated by children from lower-income homes. Many had performed dreadfully poorly on end-of-year kindergarten testing. Many seemed to have had few book and print experiences before they came to school and, unfortunately, too many had had few such experiences in a kindergarten

Wonderful Sources for Powerful Comprehension Strategy Lessons

Beck, I. L., & McKeown, M. (2006). *Improving comprehension with questioning the author.* New York: Scholastic. (www.scholastic.com)

Dorn, L. J., & Soffos, C. (2005). *Teaching for deep comprehension.* York, ME: Stenhouse. (www.stenhouse.com)

Duffy, G. G. (2009). *Explaining reading: A resource for teaching concepts, skills, and strategies* (2nd ed.). New York: Guilford. (www.guilford.com)

Harvey, S., & Goudvis, A. (2007). *Strategies that work: Teaching comprehension to enhance understanding* (2nd ed.). York, ME: Stenhouse. (www.stenhouse.com)

Taberski, S. (2011). *Comprehension from the ground up: Simplified, sensible instruction for the K–3 reading workshop.* Portsmouth, NH: Heinemann.

Tovani, C. (2001). *I read it, but I don't get it: Comprehension strategies for adolescent readers.* Portland, ME: Stenhouse. (www.stenhouse.com)

Wilhelm, J. D. (2001). *Improving comprehension with think-aloud strategies.* New York: Scholastic. (www.scholastic.com)

program that focused on a "letter-of-the-week" curriculum plan with lots of worksheets and letter-naming drills but few story or book experiences.

The children in this classroom also represented a variety of ethnic groups and cultural traditions. The teacher seemed to know that not all cultures value the same type of story summary (Au & Jordan, 1980; Cazden, 1988; Delpit, 1995). Nevertheless, there is only one way to retell a story in school. That way is well represented by the story elements strategy. It is a "just the key facts" retelling with "key" defined by the several story elements. Children who arrive at school (or first grade) with few experiences with books have had few opportunities to acquire story summary proficiencies. Children who arrive in first grade with little experience with the "school way" of summarizing stories are at a disadvantage. They remain disadvantaged unless we create classrooms that level the field by providing useful and explicit strategy instruction that develops the needed proficiencies. This classroom provides such powerful instruction. The performances of the children illustrated just how useful such instruction can be.

But it isn't just story, or narrative, summary that is important. Many students need similar lessons for summarizing informational texts and other types of reading materials. There are wonderful resources available for planning such lessons. And, of course, there are proficiencies beyond summarizing that students must develop. The key features of effective comprehension strategy teaching remain largely unchanged, regardless of the strategy to be taught.

In truth, children need to learn how to employ the several important strategies almost simultaneously as they read. In other words, as stories become more complex and present new and unfamiliar settings and eras, activating prior knowledge, visualization, question generating, predicting and verifying, and thinking aloud all become useful, necessary strategies to be implemented on appropriate occasions. Bergman (1992) describes how such strategy use is supported in a third-grade classroom in one school district that has implemented well-researched strategy instruction. She makes it clear that teachers must provide, almost continually, explicit and implicit support for strategy use. The feature box on this page illustrates a classroom chart that is posted for students in one classroom. But strategy use isn't

Questions I Can Ask as I Read

To Get the Gist of What I'm Reading:
What is the story about?
What is the problem?
What is the solution?
What do I need to know more about?

To Predict-Verify-Decide:
What's going to happen next?
Is my prediction still a good one?
Do I need to change my prediction?
What makes me think so?

To Visualize-Verify-Decide:
What does this (person, place, or thing) look like?
Is the picture in my mind still good?
Do I need to change the picture?
What makes me think so?

To Summarize:
What's happened so far?
Who did what?
What makes me think so?

To Think Aloud:
What am I thinking right now?
Why?

**To Solve Problems When
I Don't Understand:**
Shall I stop and review? Reread and look back?
Ignore and read on?
Why?

Source: Adapted from Bergman (1992).

left to the students alone. Instead, the teacher refers to the chart when working with students, highlighting the queries and strategies they might focus on, given the problem they are facing with a particular text. All this highlights the sort of self-monitoring that good readers constantly do.

Similarly, Beck and colleagues (1997) provide extended classroom examples of the implementation of a technique they call Questioning the Author (QtA). One example illustrates how a teacher and her students puzzle through a social studies book using the general QtA queries as a guide. These queries include:

Initiating Queries
- What is the author trying to say here?
- What is the author's message?
- Why is the author telling us that?

Follow-Up Queries
- What does the author mean here?
- Does the author explain this clearly?
- How could the author have said things more clearly?
- What would you say instead?

Beck and colleagues (1997) detail a classroom episode where the students were reading from their social studies textbook and encountered this passage:

Washington gave the Governor's letter to the French leader. No one knew this, but Washington made a drawing of the fort. Washington saw that the French planned to make war on the English. At last, the French leader gave Washington a message for the Governor. He said the French would not leave Pennsylvania. (p. 42)

After reading this, the teacher asked, "What is the author's message?" One student replied, "That the French aren't gonna leave Pennsylvania. They just plan to keep it."

The teacher restated the comment and then asked, "What does the author say to make Quianna think that?" Another student responded, "They were planning to stay, and I think that they're bound to have a war." The teacher restated the comment and then asked, "What do you think gave Dorelle that idea?" Another student replied, "Because the Governor knew that the French were staying because, um, I think he knew the French wouldn't just let the English have it without having a war." The teacher again restated the student comment and said, "I think Leah is right—there is too much at stake and there would probably be a war." Another student agreed, "They have soldiers, so why would they leave when they have soldiers there to fight?"

Now that the students have understood the possibility of an impending war the teacher drew their attention to that portion of the text that tells that Washington made a drawing of the fort. She asked, "Why do you think the author tells us this? What is the drawing of the fort all about?" A student replied, "'Cause when he gives the message to the Governor . . . the reason is he wants him to know what the fort looks like." The teacher again restated the student's comment and again turned the responsibility for figuring out why the Governor might want the drawing back to the students. "But why would he want to show the Governor what the fort looked like anyway?"

One student responded, "Maybe because the Governor would need to know what the fort looked like, like how big it was." Another student chimed in with, "Yeah, so when he attacked, he'd know where to attack and how many soldiers and stuff he'd need to do it."

Thus, the students are led to a deeper understanding of the implicit message in this text. In fact, Beck and colleagues (1997) continue with their presentation of this lesson segment by noting that one student commented how authors often don't tell you everything, how sometimes you have to figure out a lot all by yourself when you are reading. The QtA is a well-researched instructional technique that provides students with a set of useful thinking strategies to employ when reading. It helps students understand that an author is attempting to communicate something and that sometimes authors are not very successful in their attempts.

QtA is a powerful strategy for helping struggling readers not only better understand the texts they read but also understand that some texts are just hard to understand for any number of reasons. This "blame the author" feature—she just didn't write it very clearly—can be empowering for struggling readers.

Summary

The potential of effective strategy instruction to improve students' performance on school comprehension tasks is well documented. Unfortunately, too few classrooms routinely offer the sorts of strategy teaching that produces better comprehension. Likewise, the lessons in core reading programs offer little support to the teacher who wants to teach effective comprehension strategy use. In order to enhance reading comprehension, more children need regular access to the sort of teaching described earlier. However, a caution should be heeded: Children and adolescents also need to read a lot. Do not get so taken with strategy instruction that the classroom gets out of balance in terms of time spent reading versus time spent on the other things.

Developing Thoughtful Literacy

Thoughtful literacy is more than remembering what the text said. It is engaging the ideas in texts, challenging those ideas, reflecting on them, and so on. It is responding to a story with giggles, goose-bumps, anger, or revulsion. Earlier I discussed the notion of "literate conversation"—the sort of talk around texts that literate adults routinely engage in. It is the development of this sort of proficiency that is desperately neglected in schools today. So where to begin?

Well, we could begin in kindergarten, actually. Building on her research in preschool and kindergarten classrooms, McGill-Franzen (McGill-Franzen, Lanford, & Adams, 2002; McGill-Franzen, 2006) examined kindergarten teachers' talk around the books they read aloud. She noted that the nature of the teacher talk not only contributed to growth in vocabulary and language knowledge, but also shaped children's understandings of what it means to be literate. By helping kindergarten teachers learn to engage children in a richer talk environment during and after a story read-aloud, she demonstrated the substantial impact that such shifts can have on kindergarten children's early literacy development (McGill-Franzen et al., 1999). In this case the focus was on helping kindergarten children make text-to-self and text-to-text connections as books were read across the year. Although the elaborated book reading was only one feature of this kindergarten intervention, it was an important component in predicting whether the urban kindergartners were well prepared for first grade.

One way to begin to foster literate conversation in your classroom is to consider helping students develop the text-to-self, text-to-text, and text-to-world connections (Keene & Zimmerman, 1997). You might begin by offering your own text-to-self connections with texts you read aloud to students or even with texts they are reading (even basal excerpts). For instance, if I were to read aloud (or have students themselves read) *The Barn* by Avi (Orchard Books), I would comment on my own text-to-self experiences growing up on a midwestern dairy farm in the 1950s. Although I never attended a barn raising, as in the Avi book, I could talk about how the farmers in my rural community gathered together at harvest time to assist each other. I would tell about the meals at noon under the maple trees, about making "sun tea" and cooling the jug in a fresh water spring. I would ask students about times when members of their families or their neighbors might get together to help complete a job of one sort or another. I might ask them to compose a journal entry on this link, or to draw a picture of it and then have them describe the pictured event to a partner.

I observed one of our exemplary fourth-grade teachers make text-to-text connections as his students read a piece of historical fiction set in the era of the California gold rush. In this case he elicited a variety of connections between that text and texts read earlier, ranging from the social conditions of the era to the fact that school and schooling for children was very different in that time period compared to today. Some children noted very literal connections—the role of horses as transportation, for instance—but one commented that poverty and the hope for wealth seemed a connection that linked much of the movement westward.

In a middle school classroom the teacher connected her visit to the Gettysburg National Park with Murphy's historical book, *The Boys' War* (Clarion Books). One student connected that text to the film *Glory,* the story of the African American Massachusetts Fifty-Fourth Regiment. This led to an amazing class discussion of how it was that children their age could be allowed to join an army, and how anyone could shoot a drummer boy even if he was "the enemy." Finally, another student connected a recent TV news account of child soldiers in the Far East and Africa to suggest that "boy soldiers" weren't just a terrible historical mistake. These text-to-world connections fostered much more interesting journal responses, as well as greater student engagement in the texts being read and discussed.

Finally, in another classroom the teacher read Johnson's *Tell Me a Story, Mama* (Orchard Books) and then asked, "Does anyone in your family tell stories about growing up?" A dozen hands shot up as students wanted to tell about Uncle Jerome or Grandma Dykstra. This led to a writing activity that involved the students describing both the relative and the stories they told. These text-to-world connections produced a number of hilarious episodes that were later shared with others at their tables and in their journals.

Similarly, Duthie (1996) describes how effective having her first-grade students develop "How to" books was in fostering not only thinking but conversation as students attempted to follow the directions their peers had written. The activity also made it clear just how difficult it is to write clear directions, even for something as common as making a peanut butter sandwich or displaying appropriate manners at a wedding reception. Her lessons often focused on students' various expertise—and every student was an expert on something. Being the class expert on something allowed for all children to assume the principal role in some discussion. In other words, "Let's ask Jimmy. He's the expert on farms (or butterflies, or stomper trucks, or dinosaurs)."

Jenkins (1999) focuses on the use of one sort of text sets, in this case author studies, to foster thinking and conversation. She provides the example of students reading several books by Cynthia Rylant, along with her autobiography *But I'll Be Back Again* (Dell). Different teachers used sets of Rylant's books for different sorts of study but in each case the goal is the fostering of more literate conversation about the author and her books. But other sorts of text sets can also be useful tools for engaging students in text-to-text literate talk. For instance, one might use Hunt's *Across Five Aprils* and Beatty's *Turn Homeward, Hannalee,* to contrast the similarities and differences in young women of different circumstances during the Civil War. These text-to-text comparisons could be supplemented by text-to-self

Below these various book bin collections is a poster that provides prompts for students as they write about what they've read.

comparisons: How is your life different from the lives of these young women? Are there any similarities between your life and theirs?

Another technique for fostering conversation about texts is to provide students with "sticky note" pads to use as they read (Cunningham & Allington, 2011). Those ubiquitous sticky notes can be used by students to record text-to-self, text-to-text, or text-to-world connections as they read. The technique requires that students are first familiar with the text-to-_____ connections process. The method of making connections to text should first be introduced and practiced for a time conversationally. Once familiar, the students simply use the sticky notes to record when they make the connections while reading. I would have them use the simple abbreviations of *ts, tt,* and *tw* to represent the different types of connections. They might also jot a brief comment on the note to remind themselves later of the connection they made. What makes sticky notes especially useful is that they allow students to "mark" the connections in their copies of the texts, which makes it easier at a later discussion group to reactivate the connections that were made.

Literate Conversations

Finally, we come directly to a topic I have indirectly addressed throughout this chapter: literate conversations. Consider that there is little research that supports the too common classroom scene where every child is working on the same low-level worksheet, alone. If we want to foster thoughtful literacy, then classrooms must become noisier places than most I visit. Noisier because conversation is noisier. Noisier because learning is noisier.

A good first rule of thumb at creating a conversational classroom is this: *Never ask a question you already know the answer to*. In other words, ask children only authentic questions. A second rule is this: *Never ask questions that can be answered in one word*. For instance, here are the sorts of questions we observed the exemplary teachers asking children before, during, and after they had read a text.

What do you think this book/story is about?

Why did you select this book/story to read?

Was there anything/anyone you wanted to know more about?

Did it remind you of any other book/story that you've read?

What did you think about when you finished the book/story?

Who else do you think might like this book/story?

Remember that these questions are just a few of the questions that teachers asked to get a conversation going. In each case a teacher would likely expect different answers from different children. None of these questions lend themselves to a simple "Correct" response from the teacher. Most of these questions will lead to another follow-up question or the possibility of a challenge from another student who will have a different answer. But that is the nature of literate conversations.

Literate conversations do not have to begin with a teacher question. They might begin with a teacher (or student) comment about what is being read. What we heard in the classrooms of exemplary teachers were phrases and tags such as the following:

Did anyone else notice . . . ?

How could we check that?

I wonder whether . . . ?

Are there any other ways we can think about that?

Why would an author . . . ?

Johnston (2004) documents the sorts of conversations we heard and notes how these teachers created *collaborative* classrooms, not *competitive* classrooms. By this I mean that students were prompted to assist each other in understanding a text. They were not competing to see who could come up with the "right" answer.

In the end we need to work harder at creating more conversational classrooms. We can begin by trying to limit the amount of interrogation we do, such as asking fewer questions to which we already know the answers. Literate conversations, though, are largely only possible when the text is interesting enough to stimulate

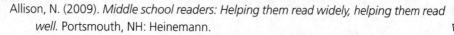

Wonderful Ideas for Fostering Thoughtful Literacy

Allison, N. (2009). *Middle school readers: Helping them read widely, helping them read well.* Portsmouth, NH: Heinemann.

Cunningham, P. M., & Smith, D. R. (2008). *Beyond retelling: Toward higher level thinking and big ideas.* Boston: Allyn & Bacon.

Duthie, C. (1997). *True stories: Nonfiction literacy in the primary classroom.* York, ME: Stenhouse. (www.stenhouse.com)

Jenkins, C. B. (2000). *The allure of authors: Author studies in the elementary classroom.* Portsmouth, NH: Heinemann. (www.heinemann.com)

Johnston, P. H. (2004). *Choice words: How our language affects children's learning.* Portland, ME: Stenhouse. (www.stenhouse.com)

Tovani, C. (2004). *Do I really have to teach reading? Content comprehension, grades 6–12.* Portland, ME: Stenhouse. (www.stenhouse.com)

Wilhelm, J. D. (1998). *"You gotta be the book": Teaching engaged and reflective reading with adolescents.* New York: Teachers College Press. (www.tcpress.com)

thinking. Too often the texts used in schools, and especially the texts used in intervention programs, are simply boring. Worse, they are not authentic texts that someone wrote to stimulate thinking. Instead, we have too many school texts that were especially written to practice a specific skill. Think about it. How many texts did your students read today that stimulated their thinking? How many questions were they asked that required them to think (as opposed to remember what they read)? The time to begin changing classroom environments and reading lessons is now.

Summary

If we wish to help children and adolescents become thoughtfully literate, classroom talk around texts is critical. Fostering thoughtful conversation often requires a rather dramatic shift in classroom practice. But proficiency in literate conversation can be developed and must be developed. I have not mentioned in this chapter the potential of activities such as Readers' Theater or other techniques that engage children in dramatic response to stories they've read, but these too can assist readers in becoming thoughtfully literate.

Summary

Let me close this chapter by simply noting that struggling readers have the greatest needs for lessons that foster thoughtful reading. It is these readers that too often are "flatliners" when it comes to reading. If we could elicit some sort of read-out of mental activity during reading, I fear that the readouts for many struggling readers would too often look like the flat EKG line so often depicted in television death scenes.

Kids need to read a lot to become proficient readers. They need books in their hands that they can read accurately and fluently and that are of interest to them. Once we have met all these conditions, we must help all readers become more thoughtfully literate. Some will need extensive assistance in this regard, in some cases because they are exposed to little thoughtful literacy at home. These are the children who depend on good instruction the most. However, all children benefit from good instruction—lessons that provide the sorts of demonstrations and supports that I have tried to describe in this chapter. For too long we have relied on the assign-and-assess lessons and provided too little useful strategy teaching and offered too few opportunities to engage in and develop literate talk. Changing in-school reading environments so that thoughtful literacy is fostered is one of the things that really matters for struggling readers.

Chapter 6

Where to Begin: Instruction for Struggling Readers

I really do wish that some "quick fix"—one effectively addressing the problems of struggling readers—had been discovered.

As far as I can tell this goal is still just a goal, but we do have good evidence that we can create schools where every child is reading on level by the end of grade 1 and remains on level through third grade (Mathes et al., 2005; Phillips & Smith, 2010; Scanlon et al., 2005; Vellutino et al., 1996). It was these studies, especially, that led Congress in 2001 to set the No Child Left Behind achievement bar such that 98 percent of all students are to be reading on level by 2014. At this time, Congress is considering reauthorizing NCLB and nothing suggests that they will lower the achievement bar. In fact, the evidence is quite the opposite. States are now competing for federal funding under the Race to the Top Act (RTTT), and central to this competition is enticing states to raise the proficiency levels that have been established for their state testing program. In addition, states are being enticed to tie student achievement gains to estimates of teacher quality. Gains will be measured by state tests of reading proficiency. All of this suggests that schools will be under continued pressure to teach virtually every child to read. Schools will have to decide whether to continue to classify children as exhibiting a disability if they have reading problems. Even if identification continues, federal law now says schools will bring these children's reading levels up to par also.

The case for the federal standards and expectations was put quite bluntly by two senior scholars (Vellutino & Fletcher, 2005), both of whom have generated hundreds of thousands of federal dollars to study learning disabilities and dyslexia. They wrote, "Finally, there is now considerable evidence, from recent intervention studies, that reading difficulties in most beginning readers may not be directly caused by biologically based cognitive deficits intrinsic to the child, but may in fact be related to the opportunities provided for children learning to read" (p. 378). In other words, their research has demonstrated that virtually all children can be taught to read, even those with a supposed learning disability or dyslexia. Their paper basically suggests that a better term to replace *learning disabled* would be *teacher disabled*. We know from other research that roughly 25 percent of classroom teachers account for 75 percent of all referrals to special education and recommendations for retention in grade. These teachers typically make multiple referrals every year and often recommend retention in grade for several pupils. Another 25 percent of classroom teachers make less than one referral or recommendation for retention per every five-year period. The remaining half of the classroom teachers refer and retain the remaining children but basically these teachers have problems with only one or two children each year.

We also know what good early intervention looks like. Key elements of researched-based interventions include:

- Improving classroom instruction
- Enhancing access to intensive, expert instruction
- Expanding available instructional time
- Availability of support for older struggling readers

In the remainder of this chapter, each of these elements will be discussed.

Improving Classroom Instruction

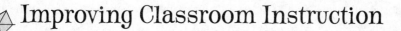

The most powerful feature of schools, in terms of developing children as readers and writers, is the quality of classroom instruction. Effective schools are simply schools in which there are more classrooms where high-quality reading and writing instruction is regularly available. No school with mediocre classroom instruction ever became effective just by adding a high-quality remedial or resource room program, by adding an after-school or summer school program, or by purchasing a new reading series. For too long we have ignored this fundamental aspect of schooling. We have added more support programs, more instructional aides, more specialist teachers, and more computers and software programs, while ignoring the powerful evidence on the importance of high-quality classroom teaching (Allington & Johnston, 2002; Bembry et al., 1998; Ferguson, 1991; Nye, Konstantopoulos, & Hedges, 2004; Pressley et al., 2001).

So how might improved classroom instruction be accomplished? In my view, it won't be accomplished by purchasing a different basal reader series or by just adding a souped-up technology component (e.g., Waterford Reading, Accelerated Reader, Fast Forward, etc.). Such tools simply will not do much to improve teaching quality, nor do they improve reading achievement (Campuzano et al., 2009). Teachers teach what they know and expanding what teachers know produces a substantial impact on students, as Linda Darling-Hammond (1998) noted in summarizing the research on improving teaching. Perhaps the most interesting recent research is that done by Scanlon and colleagues (2010). This study found that providing high-quality professional development for classroom teachers was as effective as providing expert tutorial support for struggling readers. In other words, creating more effective classroom reading lessons literally eliminated the need for specialist teachers to work with struggling readers. However, few, if any, school systems currently provide such effective professional development. Instead, these schools blame the students or their students' parents for the problem of underachievement in reading. It is now clear that we can teach everyone to read and that we can do that without adding the exepense of extra specialist teachers and their interventions.

Supporting Professional Growth

So, a good first step in developing more effective instructional programs for struggling readers is developing a plan for continually upgrading each teacher's expertise (Duffy & Hoffman, 1999). There can be few less organized aspects of education than professional development. School districts have five-year plans for replacing roofs, for upgrading athletic fields, for purchasing buses and new textbooks. But the same districts with these longer-term plans for buildings, grounds, textbooks, and transportation rarely have a five-year professional development plan—even for new teachers. Few school systems seem very concerned about professional development, even though opportunities abound for developing the capacity of teachers to deliver high-quality instruction.

For instance, in most schools teachers are in the building but not with children for two or more hours every day—before school begins, after school ends, during scheduled planning periods, and so on. In most districts little of this time is captured for professional development. Instead, most school districts schedule several professional days before the beginning of the school year and a couple during the school year—the ubiquitous Superintendent's Days—and consider this their professional development investment. Only rarely is there a comprehensive plan for targeting how these days will be used or focusing on specific instructional competencies that will be fostered—plus, teachers repeatedly complain about the ineffectiveness of such experiences. Researchers, meanwhile, routinely demonstrate the very limited impact of such activities (Birman et al., 2000). And year after year the same pattern is repeated. Yet every day, all year, teachers could be supported in their learning. It is time to rethink professional development.

Most teacher learning occurs on the job, not at workshops. My point here isn't to argue against the traditional workshop, as much as it is to argue for a much broader conceptualization of how we might foster the development of

The Impact of High-Quality Teaching

Recent studies have demonstrated the enormous impact of high-quality classroom instruction. For instance, in an analysis of the impact of higher-quality instruction, Bembry and colleagues (1998) found that students enrolled in classrooms offering higher-quality instruction achieved standardized reading tests scores after three years that were approximately 40 percentile ranks higher than students enrolled in classrooms with lower-quality instruction. In Pressley and colleagues' (2000) study of exemplary first-grade teachers, the lowest-achieving students in the exemplary teacher classrooms performed at the same level as the average students in the typical classrooms. These studies, and others like them, simply point to the incredible power of providing children with high-quality classroom instruction. In fact, both Ferguson (1991) and Snow and colleagues (1991) found that nothing was as powerful as the quality of the teacher in predicting the achievement of children. Neither parents nor socioeconomic status of the family was as powerful as good instruction in shaping the academic futures of students.

teacher expertise (Richardson, 1994; Taylor et al., 2005). Professional development should be a personal professional responsibility as well as an organizational responsibility. In other words, each teacher has a professional responsibility to continue to become more expert with every year of teaching. Each district has an organizational responsibility to support the professional development of each member of the faculty.

Every school system, or its teachers, should consider alternatives to a heavy reliance on the traditional "talking head" workshop approach to professional development. I recommend that schools support both teachers as professional education readers (TAPER) and teacher inquiry projects (TIPs).

Teachers as Professional Education Readers

In TAPER professional development, it is professional texts that become a focus for extending professional expertise. Professional books, magazines, or articles are read by the TAPER group and then discussed in a collegial setting.

During the discussion the primary focus is on responding to five questions:

- What was the author arguing for?
- Does the text seem to offer useful ideas for our school/classrooms?
- What do we need more information about?
- Who has tried to implement one or more ideas in their classroom?
- Does it make sense to support additional applications of these ideas?

As with the arguments I made about student book discussions in Chapter 5, group members discuss these questions in order to help each other develop deeper and broader understanding of the ideas offered in the books.

I would not suggest that a whole school faculty engage in a single TAPER activity. But I can see how a school might have several TAPER initiatives operating at any given point, each with perhaps three to seven members. Someone has to select the text(s) to be read. This could be a group or individual decision (assuming the group is willing to accept the decision of the selector). A period of time for completing the reading is agreed on with a completion date set. Soon after that date the readers agree to meet for a short period (say 30 to 45 minutes at the end of the school day) and talk together about the text read (Hoerr, 2009).

But how will a TAPER group (or group leader) find the texts to read? In many cases there will be more suggestions than can be easily handled, in other cases one person will have lots of suggestions, and in some cases no one will have a suggested text. The latter is especially true if the TAPER group decides to read on a specific topic (e.g., research on flunking, developing expository writing, etc.).

In the following list are several sources that might be investigated when looking for good professional books:

1. Call or visit your local professional education bookseller and ask for advice.

2. Check out the professional book review columns in educational journals.

3. Brainstorm with each other.

4. Visit websites with professional book reviews (www.teachersread.net, www.reading.org, www.ncte.org, and www.ldonline.org all offer reviews of books on literacy education).

5. Peruse the professional texts recommended throughout this book.

When recommendations have been gathered, you might want to visit websites of booksellers for additional reviews. (For instance, www.amazon.com and www.bn.com offer teacher reviews, primarily, of educational texts.) In an ideal world, school district budgets would include funds for purchasing TAPER books (Allington & Cunningham, 2006). However, not all of us work in ideal school districts (or universities). Still, I have found school and district administrators generally receptive to the idea of allocating funds for professional texts when they are approached with a TAPER project plan that indicates the books to be read and the group members. Begin small, with perhaps one book in the fall, another in spring semester, and a third to read over the summer.

Don't, however, select traditional textbooks for TAPER activities. Many texts meant for the college textbook market suffer from the same limitations that traditional content-area textbooks have suffered from—they are too broad, too shallow, and written with no voice. Luckily the past decade has seen an explosive growth in powerful professional texts that are readable, engaging, and practical. Often these texts focus on a slice of literacy and classroom life rather than attempting to cover the field, and they are frequently a bit sassier than the droll textbooks we all read as undergrads.

The goal of TAPER activities is to develop individual expertness and foster the development of shared knowledge among members of the group. Some have complained that TAPER activities are too unstructured for their tastes. I will suggest that too often too much structure—all-day workshops with one presenter for a K–12 faculty, for instance—has been the real problem. Teachers within a school differ widely in their expertise, professional needs, commitment to professional growth, and so on. It is as hard to construct a single workshop that meets the needs of all teachers as it is to construct a lesson that meets the needs of all students (imagine designing a single lesson in any subject for a K–12 group of students). Rather than considering TAPER activities unstructured, I'd prefer to think of them as targeted activities that will better meet the needs of a diverse group of professionals.

Videos of Thoughtful Literacy in Action as Professional Development

Thoughtful Reading: Teaching Reading Comprehension to Adolescents and Comprehending Content: Reading across the Curriculum, Grades 6–12. These videos feature teacher-author Cris Tovani. The four 30-minute videos take you into a high school classroom where reluctant readers are learning to be "comprehension constructors." Available from Stenhouse (1-800-988-9812), $395.00 for the set. You can view videoclips from the tapes at www.stenhouse.com.

Think Non-Fiction: Modeling Reading and Research. This 30-minute video features Stephanie Harvey and Anne Goudvis working with teacher Barb Smith in her elementary classroom. Available from Stenhouse, $95.00.

Strategy Instruction in Action. This video set also features Stephanie Harvey and Anne Goudvis working in three different classrooms. Features demonstrations of reading workshop, book club discussions, and strategies for nonfiction reading. Available from Stenhouse, $395.00 for the four-video set.

What Is Visual Literacy? This 50-minute video features Steve Moline, author of *I See What You Mean! Children at Work with Visual Information,* a one-of-a-kind text on helping students use graphs, charts, timelines, diagrams, and so on. Both the text and the video are available from Stenhouse, $95.00.

Thoughtful Literacy: Key to Student Achievement. I am interviewed in this video on the topic of thoughtful literacy and how it differs from the traditional basic literacy. Skylight Professional Development, 1-800-348-4474, $19.95.

How to Turn Wrong Answers into Learning. In this 15-minute video, elementary teachers explain and demonstrate how they use an exchange of questions as opportunities for learning. ASCD, 1-800-933-2723, $79.00.

Comprehending, Composing and Communicating. This 37-minute video models the use of instructional conversations between students and teachers. Films for the Humanities and Sciences, 1-800-257-5126, $49.95.

Teacher Inquiry Projects (TIPs)   TAPER activities can lead to an interest in TIP activities (although that should not necessarily be designed into a plan). In *You Gotta Be the Book* (Teachers College Press), Jeff Wilhelm (1997) describes in detail how his teacher inquiry project provided the understandings he needed in order to restructure his middle school literacy instruction to better serve the struggling readers he taught. His engaging book-length description of how he changed his instructional practice might serve as the impetus for others to experiment with a similar system in their classrooms. In many respects, Christie Duthie's (1996) *True Stories* (Stenhouse) is a book-length discussion of how she came to see how powerful nonfiction texts can be in developing the reading and writing of primary-grade students.

I suggest the use of teams in inquiry projects because it is through teamwork that shared knowledge is fostered and professional conversations develop (I find it generally hard to have an extended conversation with myself). Inquiry teams (even two-member teams) provide sources for reflection, revision, and interpretation of information. The old "two heads are better than one" idea seems an appropriate way of thinking about researching classroom practice or organizational patterns. And I have become convinced that local research, teacher inquiry, is a necessary component for enhancing the instructional capacity of schools. It is the thoughtful reflection on the complications of teaching the students in our classrooms that exposes quick-fix solutions as largely offering mythological advantages. The advantage of TIP activities is in the attempts to see more precisely just what the problem

Teacher Inquiry Projects Guidelines

There are several hands-on texts that provide an introduction to TIPs. A TAPER group might want to read one or more of these before beginning a TIP.

Allen, J., Cary, M., & Delgado, L. (1995). *Exploring blue highways: Literacy reform, school change and the creation of learning communities.* New York: Teachers College Press. (www.tcpress.com)

Anderson, G., Herr, K., & Nihlen, A. (1994). *Studying your own school: An educator's guide to qualitative practitioner research.* Thousand Oaks, CA: Corwin Press. (www.corwinpress.com)

Hubbard, R., Power, B. M., & Hubbard, R. S. (1999). *Living the questions: A guide for teacher-researchers.* York, ME: Stenhouse. (www.stenhouse.com)

is and to evaluate more specifically how shifts in instruction or organization impact those problems. When teams of teachers explore these questions together, a better understanding of the problems, limitations, and complexity of any proposed solutions become clearer. One result of this improved clarity can be improved instruction or improved organization of school programs.

A second argument for supporting TIP activities in the quest for improving instruction is that the most powerful source of evidence for the benefits (or lack thereof) of an instructional shift (or a shift in organizational patterns) is the data gathered by teachers in their classrooms. For instance, McGill-Franzen and colleagues (2002) describe how a teacher inquiry project that focused on the longer-term effects of retention led to a shift in school flunking practices. The availability of a considerable and consistent set of research studies illustrating the negative impact of retaining students (c.f., Shepard & Smith, 1989) was unconvincing to many faculty members in this school (as it seems to have been to governors, mayors, and other politicians). But when the longer-term impact of retention on *their* students was examined, the evidence, also negative, was considered important enough to shift away from the widely practiced tradition of flunking students.

Professional Conversation   In our research on effective schools, it has been the number and quality of professional conversations available that predicted teacher development (Johnston et al., 1998). Most of these professional conversations were private and personal, and most were one-to-one or small group conversations about teaching. In the schools we studied that had better adapted instruction to meet the needs of struggling readers, more professional conversations occurred and they involved, overall, many members of the faculty. In the schools that were floundering in their efforts to meet the needs of struggling readers, we found fewer conversations involving far fewer teachers.

So what accounted for the differences? Well, the more successful, more conversational schools had more decentralized decision making. In other words, teachers made more decisions about curriculum, instruction, and assessment—teams, clusters, committees, and task forces of teachers decided much of the what and how of instruction. In the less successful, less conversational districts, teachers were more often told what they would do—in some cases, down to which pages in which textbooks would be completed on which days.

When teachers work under conditions of low autonomy they do not seem to develop the very expertise that will be necessary to teach expertly. Under such conditions many teachers simply follow the rules and offer a standard form of instruction. But no school ever became an effective school by having teachers follow a script or having teachers provide one-size-fits-all instruction. Valencia and colleagues (2006) describe certain school environments that undid what new teachers knew how to do and how other school environments fostered greater expertise in beginning teachers. When schools offered teachers mandates of what to teach and how to teach, right down to which pages should done each day, some teachers became passive and just followed orders (mandates). These teachers took little responsibility for providing differentiated instruction, instead indicating that was the role of reading or learning disability specialists. Teachers who began work in schools where their autonomy was honored, where principals asked them what they needed to teach effective reading, not only accepted responsibility for teaching reading to every child but actually provided that differentiated instruction every day. Scharlach (2008) provides further evidence that teachers differ substantially in their beliefs about their professional responsibility. In Scharlach's case two-thirds of the new teachers she studied accepted no responsibility for teaching struggling readers. As was the case with the teachers studied by Valencia and colleagues, these teachers believed it was the responsibility of the reading and learning disability specialists to provide reading instruction to struggling readers. One-third of the teachers, on the other hand, believed it was their responsibility to teach every child to read and they provided struggling readers with the sorts of lessons they needed. The situation in U.S. schools today seems to be one in which principals and experienced teachers will need to clarify the expectations about teaching *all* children. Additionally, some teachers, many teachers in some schools, will need to acquire the expertise to provide the high-quality reading lessons that all children, including struggling readers, need.

I believe the evidence on the power of professional conversation in developing teacher expertise is sufficient to warrant initiatives that work to foster more such conversation. Although TAPER and TIP activities generate professional conversation, there are other ways to get folks talking productively with each other. Thus, the following three ideas should be considered if little professional conversation exists in your school (Allington & Cunningham, 2006).

- *Hold faculty or grade-level team meetings in classrooms.* At the beginning of the meeting, the "teacher-host" gives a 5-minute tour of his or her room. This simply involves pointing out work areas, student projects, special displays, neat ideas, and such. Then the meeting proceeds as normal. This public sharing opens the door to further conversation about the classroom environment, teaching practices, projects, and the like.

- *Hold grade-level team meetings at least weekly.* These can be before school, after school, or during a combined planning period (assuming the school has common planning blocks across grade levels). The main topic of conversation is who is doing what this week. This strategy again produces greater shared knowledge, which by itself increases professional conversation among teachers of the same grades.

- *Web-based lesson plans.* In some schools, teachers now post their weekly (or longer) lesson plans on the school's website. This is often done so that parents can access the lessons and see what sort of assignments their children have. But these lesson plans can also serve as a basis for professional conversation among teachers, especially if collegial lesson plan review or collegial planning is an expected responsibility.

Schools that improve over time foster collegial sharing and support. Enhancing the frequency and usefulness of the professional conversations in your school is a good first step to becoming a school that serves all children better.

Class Size

There is now good evidence that smaller classes, at least in elementary schools, make better teaching possible. This is the primary reason why children in smaller classes demonstrate higher achievement (Achilles, 1999). But smaller classes with more expert teachers in better organized schools produce higher achievement than smaller classes with less expert teachers in schools that are badly managed. Smaller classes produce larger achievement gains in children from low-income families than with more advantaged children—not a surprising finding.

If schools are to develop high levels of reading and writing proficiency in virtually all children, then funding schools so that class sizes of 20 or so are common would be a good first step. But smaller classes are even more effective when the teacher is more expert about teaching children to read and write.

At the same time, remember that the effects of individual teachers was two to three times as large as the effects for smaller class size (Nye et al., 2004). In a world driven by research findings schools would be investing at least as much money in teacher development each year as it would cost to lower class sizes. This is because, in the end, the reading growth of pupils is largely a function of the quality of the reading lessons they offered. Small classes is a good idea, but more expert teachers is an even better one.

Access to Appropriate Instructional Materials

Effective instruction is characterized by adaptation of the standard form of instruction in ways that better meet the needs of individual students. For example, too many curricular plans are organized around the single-source curriculum material. In these plans every student has the same curriculum materials, regardless of her or his level of proficiency. In reading plans of this sort, every child reads in the same basal reader or the same trade book; in social studies plans of this sort, every child reads from the same social studies textbook; and in spelling, every child works with the same spelling book. I know of no evidence that suggests that any curriculum plan that had all children working in the same books all day, all week, all year, ever produced high achievement in all children, or even in most children (Allington, 2007).

A key to effective classroom reading lessons is finding books that fit the various children. Chapter 3 provided an extensive discussion of the scientific research available on the importance of this principle. Developing expertise in fitting the books to children might be one important focus of professional conversations. Most teachers have received some initial training on how to assess the match between books and children, but they have often worked in schools where the organizational mandate was the single-source lesson plan—everybody in the same book. When confronted with 25 students and 25 copies of the same text- or trade book, it isn't surprising that few teachers seemed to use the book-matching skills they had learned. So, we might begin by focusing on supporting teaching within a multisource, multilevel lesson plan.

I will repeat: Although school plans might have some common texts that all students use, my advice is that common texts—single-source lessons—be used no more than 20 to 30 percent of the time. And when common texts are used, teachers must still adapt instruction so that these texts are accessible to all students. There are a variety of techniques that teachers can use to this end: Shared reading, reading the text to students as they follow along, audiotape recordings of the texts, and so on, can work to enhance the usefulness of more difficult texts to lower-achieving students. But all students need books in their hands most of the day that they can read, accurately, fluently, and with comprehension.

Supplying classrooms with books that fit the students may not necessarily require more money to be spent on texts. When schools adopt the book room plan, easy access to a large supply of different texts becomes economical. When schools order fewer copies of a larger number of texts, variety is increased while expenditures are not. But when education dollars are allocated to purchase 100 copies of single fifth-grade basal or social studies text, there is often little money left to expand the supply of texts available. Likewise, when every fourth-grade teacher receives 25 copies of the same four trade books, there is often little money left to expand the variety of books. Thus, a first step in creating effective, adaptive classrooms is planning for using available funding to enhance the variety of texts available. We should not be surprised to find teachers planning single-source lessons if the school has allocated its funds to fill every classroom with multiple copies of the same book.

Honoring Instructional Time

So once we have the variety of texts needed to plan multilevel, multisource lessons and once the teachers have refined their fitting techniques, we can get on with effective teaching. But such teaching will also take time—blocks of uninterrupted time. The school schedule may need adjustment so as to capture as much of the academic time as is possible. If we can organize schools intelligently and protect every minute of official instructional time—no attendance taking; no milk, lunch, book, or candy sales money collecting; no public address announcements; no unpacking or packing up to leave during the instructional day—we can expand the time teachers have to teach well.

Summary

All this seems minimally necessary in order to create effective classrooms. Teachers need support in order to become more expert with every year of teaching. In my view it is an organizational responsibility to provide such support every single day of the school year. Similarly, teachers cannot be expected to adapt and differentiate their lessons if they are provided with lots of copies of a single text and almost no other books. Nor can teachers be expected to design school days so that much reading and writing is accomplished if they have few books and an instructional day that is effectively reduced in length by bad organizational plans that nibble away, and sometimes gobble up, instructional time. Schools must be organized so teachers and students have every possible minute needed for instruction. None of this is rocket science; all of it is based in scientific studies of effective schools, classrooms, and teachers.

Enhancing Access to Intensive, Expert Instruction

Once we are satisfied that the basic organizational responsibilities for creating effective classroom instruction are in place (appropriate teacher expertise, multiple curriculum materials, effectively operating school schedule, and reasonable class size), planning for enhancing students' access to additional intensive, expert instruction is the next logical step. It makes little sense, however, to focus on this aspect of schooling without also focusing on effective classroom instruction. The purpose of support programs offering intensive, expert instruction should be to meet the needs of those children who will need more than effective classroom teaching in order to learn to read well. If ineffective classroom instruction is contributing to the problem of low achievement, fix that problem directly. Support programs should not be viewed as a way of bypassing the problem of ineffective classroom teaching. But even with effective classroom instruction, it is likely that a few students will need more expert and more intensive instruction than we can expect classroom teachers to provide.

We can expect that classroom instruction will be adapted to better meet the needs of low-achieving students. Such adaptations will be helpful, but often they are insufficiently intense or insufficiently expert to accelerate struggling readers' reading development.

Intensity

I think of intensity primarily in terms of teacher–pupil ratio, scheduling, and pacing. On the first feature, tutoring tops the intensity scale. Very small group instruction comes next in intensity. The evidence available indicates that both tutoring and very small group instructional support is more commonly effective than the traditional larger group (four to seven students) remediation (Allington, 2004a; Camilli & Wolfe, 2004; Shanahan, 1998; Wasik & Slavin, 1993). Daily support lessons are more likely to impact achievement than lessons scheduled less frequently. Tutoring or very small group lessons that are paced to take advantage of every minute of time available are more effective than lessons that doodle along.

Although tutoring has a long history, its potential for accelerating the literacy development of struggling readers seems too often overlooked. In the Camilli and colleagues' (2003) reanalysis of the research reviewed by the National Reading Panel, tutoring was found to have a greater impact on reading development than systematic phonics instruction. A recent meta-analysis of 36 studies of Reading Recovery (D'Agostino & Murphy, 2004) found that this tutoring program brought struggling readers up to the reading level of their classmates in a short period of time. They concluded, "It seems that RR was reaching its fundamental goal of increasing the lowest performing first-graders' reading and writing skills to levels comparable with their classroom peers" (p. 35). The federal What Works Clearinghouse (www.whatworks.ed.gov) agreed: Reading Recovery was the only reading program (out of 150+ reading programs studied) awarded the ranking of "strong research evidence" supporting its use to foster reading growth.

Interestingly, I noted that the very studies that are often cited as the evidence that supports the No Child Left Behind (NCLB) goal of all readers reading on grade level *all employed tutoring,* some for as long as 2½ years (Allington, 2004a). In these studies, about half of the tutored students achieved grade-level reading proficiency, but almost all moved closer to average achievement. However, I also observed that implementing tutoring on the scale found in these studies could cost as much as

$250,000 per school and noted that no legislation provided funding of this sort. Nonetheless, the evidence is clear that expert tutoring is a powerful intervention that needs to be made available more often.

In general, we might consider the following guidelines when designing interventions for struggling readers. First, the research demonstrates that as the expertise of the teacher/tutor increases, so does the likelihood that the intervention will accelerate reading development. Second, the research also indicates that as the size of the instructional group decreases, the likelihood of acceleration increases. Thus, the most effective designs employ the most expert teachers and have them tutoring or working with very small (two to three students) instructional groups. The more needy the readers, the more benefits that accrue from providing expert, intensive instruction (Wasik, 1998; Wasik & Slavin, 1993).

Thus, if I were to develop an intervention plan that provided struggling readers with more intensive instructional support, I'd organize the intervention around these principles. But for such a plan to work, classroom instruction would have to be genuinely effective for most students, including the struggling readers. The intervention wouldn't replace ineffective classroom instruction but would expand on effective classroom lessons. Struggling readers need good instruction all day long.

One substantial shift that is needed immediately in most schools is redesigning the use of instructional support personnel such that intensive interventions can be offered. In too many schools for too many years (Allington, 1987), the reading specialists, resource teachers, speech therapists, and special program paraprofessionals have been assigned to work "nonintensively" with kids who need intensive interventions. In other words, I commonly see reading specialists working with 50 or more students a day in groups of 7 or more children. These groups meet briefly—30 minutes seems common—every other day or so. The same pattern is often repeated with special education teachers and other specialists. But one reason such plans hardly ever produce the sorts of gains we need is that the intensity is so low that little benefit can be expected.

Instead of working all year with 50 students in large groups (5 to 9 kids) for a few short sessions each week, consider restructuring the work assignments so that more intensive interventions of less than a year's length are offered. For instance, offer half the students twice as intensive instruction for a single semester. Or offer half a 10-week more intensive intervention and then 10 weeks off, followed by another 10-week more intensive intervention. Even Individual Education Plans (IEPs) required for every pupil with a disability can be written to support interventions that offer greater intensity of this sort (300 minutes weekly for a semester rather than 30 minutes daily all year).

Key to more effective support programs is the likelihood that participation will provide access to expert, intensive instructional support designed to quickly accelerate literacy development. Research (Mathes et al., 2005; Phillips & Smith, 2010;

Response to Intervention (RTI)

In 2004 Congress passed legislation that allows states and schools to identify pupils with a learning disability in a new way. The approach the federal education agency now supports is called Response to Intervention (RTI). The RTI program is a general education initiative that is to be funded, at least in part, by using 15 percent of a district's special education funding. That is, general education personnel simply remove those funds from the special education funds and use the money to begin to fund the RTI process. That procedure is reasonably simple. Schools would provide additional, expert, intensive reading instruction for children struggling with reading. Response to Intervention programs would typically begin in kindergarten and provide at-risk kindergarten students with tutorial or very small group reading lessons. In fact, to date there are few published studies of the RTI process above grade 3. Most typically these lessons would be taught by reading specialists. If providing this instruction does not accelerate reading development after a year or two, then the child would be identified as exhibiting a learning disability. Here are a few recent books on RTI that may be useful in designing your RTI plan.

Allington, R. L. (2009). *What really matters in response to intervention: Research-based designs.* Boston: Allyn & Bacon.

Howard, M. (2009). *RTI from all sides: What every teacher needs to know.* Portsmouth, NH: Heinemann.

Johnston, P. H. (Ed.). (2010). *RTI in literacy: Responsive and comprehensive.* Newark, DE: International Reading Association.

Scanlon et al., 2010; Vellutino et al., 1996) demonstrates that such intensive interventions work faster and more reliably than the longer-term, less-intensive interventions that now dominate school programs. Some students will need instruction at a level of intensity that is difficult, if not impossible, to provide in the classroom. Rethinking how we design remedial and special education support is needed in most schools.

Expertness

Every school needs teachers who are more expert on some topics than most teachers. We cannot expect every classroom teacher to be expert on every relevant educational topic. Thus, schools will always need some teachers who are more expert at sorting out why Brittney is struggling with learning to read, even with good classroom teaching, or why Keyshaun has such a difficult time with fractions, or how to help Dom control his anger.

However, consider this: If Dom's anger comes from sitting in a classroom in which he is confronted all day every day with work he cannot do, then the specialist should not be working with Dom but with his teacher. Dom's anger is justified, and if we don't solve the classroom problem that Dom is facing, then we can expect to see more and more children who need anger therapy. In too many schools, the expert teachers are working with the wrong clients—the kids instead of the teachers. In my view, if the expertise of a reading specialist, a Reading Recovery teacher, or a resource teacher has little impact on improving the quality of classroom instruction across the school, then the expertise is largely wasted. If instructional expertise available in any school does not improve the classroom instruction, then it is typically uneconomical.

We do not need experts who just fix kids and return them to ineffective or inefficient classrooms. Sending a fixed student back into broken classrooms just means that the student will likely need fixing again. Often, the student never gets fixed, even though he or she was provided with the usual low-intensity support instruction. Unfortunately, that common finding in the research on remedial and special education programs is not difficult to explain (Glass, 1983).

In too many schools the remedial and special education programs are designed so that it will be unlikely there will be any large impact on struggling readers' achievement. Add to that the unfortunate fact that many children served in these programs languish daily in classrooms with no appropriately adapted instruction, and it is not difficult to see why remedial and special education interventions have often not worked to accelerate the reading development of struggling readers (Allington & McGill-Franzen, 2009; O'Connor et al., 2002; Puma et al., 1997; Vaughn & Linan-Thompson, 2003).

In school designs in which too many students are scheduled for special instruction for too little time, reading specialists and resource teachers often simply cannot act on their expertise because the limited contact with large numbers of students means it is unlikely these support teachers know any of their students well. And knowing your students well is critical to good teaching. Many support teachers work with students from 12 to 20 classrooms, making coordination with the classroom instruction difficult and collaborative planning with the classroom teacher almost impossible. My point here is simple: We can design interventions that are expensive and unlikely to work, even when the intervention personnel are quite expert. Not only *can* we design interventions that are unlikely to be successful, but many schools *do*.

In addition, we often design interventions where the important role of instructional expertise is largely ignored. The now widespread practice of employing paraprofessionals to work with struggling readers is one example of this. There is much evidence that paraprofessionals' lessons rarely exemplify even modestly effective

Who Are Reading Coaches and What Do They Do?

With the implementation of NCLB, many states have moved in the direction of encouraging schools to employ reading coaches. However, to date only a few studies of well-designed coaching projects have been published (Sailors & Price, 2010). There is a small body of evidence focused on the key characteristics of a good coach, but not much evidence that employing coaches who fit that model reliably improves student reading achievement. Nonetheless, the International Reading Association (www.reading.org) provides reasonably clear guidelines on the qualifications for reading coaches.

- Reading coaches hold a reading teacher/specialist certificate.
- Reading coaches are excellent teachers of reading, preferably at the levels at which they are coaching.
- Reading coaches have in-depth knowledge of reading processes, acquisition, assessment, and instruction.
- Reading coaches have expertise in working with teachers to improve their practices.
- Reading coaches are excellent presenters and group leaders.
- Reading coaches have the experience or preparation that enables them to model, observe, and provide feedback about instruction for classroom teachers.

The International Reading Association statement then goes on to note that no single role definition currently exists for reading coaches, but there is agreement around the central theme that it is the in-class instructional coaching provided by coaches that distinguishes coaching from other roles. However, it is common to find coaching definitions that include various other professional development roles as well (e.g., developing and delivering workshops, organizing TAPER and TIP groups, managing grade-level team meetings, etc.). For a concise article on coaching, go to www.edletter.org/past/issues/2004-ja/coaching.shtml.

instructional practices and much evidence that, because of this, struggling readers rarely make much progress when instructed by aides (Allington, 1991; Gerber et al., 2001; Rowan & Guthrie, 1989). In fact, the research on the use of paraprofessionals is an example of how expensive a bad idea can be. But the numbers of paraprofessionals employed in remedial and special education programs has continued to rise.

Meanwhile, data from the National Center for Education Statistics (2004) indicates that there are only enough certified reading specialists to place one in every tenth school! One would think that any school system serious about improving reading outcomes would employ one or more certified reading specialists. Instead, schools employ certified teachers, but not reading specialists. Schools employ paraprofessionals, but not reading specialists. Schools employ special education teachers, most of whom have but a single course in teaching reading, but not reading specialists. I could go on naming the folks schools employ but my point is this: Someone in every school needs to have developed the types of expertise commonly associated with earning the reading specialist certification.

Finally, instructional support programs must work to enhance the likelihood that participating students receive larger amounts of appropriate instruction across the school day. In order to achieve maximum progress, students need appropriate texts in their hands *all day long,* not just when they are participating in instructional support programs. Thus, one other role for reading specialists is assisting classroom teachers in locating texts of an appropriate level of difficulty for use in classroom reading, science, and social studies lessons.

Summary

Some students need more expert and more intensive instruction in order for their learning to keep pace with that of other children. Schools must enhance classroom instruction so that the number of struggling readers is minimized and then put into place an organizational strategy that ensures that the children who need intensive, expert instruction receive it. Ensuring that such services are available will not necessarily be any more expensive than current, less effective, less intensive efforts. The research demonstrates just how powerful expert tutoring is (Camilli et al., 2003; Mathes et al, 2005; Phillips & Smith, 2010; Scanlon et al., 2005; Vellutino et al., 1996). Effective interventions that solve the problems of struggling readers are inexpensive in the long run when compared to less intensive interventions that produce only modest gains. This is the potential of the Response to Intervention (RTI) legislation, but it will be up to schools to implement RTI plans that accelerate reading development, beginning with interventions in kindergarten.

For instance, much concern about the role of the development of phonemic segmentation in beginning reading has been offered in both the public and professional media in the past few years. My interpretation of the research suggests that although most children develop adequate phonemic segmentation in the course of routine beginning reading instruction, a small proportion of students fail to acquire the understandings and strategies that underlie this skill. These students do not seem to acquire phonemic segmentation from classroom lessons and this lack of development seems powerfully related to their difficulties in learning to read. But the research also points to the power of tutorial and very small group instruction offered by an expert teacher in fostering the development of this important skill. In other words, most of the children who fail to develop this skill will develop it with only a few weeks (6 to 12) of appropriately intensive, expert intervention (Torgeson & Hecht, 1996).

What this suggests to me is that schools need to ensure that (1) classroom lessons feature activities that foster development of phonemic segmentation (such as daily invented writing with application of "sound stretching" strategies); (2) an early warning system will identify those students having difficulty (perhaps monitoring their invented spelling development for evidence of phonemic segmentation); and (3) an intervention plan will target, by the middle of the first-grade year, any student who has failed to develop this skill, and will provide that student with expert, intensive instruction (McGill-Franzen et al., 1999; Scanlon & Vellutino, 1997; Snow et al., 1998; Troia, 1999).

A similar scenario for students who fail to develop self-monitoring, fluency, big-word decoding, narrative comprehension, persuasive composition strategies, and so on should be in place in every school. This sort of targeted assistance, offered more intensively, by expert teachers, should replace the currently popular plan of providing low-intensity, low-expertness, general remediation.

Expanding Available Instructional Time

A third class of intervention plans focuses on expanding available instructional time. I have seen three variations within this category. First, there are plans that add a second daily reading lesson during the regular school day. This might be offered by the classroom teacher or by a specialist teacher, and might occur in the classroom or at some other location. Second is the development of extended day programs where the extra lessons are offered in before- or after-school programs. Again, these lessons might be offered by the classroom teacher or a specialist teacher. Third are the extended week/extended school year plans. In these plans extra lessons are offered in Saturday school or summer school settings. Again, the lessons could be offered by classroom or specialist teachers.

The theory behind each of these is one that is linked to the time-on-task research reviewed in Chapter 2. Fundamentally, the argument is that some children simply need a larger amount of instruction and greater opportunities to practice reading. There is good research evidence that such added instruction can foster accelerated reading development, but, again, the most powerful extended time interventions provide more intensive, expert instruction during the added time.

Each of these three classes of extended time efforts should be part of the school plan to meet the instructional needs of struggling readers. In each case, planning such interventions around research-based principles will enhance the likelihood of success.

Adding a Second Daily Lesson

The additional daily instruction might be offered in the classroom by the classroom teacher. In some cases (Connor et al., 2007; Cunningham & Allington, 2011; Taylor et al., 1992) this might be offered while other students are engaged in self-selected reading. This seems an especially good time for students who seem unable or unwilling to read independently. But caution is needed—as you recall, the volume of reading is important and if a second reading lesson limits the quantity of reading, then the effort seems misguided. However, a second guided reading session has been shown to be useful, especially in the early grades when independent reading is more difficult because of limited reading proficiencies.

Traditional remedial reading programs were intended to provide a second daily lesson but often did not (Allington, 1987). The federal guidelines for the Title I remedial reading program have always required that the remedial lessons supplement the daily classroom reading lessons. In other words, the remediation was to be *in addition to* classroom instruction. And classroom instruction was to be adapted to meet the needs of the students who participated in the remedial reading program. A similar model guides federal plans for special education interventions. However, the research indicates that in many schools the guideline was (and still is) routinely ignored.

What Are Supplemental Services under NCLB?

In the second year that a school fails to make adequate yearly progress (AYP) under the provisions of NCLB, parents must be provided the option of enrolling their children in after-school intervention programs (and Saturday school programs, if available). Up to 20 percent of federal Title I funds allocated to the district must be used to fund the supplemental services and transportation to and from the site where those services are offered.

The rationale for mandating the supplemental services seems to set largely in the notion of expanding instructional time. That is, supplemental services as defined under NCLB extend the school day. Thus, instead of offering remedial or special education services during the day, which adds no additional instructional time, after-school programs should reliably increase the amount of instruction students receive each day.

Under NCLB, supplemental services can usually be provided by the school district or by private providers or both. When both are available, parents elect which option to use.

The most common schedule for remedial or resource room instruction has been during the classroom reading instructional period. Thus, in many cases, participating in remedial or special education programs neither increased the quantity of reading instruction nor the volume of reading (Allington, 1984b; Allington & McGill-Franzen, 1989, 1996). In addition, the research also indicated that many classroom teachers failed to offer any adaptations to the whole-class lessons that

Effective Classroom Programs for Struggling Readers

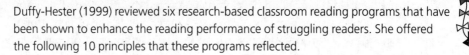

Duffy-Hester (1999) reviewed six research-based classroom reading programs that have been shown to enhance the reading performance of struggling readers. She offered the following 10 principles that these programs reflected.

- Reading programs must be balanced, drawing on multiple theoretical perspectives.
- Be sure there is a practical and theoretical justification for every component and element in the reading program.
- Teachers should teach word identification, comprehension, and vocabulary strategies explicity in conjunction with authentic reading and writing tasks.
- Teachers should read aloud daily from a variety of genres.
- Reading instruction should be informed by and based on meaningful reading assessments.
- Teachers should be decision makers, using their practical, personal, and theoretical knowledge to inform their reading instruction.
- Staff development must provide opportunities for teachers to reflect on their practice.
- Reading programs should be based on multiple goals for student success—that is, enhancing voluntary reading, discussion, genre knowledge, and other goals beyond improved test scores.
- Reading programs should provide work on multiple types of tasks and engage in multiple talk structures.
- Reading programs must be designed to support the reading growth of all children, both struggling and nonstruggling readers.

were offered. If support instruction fails to enhance the quality of classroom reading lessons and also fails to expand the amount of reading instruction, it isn't surprising that many remedial and special education programs produce only small improvements in reading, at best.

One reason that politicians from both parties voted for the No Child Left Behind Act, with its requirement to eliminate the achievement gap between various subgroups, was the 40-year history of failure of Title I and special education programs to achieve this end.

Nonetheless, it is possible to design interventions whereby a classroom teacher or specialist teacher provides a second daily reading lesson for struggling readers during the school day. To do this, however, requires making a decision about just what classroom instruction will be replaced by the remedial or special education intervention. In other words, what classroom instructional activities will be sacrificed to provide the second reading lesson? For the second daily lesson to be most effective, it cannot replace part of the classroom reading instruction.

The "After Lunch Bunch" second reading lesson occurs while most children are engaged in an independent reading activity (Cunningham & Allington, 2011). Here, a second guided reading lesson is offered. But we have to be sure that this lesson is more powerful than just reading during independent reading time. Ideally, the After Lunch Bunch varies on a daily basis with not every struggling reader attending and some not-struggling readers involved. In the Early Intervention in Reading (EIR), a second daily 20-minute reading lesson was again proven successful in raising the achievement of primary grade students (Taylor et al., 1992). In other projects, the reading teacher provides the second lesson in the classroom while the classroom teacher works with other students.

Designing Extended-School-Day Efforts

As states have raised both the achievement standards and the stakes for students (and their teachers) who don't meet those standards, there has been an increased interest in, and use of, after-school program designs in an attempt to enhance the achievement of struggling readers. There are four basic designs that seem most popular:

- *School-based remedial assistance with expert instruction.* In this design, targeted students work with reading and special education teachers for an hour or more after school to accelerate literacy development.

- *School-based tutoring from trained community volunteers, high school, or college students.* These efforts sometimes involve only once or twice weekly sessions, although some do provide daily instructional support.

- *School-based homework help/child care/recreation with paraprofessional or volunteer support.* Here, the targeted students work mostly on homework help with the addition of organized and free-play activity, with only modest attempts of instruction.

- *Community-based homework help/child care/recreation.* There are actually fewer school-based than community-based after-school programs currently operating. These programs are sponsored by the YMCA, Boys and Girls Clubs, churches, and other community groups.

It is important to acknowledge that we can design after-school programs that produce accelerated reading development. But to achieve this outcome, the program has to be well designed for that purpose. In other words, the key elements of powerful literacy instruction described in the first five chapters of this book are essential in the design of after-school programs. But to develop a powerful after-school program there are a number of other issues that need to be addressed.

Staffing   Not surprisingly, after-school programs where instruction is offered by certified teachers seem more effective in fostering achievement than programs using other staffing patterns. But most after-school programs operate with only one or two certified instructional staff members (Seppanen et al., 1993). One problem, of course, is funding, and certainly the use of noncertified staff does reduce costs. When after-school programs are focused on homework help, child care, and recreation opportunities, then wider use of noncertified staff may be reasonable. However, when accelerating the literacy achievement of struggling readers is the goal, we must be more concerned about effectiveness than costs.

There are funding sources for after-school programs that have gone largely untapped. Title I funds, for instance, were historically used to support less than 10 percent of after-school programs (Seppanen et al., 1993). Special education funds were not even noted as a source. In fact, most after-school programs were funded by parent fees. This may account for the fact that such programs are more common in higher-wealth communities than in the lowest-wealth communities (Halpern, 1999).

Flextime, another strategy for providing certified professional staff for after-school programs, seems little used (Allington & Cunningham, 2006). In flextime models, a school's specialist teachers—reading, special education, speech therapists, physical education, art, music, and computer teachers—along with other non-classroom teaching staff—librarians, counselors, psychologists—work on a different daily schedule from that which the classroom teachers follow. For instance, if the school day begins at 8:00 A.M. and ends at 3:00 P.M., then classroom teachers might arrive at 7:30 and depart at 4:00. Specialist staff, however, might arrive at 9:00 and depart at 5:30. These staff would provide the core staff with an after-school program that would run from 2:30 to 5:00 (although not all students would necessarily remain for the full 2½ hours).

Although certain staff might be providing tutorial and small group instructional support during the after-school hours, others would offer recreational activity, homework support, and general supervision. Some of the recreational activity might be linked to the reading instruction provided—for instance, art, drama, or music activities linked to books being read. Physical activity should be a regular component of after-school programs that extend more than an hour in length. The after-school program would have a variety of large group, small group, very small group, and tutorial activities occurring simultaneously.

Use of community volunteers, paraprofessionals, and high school and college student tutors are common in many after-school programs. Although Wasik and Slavin (1993) found that programs using certified teachers were substantially more effective than programs using noncertified personnel, others have reported fairly powerful results with programs staffed by noncertified personnel (e.g., Davidson & Koppenhaver, 1993; Invernizzi et al., 1997; Wasik, 1998). The key here seems to be providing noncertified personnel with strong training, structured tutorials, and ongoing supervision and support.

For instance, in the *Reading Buddies* after-school program (Invernizzi et al., 1997), community volunteers receive initial training in a four-step tutorial lesson plan. A site coordinator also provides daily lesson planning assistance for each tutor. Site coordinators are certified reading teachers and supervise no more than 15 volunteer tutors. The tutors follow a 45-minute structured lesson format that includes the following:

10 to 15 minutes of rereading a familiar book;

10 to 12 minutes of word study from a developmental spelling perspective;

5 to 10 minutes of writing for sounds; and

10 to 15 minutes of introducing a new book including an echo reading, if needed.

The coordinators select the texts for tutors and identify lesson elements that are to be worked on. During tutoring sessions they observe the tutors and later offer advice on improving their instructional activities. The *Book Buddies* program has proven quite successful as part of the Charlottesville, Virginia, schools' commitment to helping every child read on level by third grade. The gains children have made are impressive, especially those who participate in 40 or more tutorial sessions. The annual cost is estimated at approximately $600 per student served (this includes a professional wage for the supervisors and materials used).

Davidson and Koppenhaver (1993) describe another successful program that uses high school and college students as tutors in a program targeted at improving

Cautionary Advice on Extended-Day and Extended-Year Efforts

Before penalizing children by taking away normal childhood free time, it is incumbent on schools to ensure that very nearly 100 percent of the school day's instruction is appropriate to each child's needs. Creating after-school or summer school programs is professionally unethical unless we are absolutely sure that all children receive optimal instruction all year long *during* the regular school day. All of us need to focus our primary efforts on ensuring that children have access to high-quality teaching in their classrooms before we consider adding extended-time interventions.

the achievement (and ultimately reducing the dropout rate) among Native American elementary school students in a northwestern school district. The two certified instructional staff members train tutors and supervise the tutoring of the 75 or so students, mostly fourth- through sixth-graders struggling with reading. Each student receives two 1-hour tutorials each week. Tutors are drawn from local high schools and colleges, and are provided with 8 hours of training before they begin tutoring. Again, the tutoring sessions are structured for the volunteer tutors (some of whom are former tutees). Tutors work on a particular reading/spelling/writing skill with students (based on analysis of student development by supervisors) for 10 to 15 minutes, then they work on building sight vocabulary of words the student has had difficulty with for another 10 minutes; the remainder of the session is spent reading a student-selected book, often in a partner reading format, and discussing the story being read. Each student also receives approximately six books each year through the Reading Is Fundamental program. These books are often the focus of the shared reading.

Many of the most effective programs described in the literature have worked hard to create after-school programs that are not only powerful but also that do not mimic the typical school-day lessons. Students seem more often to have the opportunity to choose the material they read, they have up-close and personal interactions with their tutors, and they are more often actively engaged (as opposed to sitting alone passively completing worksheets). One potential advantage of using community volunteers and high school and college students (besides the inexpensiveness) is that these folks seem to find it easy to deliver instruction that is less formal while still powerful.

Staffing after-school programs is important, as is cost. But so is the effectiveness of the program in solving the problems of struggling readers. It seems unlikely that we will soon have the funding to provide tutoring from certified, expert teachers to every child who needs it. Therefore, one can easily understand the importance of focusing on how to create after-school programs without a full staff of certified, expert personnel.

Scheduling

At first glance this issue seems like a no-brainer: After-school programs are scheduled after the school day ends. But there are other scheduling issues to consider. Will every student be expected to attend every day, or only some days (say, Tuesday through Thursday or Monday and Wednesday)? Will different students be provided different schedules for attendance (some twice weekly, some every day)? Flexibility in scheduling should be a given, since some students would seem likely to benefit from more intensive and more frequent attendance and others might do quite well while attending less often. Will every student be tutored every day, or only some of the neediest students, with others being tutored twice a week? Will some students be tutored by expert staff and others from volunteers? How will this be decided?

How long will the after-school program run—one hour, two hours, three hours? Will all students stay the full period? What sorts of activities will be available during the after-school program? Will it begin with a large group aerobics session to allow kids to get active for a few minutes before settling in for lessons or homework help? Will there be a small snack available? Will each day include large group, small group, very small group, and tutorial sessions? For all or only some kids? Will there be active time as well as quiet time? Social time as well as academic?

I can envision an after-school program that rotates students among large group, small group, and tutorial activities throughout a 90- or 120-minute period. I can envision students selecting from art, drama, music, and physical education activities as well as choosing particular themes (e.g., pirates, mammals, mysteries, weather, comic books, scripting, etc.) about which they will read, write, and create. I can see large groups of children snuggled about with books or magazines they have selected to read for the next 30 to 45 minutes. I can see groups of five to seven students working on a script developed from a novel they've read, readying themselves for a short dramatic enactment. And all the while some children come and go from their tutoring sessions.

In short, I can envision an after-school program that accelerates literacy development by engaging students in substantial quantities of joyful reading and writing activities. But few after-school programs currently resemble my envisioned program, and I know we can do better than we typically have.

Homework

Like many parents, I worry about creating "pressure cooker" environments that rob children of childhood play time. But I also worry about children who are struggling in their attempts to learn to read—especially given the stakes that are now being tied to failing to attain grade-level achievement (e.g., flunking). Designing after-school programs that balance these concerns is important. I happen to believe that learning to read can be a joyful experience and that after-school programs need to work toward achieving this end. Thus, we have the problem of homework assigned to struggling readers. Homework becomes problematic when it is (1) inappropriately difficult, (2) incredibly boring and trivial, and (3) assigned in immense quantities (more than 30 minutes daily). Such homework becomes a problem because it often interferes with our attempts at providing high-quality instruction in after-school programs.

So what to do about homework? First, check on the appropriateness of the assigned homework for struggling readers attending the after-school program. In an ideal world, the homework will be useful and extend the learning opportunities for the student. In such cases, make time in the program for homework completion. This might be either before or after tutoring or small group instruction designed to accelerate literacy development. Homework completion can be accomplished in a larger group setting and appropriate homework should not require much assistance.

But when the assigned homework is not appropriate—too much, too hard, too trivial—then I think negotiations with the classroom teacher must be scheduled. The negotiations will differ depending on the problematic aspect of the assigned homework. Replacing the assigned homework with something more appropriate is one possibility. Eliminating the assigned homework in lieu of after-school–linked assignments is another. But spending valuable after-school-program time on inappropriate homework assignments must be avoided. Remember, homework has no research suggesting that it improves achievement—at least not below the ninth-grade level. As Cooper and colleagues (2006) noted in their review of the research on homework, "No strong evidence was found for an association between the homework-achievement link and the outcome measure or the subject matter" (p. 1). Homework is a tradition in American schools but a tradition that perhaps needs reexamination.

Summary   We have a choice: We can create powerful programs that accelerate literacy development or create something else. After-school programs need to be guided by the same principles as effective classroom programs. I would argue that access to appropriate texts, access to powerful, personalized strategy instruction, and the opportunity to select the sorts of texts to be read are critical features of the design of after-school effort to accelerate literacy development. Perhaps the best measure of the success of after-school programs is the number of children who yearn for the end of the school day so they can go to the after-school program. The nice thing about after-school programs is that they are not constrained by the same sorts of rules and regulations as the typical school-day program is—so be creative, loosen up. Remember, though, that acceleration of literacy development is the goal, but within a design that fosters engagement and joy.

Crafting Powerful Summer Programs

When thinking about summer programs it is useful to differentiate among programs designed to achieve different outcomes. For instance, if we wanted simply to attempt to stem summer reading loss—that phenomenon that seems to impact primarily both lower-achieving readers and students from lower-income communities (Allington & McGill-Franzen, 2003; Cooper et al., 1996; Puma et al., 1997)—then we might design an intervention that simply increases student access to reading materials over the summer months. We did just this in setting up spring book fairs where children from low-income families could select 12 titles that would be ordered for them. Then on the final day of school we gave these children the 12 books they had ordered. The books were simply sent home with these children—sent home to ease access to books they could read and books they wanted to read. We ran this study for three consecutive summers with children who were completing first or second grade when the study began. Our findings indicated that the children we gave the books to increased their reading skills at the same rate as children attending summer school (Allington, McGill-Franzen, et al., 2010). Given that our costs were approximately $45 per child per year, it is obvious that many schools could afford this economical and practical approach to eliminating the rich/poor reading achievement gap.

On the other hand, if we hoped to accelerate the development of reading and writing proficiency during the summer, then we would design an intervention that provided students not just reading materials but also intensive, expert instruction. And if we simply wanted to keep students entertained (or even just busy), then we might design a program with little attention to enhancing access to either reading materials or expert instruction. In addition, the design would be influenced by many of the same decisions one makes in designing after-school programs—budget, staff, schedule, and so on. The following sections will focus on the design of programs of the first two types—minimizing summer reading loss and accelerating literacy development.

Minimizing Summer Reading Loss

Researchers have noted that approximately 80 percent of the rich/poor reading achievement gap is attributable to what happens, or doesn't happen, during the summer months when schools are not in session (Alexander et al., 2007). Research has demonstrated the relationship between access to reading materials and volume of reading and the relationship between volume of reading and reading proficiency. Thus, it seems obvious that one proactive preventive measure that schools should take is to ensure that all students have access to books during the summer months. Remember that students from lower-income families are those least likely to have easy access to appropriate books in their homes (or their neighborhoods). These students generally have the most limited access to books in their schools as well (Guice et al., 1996; Neumann & Celano, 2001; Smith et al., 1997).

Access to School Library Collections

I would suggest that the least expensive intervention that a school might offer, especially a school that serves students from lower-income families, is simply to make the supply of school library books available to students over the summer. For instance, any student who so desired might be allowed to check out, say, 10 books from the school library for the duration of the summer. However, parents with few financial resources will be wary of allowing their children such a privilege if they worry about a potentially large bill should the books be damaged or lost. To combat this, schools could set up "night return" receptacles such as those found at most public libraries and video stores. Students could then return books as they were completed, which should stem losses. But I believe we worry too much about protecting books from children—allow the children to take the books and hope for the best.

A better suggestion, of course, would be to keep the school library open during the summer, at least one or two days each week. In this case, students could check out one or two books each visit, which would again minimize loss as well as provide access to more books over time. But keeping the library open during the summer adds costs not present when students simply check out summer reading books on the last day of school. Still, a handful of schools across the country keep their libraries operating during the summer months—perhaps 1 of every 100 or so school libraries, based on the responses of teacher-audiences I've asked over the past few years. But if we adopted flextime models we might close the library on Mondays during the school year and use those staff days to open the library four days a week over the summer. Thus, the school librarian would work no more days but would instead work the contractual days across the whole year, not just during the traditional academic year.

Another strategy would be to distribute classroom paperback collections to students for summer reading. You may need to open up the selection so students can choose books from all classroom libraries, which won't be a popular idea if many of the books in classroom libraries are teacher-purchased and if classroom libraries vary substantially because of that. Nonetheless, the importance of access to books is great enough to ask why any school-purchased books should remain in the building over the summer if there are students who want to read them and who have little alternative access to books.

If we were a bit more ambitious (and had a bit more money) we might consider promoting reading clubs during the summer months and organizing opportunities for students to meet and talk about the books they've read. We might link this to opportunities to perform—reenact scenes, display artwork developed from the

Creative Summer Interventions

Too often when we think of summer school, we imagine the traditional summer school with its skill-and-drill emphasis. There are alternatives to this model that have demonstrated their impact on struggling readers' achievement. Here are three of these alternatives.

1. *Ring Me Up.* Willman (1999) asked her 26 struggling readers to call her voice mail and either read to her for three minutes from a summer book or summarize the chapter they had just completed reading. She received about 100 calls, and none of the children who called registered a setback in reading during the summer vacation period.

2. *Check the Mail.* Crowell and Klein (1981) mailed 10 easy books to struggling readers. One book was mailed each week. Increases in vocabulary were found for those children selected to get the summer books.

3. *RV Reading.* Malach and Rutter (2003) focused on transitioning first-graders. They equipped an RV as a mobile tutoring center and book mobile. Any elementary student could come and select books, but struggling first-graders received one-to-one tutoring each week and were provided appropriate books to read between the weekly lessons. The RV went to five selected neighborhoods, one each day, for eight weeks. Fall testing demonstrated that 76 percent of tutored children maintained or improved their reading over the summer.

reading, or perform skits and plays motivated by the books read. We could have students post reviews on the Internet at any of the several sites that encourage such responses from young readers. Developing these ideas would be done largely at home, not at school, although in some cases the school might need to provide some of the necessary materials or equipment or a space to rehearse. Staffing could be kept to a minimum in such a design, especially if older student volunteers are available to assist younger children in their discussions and projects.

Access to Books of Their Own

Consider gifting books to children to read over the summer, ideally allowing children to choose the books they will get. Of course such a plan would require funding to purchase the books. However, with resources such as the inexpensive books distribution program, a school could provide each student with two paperbacks for a dollar or two per student. Or we could implement a summer reading program modeled after the Sweet Home, New York, school district plan of providing students with a gift certificate redeemable at a local branch of a national bookstore chain, though we might have to offer transportation to the bookstore for some children (and their parents). Each student could be asked to donate one of the purchased books back to the school after it had been read to build book collections for future use. We could encourage students to trade books with other students after they had read them to increase the number of books available to each student.

Personally, I can't imagine any better expenditure of curriculum materials funds. The huge array of books in these book superstores, when combined with their student discounts, produces a powerful setting for helping almost any child find a book that begs to be read. Imagine if on the opening day of summer school (or the day before summer vacation begins) all students were bused to such a bookstore and given such gift certificates and two hours to shop. Imagine the excitement for the student who has no books of his or her own at home, who attends a school where classroom libraries are virtually nonexistent, and where the school library is closed all summer.

There are other variations on this theme:

- The Gainesville, Florida, newspaper reported on a similar project that provided every child, all 540 of them, with a summer book on the final day of school. In this case one teacher worked to recruit donations, many from the small business community.

- A Michigan school I visited offered a book fair during the last week of school and the PTA funded one free book for every student whose parents did not send in the requested $3.

- At an Alabama high-poverty school the principal developed a "free library" at the school's entrance. Here, there was a display of paperbacks that students could just take with them as they left the building, including books for the summer from an enhanced supply provided in the final week of school. The books for the free library came from a variety of sources, including inexpensive books programs, student-donated books, teacher- and community-donated books, and purchased books.

- A Wisconsin school asked parents to donate any children's books that were no longer being used and then filled a table with the donations so that on the final day of school students could pick up two books to read over the summer. The project is so successful that the free book table is now a permanent fixture at the school entrance.

I think the evidence (Allington, McGill-Franzen et al., 2010; Kim, 2004; Kim & White, 2008) is clear that

- Some students have few books or other reading materials at home.
- Easy access to reading materials enhances the likelihood that students will read.
- Students who read more frequently become more proficient readers and writers.
- Summer reading loss is attributable, in part, to limited reading activity.

Thus, it would seem to me that efforts to increase students' access to books during the summer months would be a priority in schools where many students have limited access to books and other reading materials outside of school. Ideally, the books made available would be books that had a high level of attractiveness to target students. That is, series books, cartoon books, scary books, everyday culture books (e.g., *Scooby Doo, Miley Cyrus, NFL Superstars*), informational books, and the like may be more attractive to some children than award-winning literature (Williams, 2008). This isn't an argument to deny access to great literature, as much as it is a plea to consider student interests when planning for voluntary summer reading.

Public Libraries and Summer Reading

Since we published our first paper on summer reading we have been contacted by public librarians who ask why we don't mention public libraries as a source of books for reading during the summer. To be honest, I usually respond to such queries by noting that (1) high-poverty neighborhoods in large cities usually don't have public libraries; (2) when they do, the hours of operation are usually short; and (3) the supply of childrens' books is typically limited. Public libraries seem most available and used in middle-class communities. I wish that weren't true but I cannot escape the sad fact that libraries are located and used wherever middle-income people live. In addition to easy access, public libraries in low-income communities must rethink the rule on replacement charges for books that are damaged or lost if only because poor people don't have money for such expenses. I can imagine rich and accessible public libraries in poor neighborhoods, but today I just seldom see them.

Accelerating Literacy Development

Developing plans to stem summer reading loss seems like a good idea to me. But some students need more than this. In fact, increasingly, students are being mandated to attend summer school because their reading proficiency falls below some normative cutoff point. These students often see summer school as a personal penalty for something over which they had little control. Unfortunately, in too many cases they seem to be right. When students who find learning to read difficult attend schools where little intensive, expert assistance is provided during the school year, it isn't surprising that many end up falling behind. When falling behind means you have to forego your summer vacation, it isn't surprising that some students resent the imposition. Imagine if these new regulations included the requirement that the teachers who taught students who failed to read well enough were also mandated to attend summer school—to teach in the summer with no additional salary stipend. It wouldn't surprise me if more than a few of the teachers were disgruntled and thought this plan to be unfair.

My point here is that mandatory summer school attendance isn't the most motivating basis for showing up at the classroom door. But here is the tricky part: Summer school programs for such students need to be both engaging *and* powerfully instructional. In fact, it is difficult to achieve the latter without the former. I worry that sometimes we attend more to the engaging aspect than the powerful instruction aspect (not all engaging things are powerfully instructional—watching the Cartoon Network or Jerry Springer or playing electronic basketball, for example). Or we get caught up in the myths of skill-drill and worksheet activities. We then create summer schools that reflect the worst of traditional remedial and special education programs.

What worries me most are summer school programs that are neither engaging nor instructionally powerful. Imagine creating a summer program where paraprofessionals supervise struggling readers completing piles of worksheets or test prep and then engaging in round-robin oral reading of inappropriately difficult texts; followed by regular spelling tests on words the students can't read, much less spell; and closing with another pile of grammar/punctuation/contractions worksheets. Sad to say, but this is not a fictitious poorly designed summer school but, rather, one I had been asked to evaluate because attendance was poor, discipline problems were rampant, and, not surprisingly, little academic progress was observed as a result of participation.

I would like to think that the educator who designed this summer school was simply ignorant as opposed to mean-spirited. In my short evaluation of the program, I asked why anyone would have thought such a design would have had a positive effect on achievement. Think about the research-based principles presented in this book. Not one was represented in that summer program. So what might a research-based summer school program designed to accelerate reading development look like?

Expert Instruction Students who struggle to acquire reading proficiency need more expert instruction than other students. Expert instruction is more likely from a well-trained teacher than from a volunteer or paraprofessional. That doesn't mean that volunteers and paraprofessionals have no role in summer programs—what it means is that we cannot expect them to provide the expert instruction that struggling readers will need to accelerate their literacy development. That is, volunteers and aides might supervise larger groups of students during independent reading blocks or organize and support a Readers' Theater activity or work to help students select new books. They might even listen to younger readers read aloud, after training in the PPP (Pause, Prompt, Praise) strategy for how to listen and support that reading.

Students don't necessarily need up-close and personal expert instruction over the whole summer school day, though. Here again, we should think flexibly in the design of a summer school day. I think that a mix of large group, smaller group, very small group, or tutorial activities should be part and parcel of summer school days. For instance, in a 3-hour morning summer school day (8:00 A.M. to noon with 30 minutes for breakfast and a 30-minute recess), I would insist on the following:

- Large group sessions where students read or write independently for blocks of time (45 to 90 minutes) once or twice each day. These could be supervised by paraprofessionals.

- Smaller group sessions for guided reading and writing lessons, for collaborative student projects, book discussions, and so on, that might last for 30 minutes. This instructional session would be conducted by teachers.

- Very small group sessions (two to three students) or tutorials that every struggling reader would participate in daily for 30 minutes. Two types of such activities—expert instructional and personalized practice—should be available with expert teachers offering the former and well-trained and supervised paraprofessionals or volunteers managing the latter.

Struggling readers need powerful summer instruction if we hope to accelerate literacy development in any substantial way. Most summer school programs should last 8 to 10 weeks. We don't expect much growth during the school year in an 8- to 10-week period. Getting serious about accelerating reading and writing development in a summer school program means that we need a daily design that produces perhaps *twice* the reading and writing these students would do during a normal school day. The research-based principles offered in this book should guide the design of summer programs—but remember the brevity factor: Only with intensive and engaging instruction can we expect to accelerate reading and writing proficiency in a few weeks (Paris et al., 2004).

Engaging Instruction   The problem that we confront in designing summer school programs looks something like this:

1. Students who have experienced difficulty in learning to read and write often demonstrate less enthusiasm for reading and writing than their peers who learned to read and write more easily and successfully.

2. These struggling readers and writers often demonstrate this diminished enthusiasm by avoiding reading and writing activity whenever possible; therefore, they are less likely to elect to voluntarily read and write or to demonstrate sustained engagement even during mildly coercive reading and writing activities such as Drop Everything and Read.

3. This is the targeted group of students who will be most likely to (a) benefit from voluntary reading to stem summer reading loss and (b) be mandated to attend summer school to improve their reading and writing proficiency.

4. But in order to stem summer reading loss or accelerate literacy development, our summer program design (or after-school program, for that matter) must involve these students in a substantial volume of reading and writing activity (Cooper et al., 2000; Paris et al., 2004).

So, in addition to access and expert instruction, our program effectiveness will turn on how successful we are in enticing our students to read and write a lot. My point here is that I think we have too long underestimated the importance of creating intervention programs focused primarily on fostering increased student engagement with books, magazines, and other texts. The recent finding from the international survey of reading abilities (Brozo et al., 2008) that children from poor families who were fully engaged readers, meaning they voluntarily read quite a bit, exhibited reading proficiencies that exceeded those of more advantaged children who were not engaged readers! The message that creating children who read voluntarily is a critical but too often ignored message.

Designing programs that foster voluntary engagement in reading actually does not seem so difficult. But the design is quite different from the traditional remedial or special education intervention design. A first difference is that a primary initial focus is finding out just what interests the student, rather than finding out which skills the student lacks. Thus, an entry assessment might include an interview rather than a diagnostic test. The interview would focus on interests, hobbies, talents, and favorite school subjects and genres of texts. We might even interview the student's classroom teacher or parents for insights into his or her interests and talents.

The results of this interview would be treated just as diagnostic test information is typically treated, as information useful in planning a summer program. We will also need to develop a good sense of the student's current reading level,

Preliminary Interview: Gathering Information on Interests

Tell me about any hobbies you have or sports you play.

What are your favorite TV programs? Video games?

Can you think of one book you really liked?

Are there any particular authors whose books you like?

Are there magazines, cartoons, or comic books that you like?

although, again, his or her classroom teacher, the school testing program, and the interview with the student should all provide information of this sort.

In addition to an interview, I would recommend that the opening day or two of summer school presents multiple opportunities for students to select reading material from a wide range of texts. Thus, I would organize collections of books of varying levels of difficulty by genre (e.g., mystery, historical fiction, biography), popular content themes (e.g., dinosaurs, pyramids, Native American peoples, machines), and everyday culture topics (e.g., wrestling, sports, television shows, entertainers, favorite series such as *Arthur* or *Sweet Valley High,* trends such as manga comic books and cartoons). Provide multiple and extended opportunities for students to select materials from these books and magazines, and have a paraprofessional or volunteer keep track of the choices each student makes, mingle with the students as they select materials, and sit to read with them (or try to).

Several times every day "bless" a few books by holding them up and telling just a bit about them or by reading a page or two from them. If the students find books that they get excited about, have them discuss and praise those books in front of other kids. Remember that most adults and most good readers get most of their recommendations for reading materials from friends and peers.

After the first day or two of summer school each teacher should be plagued by questions like: Where can I find another book or two on snakes written at a second-grade level? How about more books on the Battle of Gettysburg at the fourth-grade level? The resources offered earlier in this book will provide sources for finding needed books, but don't forget to turn to other teachers (in these examples, the school's second- and fourth-grade teachers might be sources) or the school librarian.

If truth be told, though, you are probably going to have to convince some students of their interest in a particular book, genre, or topic. In other words, part of the job will be kindling a spark of interest in reading certain texts. This becomes part of the job for two reasons. First, some students have high avoidance levels due to repeated failures with reading. Second, you will want to cluster students for guided reading and writing activities, and for very small group lessons. Although not every guided reading/writing lesson or small group support lesson requires that all students have read a common text, the use of a common text is the typical format for such instructional settings.

Most good teachers are also good actors, and so exhibiting enthusiasm for certain books is not that difficult to pull off (besides, you can always select common texts from the books you really do like). In addition, reading a bit of the book (or more than a bit) will often create an interest where none existed. Offering what we dubbed "managed choice" is another strategy that the exemplary teachers we observed routinely initiated (Allington & Johnston, 2002). *Managed choice* meant that students typically had several texts to choose from and, at times, had to come to a group agreement on which book they would read for the group sessions. At other times, students would select different books, sometimes with two kids choosing one and three others selecting a different option. The managed choice often involved choosing a book from a selection of books on a content topic or from a particular genre. As Guthrie and colleagues (1996, 2004) have so amply demonstrated, this sort of integrated planning produced greater interest and engagement in reading than did the traditional "everyone reads the same reader selection" design.

Books aren't the only texts that should be used, however. Magazines are another powerful source for engaging reading materials, as is the Internet. Especially when students are reading on a content theme, the Internet provides another ready supply of reading materials. That there already exist a number of websites that provide students with a wealth of information on content themes (and other topics of interest to kids and adolescents) can only be viewed as a positive. Many adults worry that the Internet will undermine the power of reading, but I hold just the opposite view. Few websites offer information in a manner that makes reading proficiency irrelevant.

Many educational websites offer a real-world educational activity that involves reading and writing. The Audubon Society has operated a website, for instance, where students (K–12) who live in areas where migratory birds travel count and record the birds they have seen. This creates a data bank that students can use to predict when certain birds will appear in their area. At a school in the panhandle region of Florida, elementary students operate an Internet project called *Keepers of the Coast* (www.elizabethcrowe.com). The students in Gulf Coast communities track a variety of aspects of the coastal environment and learn about everything from wildlife, to ecology, to industry in the region. They read information, much of it from websites, and write information, some posted on websites, as part of this project.

In addition, computers provide students with the tools to write better and to produce reports and stories that are incredibly more sophisticated and interesting than the paper-pencil research report. The use of software such as HyperStudio, PageMaker, and other desktop publishing and performance software can engage students who never thought writing was very interesting before.

Of course, engaging instruction is also instruction where students have books they can read accurately, fluently, and with at least general comprehension. But one real challenge we face in the design of summer school programs is that of engaging

Websites That Satisfy Curiosity (and Reading)

There is a huge amount of appropriate reading materials on the Web, some of which are even linked to school subjects. There is no way to begin to list all the interesting websites that are out there, but just as examples, visit this diverse collection of sites.

www.discoveryschool.com   Brought to you by the Discovery Channel with lots of geography, history, and science stuff for kids, this site includes games and virtual trips around the world.

www.insects.org   Advertised as "shameless promotion of insect appreciation," this site will kindle the curiosity of any kid, and especially those wondering about that bug they've just found.

www.enature.com   This is a National Audubon Society site that allows you to search for reports and images of almost 5,000 species.

www.co.fairfax.va.us/library/homepage.htm   Here, the Fairfax County Library in Virginia offers links to "Good Reading" for preschool-age children through adults.

www.zamboni.com   Just as it says, this site is dedicated to the Zamboni (the machine that resurfaces the ice at hockey games). One of my sons long aspired to be a Zamboni driver and here he could have read about the Zamboni driver of the year!

the student and enticing him or her to voluntarily read and write both in school and out. My concern is that students who are mandated to attend summer school might reasonably be expected to resist engaging very often and, instead, work harder at creatively avoiding engaging in reading and writing. Thus, our design problem is crafting powerful summer interventions that entice struggling readers to engage in the one activity that will accelerate achievement— lots of reading.

Support for Older Struggling Readers

There has been much recent emphasis on early intervention in an attempt to foster greater early school success, and the federal government has set the goal that all children will be reading on level by third grade. The thinking behind the early intervention push was stimulated by research that indicated that many children who experienced early difficulties in reading never recovered (Juel, 1994). At the same time, there have been several studies of substantial gains made by older readers when they have access to expert, intensive instruction (Davidson & Koppenhaver, 1993; Krashen, 2004a; Morris et al., 1996; Showers et al., 1998). My worry is that some educators and policy makers assume that early intervention programs will largely solve the problem of struggling readers. That is, if we could get all students off to a successful start there would be no need for later instructional support programs. But the literature is replete with studies showing that many children make adequate early progress in reading development, only to experience difficulties later on (e.g., Phillips et al., 2002, 2010).

There is the notorious "fourth-grade hump" (Chall, 1983), so called because at that grade level some children who had been making good progress begin to experience difficulties. Some attribute this to the growing use of informational texts that are often poorly written and present topics of which most children have little prior knowledge. Perhaps it is the limited use of informational texts in the early grades that makes reading informational texts an unfamiliar experience. Duke (2000) noted that primary-grade students read informational texts only 3.6 minutes per day. Students enrolled in high-poverty schools read even less informational text. Duke argues (p. 40) that the research provides four guidelines for enhancing informational text reading:

- Increase student access to informational texts.
- Increase the time students spend working with informational texts.
- Intentionally teach comprehension strategies for reading informational text.
- Create opportunities for students to use informational texts for authentic purposes.

Although I agree with these recommendations, I'm also not sure that they go far enough. I think we need far better and more powerful instruction on reading textbooks, a unique sort of informational text. Many of the powerful informational texts that one might use in the early grades share very few features with the textbooks often used in the upper grades and in middle school and high school. Of course, when we consider teaching informational text strategies and skills, including textbook reading, we need to ensure that we have texts that are the appropriate reading levels of the students (Allington, 2003).

I do think that interesting informational texts should represent roughly half of the reading early readers do. Such exposure and instruction would familiarize students with the organization of informational texts and would also provide the opportunity to build relevant world and curricular knowledge. In the international comparisons, U.S. students performed far better on tasks that involved reading narrative texts and stories than on their reading with informational texts, so there is much room for improvement.

Others (Cunningham, 2008) suggest that it is the problem of encountering a growing number of "big words": words that present decoding difficulties if children are still trying to "sound out" words letter by letter (e.g., *vignette, ideologies, misogyny, plateau, metamorphosis, inclement*). The reader also encounters more easily decodable words that are often wholly new to the reader (e.g., *pact, irony, delta, thrive, Moors*). As noted earlier, there are many reasons older poor readers go off-track with reading. Word reading is one reason, but failure to be able to pronounce new, big words may have less to do with decoding skills than with prior knowledge (Ivey & Baker, 2004). Take the word *inclement,* for instance. No matter how well developed your decoding skills might be, it is virtually impossible to know how to pronounce this word unless you have already encountered it (i.e., you have heard the word or maybe even used it). For instance, the word could be easily pronounced *in'-cle-ment* with the accent on the initial syllable (as in *detriment*), but even if allowable, that is the wrong pronunciation. The truth is that decoding words works better if the word is shorter and if you already know the word. When teaching content lessons, teachers need to consider preteaching the pronunciation of key words that represent decoding difficulty. By this, I mean teaching why the word is pronounced the way it is. Break the word apart and walk students through the pronunciation, chunk by chunk.

We cannot simply stop teaching reading skills and strategies after fourth or fifth grade if we want students to continue to develop as readers. Without continued reading instruction into the high school years, we will continue to observe the "middle school hump" in that too many successful elementary school readers exhibit little growth in reading proficiency during the middle school years (Snow et al., 1991). At the high school level (and beyond), even more students encounter their first real difficulties with reading.

I think it is critical that we recognize that there will always be students who will need continued support instruction beyond that provided in early intervention programs and that we create later intervention programs that provide older struggling readers access to expert, intensive instruction. I also think traditional notions about how to design such programs need to be reconsidered. For instance, Walmsley (1981) suggested that interventions for older struggling readers fall into one of four philosophical categories.

- *Romantic.* These programs would emphasize reading engagement and reading for personal fulfillment and empowerment. This could be a voluntary drop-in-and-discuss-what-you've-read program, or any program that focuses on voluntary, personal reading and responses to that reading. Instruction is likely to be offered but perhaps only when invited. Reading makes us human.

- *Utilitarian.* In these programs the focus is often on career enhancement or preparation of the real world and workplace literacy. Students might practice reading want ads or completing employment applications or studying manuals and technical writing. Reading makes you employable.

- *Cognitive/constructivist.* The focus of these programs is often to help students better deploy reading proficiencies in academic learning settings. There might be instruction on study skills, content text-reading strategies, and writing research papers or the traditional five-part essay. Reading makes you more successful in school.

- *Behaviorist.* Many remedial and special education interventions for struggling readers have long reflected a behaviorist approach with instruction focusing on decoding and spelling accuracy and completion of lots of low-level skills texts meant to provide practice on the imagined subprocesses of reading and writing. Reading real books is typically not a dominant theme in these designs. Reading self-selected books is even less common. Students may have reward schedules for both work completion and behavioral management. Reading is work and you should be rewarded for doing it.

My hunch is that "pure" examples of such program categories are relatively rare. I would also suggest that most intervention developers never thought much about the larger philosophical underpinnings of their programs. Personally, I am an

Decoding and Adolescents

It is not clear to me why so many remedial and special education reading programs for adolescent struggling readers target developing decoding proficiencies—unclear because we have such good evidence that for most older struggling readers decoding is not the problem. In Dennis (2009) and other studies it is estimated that approximately 10 percent of adolescent struggling readers have decoding problems. The real gaps are in vocabulary and comprehension. But various intervention programs (e.g., Wilson Phonics, Language!, etc.) continue to be used even though no reliable research has ever indicated that they improve the reading achievement of adolescents. However, virtually the same conclusion can be reached about nearly every commercial reading product targeted for use with adolescents (James-Burdumy et al., 2010). This is also true of the various and expensive computer-based reading programs (Campuzano et al., 2009).

eclectic in these matters most of the time. Programs should be designed to fit the needs of struggling readers and I can imagine older readers who would benefit differently from programs of different types. I don't have much confidence in behaviorist approaches, if only because we have tried these approaches for such a long time with so little success. Of course, some struggling readers may need instruction targeted at developing one or more of the subprocesses of reading. But at this point in my career I am quite convinced by the evidence that traditional behavioral approaches have limited utility in developing readers and writers.

If we expect all students to meet the sorts of academic standards that fewer than half of the students have historically met—and that is precisely what many of the new state high school graduation standards set as the goal—then school programs for older struggling readers will have to include plans for providing some students with access to extraordinarily intensive and expert instructional support throughout their school careers. In addition, two types of support will be needed: enhancing access to appropriate texts and maintaining/accelerating literacy development.

Enhancing Access to Appropriate Texts

The documented decline in voluntary reading that begins in the middle school years (Foertsch, 1992) seems, in no small part, related to a widening gap in the availability of appropriate materials—both curriculum materials and school-linked access to texts on topics of interest. As Chall and Conard (1991) noted, the increased reliance on single texts in middle and secondary schools increases the likelihood that students encounter texts they cannot read. The recent study of science textbooks adds to the evidence by demonstrating just how difficult many such texts are relative to student reading development (Budiansky, 2001). But it may be the critical decline in access to reading materials that are considered interesting that contributes more to the fall off in voluntary reading.

Ivey (1999), Smith and Wilhelm (2002), and Worthy and McCool (1996) report huge gaps between what adolescents report they like to read and what is available in middle and high school libraries and classrooms. They also note that there were few occasions for self-selection of reading materials—teachers almost always assigned reading materials, and rarely was there time set aside in school for independent reading. Ivey also notes that attitudes toward reading were often powerfully shaped by the nature of the classroom environments.

Finally, Wolk's (2010) research indicates that a list of the most commonly assigned books in today's high school are virtually identical to lists developed in the 1960s and 1980s. As Wolk notes, educators are assigning the same books today that were assigned before personal computers, cell phones, copiers, or the Internet were developed! The fact that all of these books were written by whites and all but one were written by now dead white males suggests just how out of touch our high school curriculum is with today's society. The net effect of the high school curriculum today is that it undermines the likelihood that adolescents will ever read voluntarily.

In earlier sections I offered a number of examples of just how a school might enhance the likelihood that students would choose to read outside of school. Although many of the examples I offered were drawn from elementary schools, I would note that this was due more to the limited number of such efforts found at the middle and high school level than to limited need for such efforts with adolescents. Yes, even middle and high school programs should worry about the extent, or lack thereof, of voluntary reading. If most students in your middle or high school do not read much on their own, it may be a good time to evaluate just what features of the school program are missing or misguided. If struggling middle and high school students in your school experience a steady diet of hard, boring (in their view) books, there is no reason to be surprised that they exhibit little in the way of literacy development (and academic progress) during the middle and high school years (Allington, 2002a).

Maintaining/Accelerating Literacy Development

The evidence indicates that some students will achieve higher standards only if they have long-term literacy support. Such support will almost necessarily have to come from teachers with expertise in meeting the instructional needs of adolescents struggling with literacy learning. My point is that even with high-quality classroom instruction throughout the K–12 span and intensive, expert literacy intervention, some students will continue to find literacy acquisition a more difficult task than most of their peers. Historically we have labeled such students dyslexic or learning disabled and then largely abandoned attempts to teach them to read. We developed what I have termed "bypass" instruction and what others have termed "accommodations." That is, we provided these students with audiotaped recorded texts, note takers, and aides who read their texts and tests to them and we often lowered the academic goals we expected these students to achieve.

For instance, there is little evidence in the research on middle school and high school special education programs that suggests that intensive, expert reading instruction is routinely offered to pupils with disabilities (Kos, 1991; Licopoli, 1984). At the same time, when such instruction is provided, many of these students exhibit substantial acceleration in the development of their reading skills. Too few adolescents attend schools that offer intensive remedial programs (and even when these programs are available pupils with disabilities often are deemed ineligible). But again, we have good evidence that intensive, expert reading interventions can accelerate the reading development of adolescent struggling readers (Davidson &

High School Reading Course Produces Big Gains

Bev Showers and Bruce Joyce with their colleagues (1998) describe the implementation of a daily reading course built into an urban, multiethnic high school curriculum that students took in lieu of other electives. Key components of the course included:

- Reading appropriate books in school and at home
- Listening to teachers read good literature
- Instruction in active comprehension strategies
- Building vocabulary through reading
- Phonics and structural analysis training
- Building vocabulary through natural language use

Each semester, students read five to six books of appropriate difficulty and interest. Both whole group and small group lessons on comprehension and big word decoding strategies are offered along with a daily read-aloud by the teacher and an interactive writing activity. Reading achievement accelerated to four times the growth observed in students not taking the course. All this points to the fact that it is never too late to design instruction that will benefit struggling readers.

Koppenhaver, 1993; Morris et al., 1996; Showers et al., 1998). I know of only a single state, Wisconsin, that has historically mandated that middle schools and high schools employ certified reading teachers in reasonable numbers. Most states do not even target funds for reading specialists at these levels.

At the very least, schools serving adolescents should have expert support available for students willing to seek it out. This might be in the form of a reading/writing center that operates during part of the school day and after school. I am thinking here of programs modeled after the college/university reading and writing support center. There is no mandate to attend, but the center is available to students who seek support when they feel they need it. Some students might attend regularly, perhaps daily, while others would drop in whenever they were confronted with assignments that produced that panicky I-need-some-help feeling. The center might even make use of peers as tutors, assuming that training on how to help is available. The center could work to foster the development of peer support and study groups for either particular types of academic needs or for particular courses or class projects. Finally, such a center might organize the training of adolescents as tutors for younger struggling readers. There is again good evidence that adolescent struggling readers benefit from tutoring younger struggling readers (and the younger readers benefit also). But both training and supervision are necessary components (Berger & Shafran, 2000; Davidson & Koppenhaver, 1993; Juel, 1996).

Other similar models emphasize voluntary reading by adolescents and their discussion of this reading with peers, who may have read the same texts (Alvermann et al., 1999; Davidson & Koppenhaver, 1993). In such programs the goal is to entice adolescent readers into participating in the very activities that seem essential for their continued literacy development—more extensive reading and engagement in literate talk about books and stories and the ideas found in them. Attendance again is typically voluntary and the sessions typically scheduled outside the normal school day. The best programs of this sort were so enticing that word-of-mouth promotion by participating adolescents produced more interested teens than could be handled given the budgets available.

Beware of Packaged Proven Programs

As struggling readers progress through school, the basis of their reading difficulties varies even more widely. Because any group of tenth-grade struggling readers will present a variety of difficulties, there is no such thing as a "scientific" or "proven" one-size-fits-all program or package. Some commercial products marketed for older struggling readers offer wide reading as their strategy, others offer decoding lessons, and so on. But struggling older readers need the same sort of diagnostic work-up as was presented earlier for fourth-grade struggling readers. Older students have no time to waste on lessons they don't need. Just remember that there is not a single program, package, or curricular material that currently meets the federal definition of "proven."

Promoters market material as "scientifically based," meaning that some science seems to support what they offer. Often this assertion is accompanied by several small developer-funded reports of how the product worked somewhere. But the federal criteria require independent studies and replication of the findings by others—all published in peer-reviewed journals. Thus far, no such studies exist that show any product has developed the reading proficiencies needed by high school students.

The middle and high school market for quick-fix solutions is growing every day. But the bottom line is that no product will be appropriate for all struggling readers and no product can overcome inexpert teaching. The best investment is to add more teacher expertise to effective reading instruction.

I would argue that some adolescents will need something akin to the traditional "reading development class"—that is, a daily 50-minute (or every other day 100-minute) class devoted to accelerating literacy development. Wilhelm (1997) and Gallagher (2009), both high school teachers, describe the sort of instruction that I imagine would be most useful. Students are engaged in some common reading that serves as one basis for strategy lessons—including class conversations—but self-selected reading plays a crucial role. Often the focus, at least initially, is on fostering "active mental activity"—or engagement—while reading. Wilhelm notes that many of the early adolescents he worked with—students who had struggled through remedial reading and learning disability classes since the primary grades—had learned to word call but had never actually read anything that stimulated active mental activity during reading. These students did not visualize characters or settings, they did not get goose-bumps or giggle when they read; they just plowed through the words, trying to get it over with.

In an ideal world, adolescents who needed tutoring would get it. Those who needed very small group instruction would have such lessons daily. In both cases, instruction would be provided by a teacher expert at puzzling through the problems adolescent readers and writers face. We are very far from that ideal today but if students are expected to achieve the new high standards, then it seems morally incumbent that access to instruction of sufficient intensity and of sufficient expertness become routinely available to adolescent students.

Slavin and colleagues (2008) provide a review of the research on reading interventions for adolescent struggling readers. However, their review also notes that little research actually exists to support the use of most products now available. Nonetheless, there are several products with evidence they do improve reading achievement but little evidence that many schools use these products.

In that ideal world, every teacher would teach reading. Every history teacher would work to help students understand the typical structure of discourse in historical texts. They would model and demonstrate how historians think as they read and write texts. They would offer powerful instruction that fostered the development of historical vocabulary. Biology teachers would do the same sorts of things with the reading and writing expected in biology. They would help students learn to read, write, and think like biologists. In all cases, content teachers would select texts for students that were well written and of appropriate levels of complexity, given the students' prior knowledge as well as their levels of literacy development. If this were to happen we would experience a "win-win" outcome—students would develop not just better reading and writing skills but they would also learn more history and biology. In my view, it is not the job of the reading specialist or the special education teacher to teach history or biology, nor to find the texts that fit the students in those classes. Rather, that is rightfully the job of the history and biology teachers. Developing content teachers' expertise in fostering the reading of disciplinary textbooks should be a primary professional development goal.

Content Support

In addition to providing literacy intervention programs, schools are going to have to rethink how content class (e.g., Global Studies, Earth Science, algebra) support will be provided. What many content teachers view as "reading/writing problems" are actually content learning problems. When students have inadequate prior knowledge of a topic under study, for instance, they cannot make much sense of a text on that topic. Content textbooks are notoriously bad on several dimensions (try to find any study of content textbooks that offers even faint praise for middle school or high school science and social studies textbooks, for instance).

As expectations for demonstrations of greater academic learning during adolescence increase (more math courses, more science courses, more history courses needed to graduate), there will arise a greater need for content tutoring. For example, neither reading specialists nor special education teachers should be expected to reteach earth science concepts and vocabulary. Such instruction should come from content specialists—in this case, teachers with expertise in earth

Websites for Improving Adolescent Literacy

For more information on innovative, research-based designs for improving adolescent literacy, visit the websites below for powerful reports.

www.carnegie.org/sns/about.html   This site provides a brief description of the Carnegie Foundation's Schools for a New Society national high school reform effort, as well as a downloadable monograph detailing the design and the research that supports it.

www.carnegie.org/sub/program/education.html   At this Carnegie web page you can download the report *The Urban High School's Challenge: Ensuring Literacy for Every Child,* which describes several model programs.

www.reading.org/resources/issues/focus_adolescent.html   Here you will find two position statements from the International Reading Association on adolescent literacy. The first, *Adolescent Literacy,* outlines the *necessary* features of any design hoping to improve adolescent literacy. The second, *Supporting Young Adolescents' Literacy Learning,* provides detailed descriptions of efforts to enhance early adolescent literacy development. The site also offers related readings and summaries of research on adolescent literacy.

science. Of course, if the basic problem is that the earth science teacher selected a textbook that many students cannot read due to their current level of literacy development, then tutoring is not the most direct solution to the problem that such decisions create (Allington, 2002a). However, it is unlikely that many reading specialists or special education teachers have much expertise in locating alternative, appropriately difficult earth science texts. But, again, the point is that not all students will grasp basic earth science concepts and understandings with any single set of lessons—some will get it; some won't. Typically, failure to get it from the standard lesson offered has meant simply that the student failed. However, now that high schools in some states are being graded based on the number of students who pass the earth science test, there seems to be more interest in attempting to develop interventions that increase the number of passing students (or increasing the number of students who know the basics of earth science).

Thus, I see a need for middle schools and high schools to develop a second support strand: content mastery programs. Such programs might operate during the school day or in after-school programs or as summer school programs (although the latter seem the most expensive and least effective option). In the high school my children attended (rated as one of the 100 best high schools in the nation by *Newsweek*), there has been an end-of-day "open" period for at least a decade. Every teacher is available every other day for small group reteaching, review, or remediation during this period. Sports teams do not begin practices until after this period. Buses do not depart until after this period is completed. Students can use the period as a study hall, for library work, or for a "second-shot follow-up" in any class they might be having difficulty in. This practice, in one of the nation's highest-achieving schools, may offer some insight as to *why* it is one of the highest-achieving schools.

Summary

Throughout this book I have focused on what I see as the few things that really matter for struggling readers. These few things are, I believe, as applicable to interventions targeted to adolescent populations as to elementary students. The 100/100 goal is appropriate for a K–12 system and not just applicable to a K–5 (or a K–3) school. We need to think long and hard about how to redesign elementary schools, middle schools, and high schools so that all students are engaged in appropriate instruction all day long. At the upper levels the programs are necessarily focused and structured differently from those targeting early grades intervention. But schools (and states) have often neglected to plan for interventions much beyond the early grades.

As of this writing, some 25 states have implemented some form of high school exit examination. Other states and districts have begun holding eighth-grade students back unless they can demonstrate on-level reading achievement, or close to it. Our national high school graduation rate hovers around 75 percent, and most of those who now drop out typically have underdeveloped reading proficiencies. Mandating reading tests and setting passing test scores is not enough. We should expect some students to struggle with reading throughout their school careers. We must plan instructional programs that continue to provide targeted reading interventions for students through twelfth grade. An emphasis on early intervention is important, but no study has ever found early intervention alone to be sufficient.

There seems to be an emerging interest in extending reading instruction, both developmental and remedial, into high school. Federal legislation providing financial support for such efforts is currently pending in Congress. The International Reading Association has an adolescent literacy task force (www.reading.org) that has offered a number of recommendations for schools, universities, and policy makers.

By twelfth grade, economically disadvantaged students read about as well as non-poor eighth-grade students (NCES, 2009). But also by twelfth grade, many of the lowest-achieving readers have dropped out so the situation may actually be worse. This four-year gap began as a much smaller gap at fourth grade and widened steadily across the middle and high school grades. We can do better—we must.

Afterword

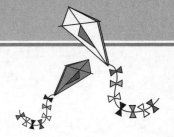

In response to an attack on the quality of U.S. schools today, a pundit is said to have replied, "Our schools are doing pretty good at what we used to want them to do but we don't want them to do that anymore!" In many ways, that simple statement pretty much sums up the current state of affairs. The levels of reading achievement have been rising for our least proficient readers; the gap between more and less advantaged students has held steady or been narrowing; and public and political interest in education seems at an all-time high. But there have been no celebratory parades or parties.

The goals for U.S. education have changed dramatically and probably for the better. Creating schools where all students acquire quite sophisticated academic understandings and proficiencies is hard to argue against. Likewise, the shift to an information economy and the dramatic shift in general information access and flow suggest that adult citizens of the future will benefit from a broad attainment of these goals. But we will have to create a type of school that has never existed before in order to attain the new goals set for K–12 education. We must also use the available research, almost none of which has been benchmarked against these new goals, in the design of new programs to meet these goals.

In my view, much of the criticism of current school programs is unwarranted, and many of the popular solutions are untested against the new goals, such that a great deal of the evangelical promotion of favorite programs is misguided at best and simply profit-oriented at worst (Allington, 2005).

No school has ever produced students who can *all* read and write and do math at the Proficient Level, for instance, on the National Assessment of Educational Progress. None. That we don't have such schools suggests the enormity of the tasks ahead. It may be possible to create such schools but there is little research that suggests just what those schools should look like. Too often, school reform research that was never benchmarked against attainment of the new standards is being touted as providing the needed guidance. What would be truly useful is research on schools where the new standards are being successfully met.

Learning from Studies of Exemplary Elementary Reading Instruction

Perhaps the best evidence available on just what high-performing classrooms might look like comes from the series of studies conducted at the National Center for English Learning and Achievement (CELA; go to http://cela.albany.edu for additional articles on these studies). These studies observed some of the nation's best teachers in a number of states (California, Florida, New Hampshire, New York, Texas, Wisconsin). Primary, intermediate, middle, and high school teachers provided a clear view of how classrooms might be organized to generate high levels of learning. In an article that appeared in *Phi Delta Kappan,* I attempted to summarize six key features of these classrooms (Allington, 2002d). I organized that summary around what I dubbed The Six T's of Effective Teaching.

1. *Time.* Effective teachers have students do more guided reading, more independent reading, and more reading in social studies and science. In many exemplary classrooms, children are reading and writing for half the day! "Stuff" does not dominate instructional time. (Stuff includes test-preparation worksheets, copying definitions, and after-reading comprehension worksheets.)

2. *Texts.* Students have books they can actually read with a high level of accuracy, fluency, and comprehension. All students, then, rarely have the same book. Students engage in enormous quantities of successful reading and become independent, proficient readers. Motivation for reading is dramatically influenced by reading success.

3. *Teaching.* Effective teachers don't simply "assign and assess"; they are involved in active instruction. Explicit demonstrations of cognitive strategies are modeled; instruction is offered in a balance of side-by-side lessons, small group lessons, and whole group lessons, but whole group lessons are brief and focused.

4. *Talk.* There's more of it, and it's more conversational than interrogational. Discussion is purposeful and personalized, not scripted or packaged. Thoughtful classroom talk focuses on making children's thinking visible and building understanding.

5. *Tasks.* Leaving behind low-level worksheet tasks, effective teachers demonstrate greater use of longer assignments, tasks that integrate several content areas, and substantive work with more complexity. Exemplary teachers provide students similar but different tasks.

6. *Testing.* Student work is evaluated based on effort and improvement. Rubrics shift responsibility for improvement to the students, so "luck" doesn't play a part. Most effective teachers use almost no test-preparation materials, believing that good instruction is what makes the difference when it comes to test performance.

However, summaries such as these always leave me worried that we "dumb down" the complex expert activity of effective teaching whenever we reduce it to a few key features. For instance, my colleagues on these studies have since extended our initial findings in several important ways. Peter Johnston (2004) has written a small book about the language of these classrooms. In my summary, I simply noted that the classrooms were more conversational. Peter goes well beyond this by showing the many ways that teacher language impels or impedes student success and their orientation to the act of reading. Michael Pressley and colleagues (2003) focused their attention on the motivational aspects of these classrooms, showing just how powerfully positive and supportive these teachers were. Their work goes well beyond simply responding to children positively and providing choices. Judith Langer (2003) noted the importance of collegial and organizational support in the high-productivity secondary school classrooms she documented. Her work shows just how hard it is to achieve effective teaching without support.

Beyond the work completed at CELA, there are the studies completed by Barbara Taylor and David Pearson and their colleagues at the Center for Improving Early Reading Achievement (CIERA). Their work adds additional evidence on the nature of high-quality classrooms and high-quality schools (Taylor et al., 2000b, 2003), as does the work of John Guthrie and colleagues at the University of Maryland (Croninger & Valli, 2009; Guthrie et al., 2000; Guthrie & Knowles, 2001; Guthrie et al., 2001).

By my count, these three research centers have so far produced at least 10 books and 40 articles reporting their findings. Thus, there is no shortage of information on what we might be doing to improve schools for poor children and for struggling readers. These studies have been cited throughout this book, but I believe that reading the original reports will be useful even for those who have nearly finished this book.

I think the following quotation from the *Phi Delta Kappan* article largely summarizes what each of these research teams have found: "In the end it will become clearer that there are no 'proven programs,' just schools in which we find more expert teachers—teachers who need no script to tell them what to do. . . . Are we creating schools in which every year every teacher becomes more expert?" (Allington, 2002d, p. 747).

I wish I could tell you that the ideas and strategies discussed in this book will turn the tide and that then all will be well in America. They won't, but I do hope

Research-Based Advice versus
Commercial Advocacy and Advertising

Jere Brophy (2000), award-winning researcher and classroom scholar, has noted:

Teachers are rightly confused and irritated by the seemingly continuous shifts and contradictions in the advice directed at them by supposed experts. However, I will submit that the problem is not being caused by researchers. . . . Researchers stay close to their data and make careful, qualified statements about implications. The kinds of overblown, polarized, and evangelical statements that cause most of the problems are coming not from researchers but from people whose policy advocacy is based on strong theoretical biases and who typically have something to sell but little or no scientific support for their claims and recommendations. (p. 177)

that they will help set us on a course more likely to lead us where we need to go. In fact, if I wasn't confident that the evidence on high-achieving schools and classrooms now available pointed to these ideas and strategies as reasonable directions for our work, I wouldn't have bothered to write this book.

For those readers hoping for a step-by-step manual for school reform, I'm sorry to have disappointed you. My basic goal has been to push all of us toward thinking more about those things that a century's worth of research and experimentation have indicated are the best bets for helping us create those schools we do not have. Developing the instructional expertise of every teacher, reorganizing schools so that supporting teacher development is, as they say, Job Number One, is the only strategy that I can endorse with any enthusiasm and the only one in which I can find substantial research support.

For those who hoped for more advice on early intervention (preschool through first grade) I have suggested a number of other available resources throughout this book. As I noted in the Preface, the emphasis on early intervention has generated a plethora of books, materials, and programs from which to review and draw ideas. I will humbly suggest that the key principles set out in this book are also critically important in early literacy instruction. But it is in grade 2 and beyond that has been much neglected in the advice offered for improving literacy proficiency. Thus, it is those grades that have been my focus in this book. As governors, presidents, and politicians, generally, have begun to recommend after-school and summer school programs as one way to meet the challenge of struggling readers, research and demonstration efforts have lagged behind. And so, I have attempted to summarize what we know about effective reading instructional designs in the hopes that students will spend this extra instructional time profitably. For those readers who wish more detail on earliest literacy instruction, I recommend both *Phonics They Use* by Patricia Cunningham (2008) and *Kindergarten Literacy* by Anne McGill-Franzen (2006).

I will close by reiterating the advice that Pat Cunningham and I offered in *Schools That Work* (one of the several books in this series): Think long and move slowly but always move forward. By this, I mean think about what you want to see happening in your school three to five years from now and begin working to get there. Change is hard. Change is anxiety provoking and necessarily slow. My own experience suggests that when we try to change everything at once, little that matters actually changes. But someone has to initiate and support the needed change. If not you, who? If not today, when?

Finally, remember that in the end it will still be teachers who make the difference in children's school lives. It is teachers who will either lead the change or resist and stymie it. The focus of school change has to be on supporting teachers in their efforts to become more expert and reorganizing all the aspects of the educational system so that they can teach as expertly as they know how. But bureaucracies rarely give up power easily and they rarely seem to improve people. In my most optimistic moments, I believe that people can change bureaucracies in positive ways. I hope that this book provides some of you with the confidence necessary to challenge bureaucratic nonsense when it arrives at your doorstep. No one knows your students as well as you do and no one knows their needs better. In the end, it is unlikely that anyone else in the bureaucracy cares more about your students than you. So fight for them when you must. Fight for the resources to create classrooms that meet, or come close to meeting, the 100/100 goal. The closer we come to achieving that goal, the closer we will be to providing what really matters for struggling readers.

Worksheet for Calculating and Organizing Accuracy and Fluency Data

Student Name: _____ **Grade:** _____

Text 1   Title: _____
Accuracy: _____%   Fluency rating: Good   Fair   Poor

Text 2   Title: _____
Accuracy: _____%   Fluency rating: Good   Fair   Poor

Text 3   Title: _____
Accuracy: _____%   Fluency rating: Good   Fair   Poor

Text 4   Title: _____
Accuracy: _____%   Fluency rating: Good   Fair   Poor

Text 5   Title: _____
Accuracy: _____%   Fluency rating: Good   Fair   Poor

Text 6   Title: _____
Accuracy: _____%   Fluency rating: Good   Fair   Poor

Text 7   Title: _____
Accuracy: _____%   Fluency rating: Good   Fair   Poor

Text 8   Title: _____
Accuracy: _____%   Fluency rating: Good   Fair   Poor

Text 9   Title: _____
Accuracy: _____%   Fluency rating: Good   Fair   Poor

APPENDIX B

Worksheet for Organizing Accuracy and Fluency Data

Enter number of texts read accurately (as number read with 98 percent accuracy or better/total number read) and enter number of texts read fluently (as number read fluently/total number read).

Student 1 Name: _____ Grade: _____

Number of texts read accurately: _____ /_____ Read fluently: _____ /_____

Student 2 Name: _____ Grade: _____

Number of texts read accurately: _____ /_____ Read fluently: _____ /_____

Student 3 Name: _____ Grade: _____

Number of texts read accurately: _____ /_____ Read fluently: _____ /_____

Student 4 Name: _____ Grade: _____

Number of texts read accurately: _____ /_____ Read fluently: _____ /_____

Student 5 Name: _____ Grade: _____

Number of texts read accurately: _____ /_____ Read fluently: _____ /_____

Student 6 Name: _____ Grade: _____

Number of texts read accurately: _____ /_____ Read fluently: _____ /_____

Student 7 Name: _____ Grade: _____

Number of texts read accurately: _____ /_____ Read fluently: _____ /_____

Student 8 Name: _____ Grade: _____

Number of texts read accurately: _____ /_____ Read fluently: _____ /_____

Student 9   Name: _____   Grade: _____

Number of texts read accurately: _____ /_____   Read fluently: _____ /_____

Student 10   Name: _____   Grade: _____

Number of texts read accurately: _____ /_____   Read fluently: _____ /_____

Tally: Number of students with 100 percent texts read accurately   _____ /10

Number of students with 100 percent texts read fluently (Good)   _____ /10

Number of students with 50–99 percent texts read accurately   _____ /10

Number of students with 50–99 percent texts read fluently (Good)   _____ /10

Number of students no texts read accurately   _____ /10

Number of students no texts read fluently (Good)   _____ /10

If most struggling readers don't have texts they can read accurately and fluently, then serious redesign of the instructional day and the intervention plan is needed.

Book Study Guide
for
What Really Matters
for Struggling Readers

Book Study Guidelines

Reading, reacting, and interacting with others about a book is one of the ways many of us process new information. Book studies are a common feature in many school districts because they recognize the power of collaborative learning. The intent of a book study is to provide a supportive context for accessing new ideas and affirming best practices already in place. Marching through the questions in a lockstep fashion could result in the mechanical processing of information; it is more beneficial to select questions to focus on and give them the attention they deserve.

One possibility to structure your book discussion of *What Really Matters for Struggling Readers* is to use the Reading Reaction Sheet on page 224. Following this format, make a copy for each group member. Next, select a different facilitator for each chapter. The facilitator will act as the official note taker and be responsible for moving the discussion along. He or she begins by explaining that the first question is provided to start the group discussion. The remaining three questions are to be generated by the group. The facilitator can ask each person to identify at least one question and then let the group choose the three they want to cover, or the facilitator can put the participants into three groups, with each group responsible for identifying one question. The three questions are shared for all to hear (and write down), and then discussion of Question 1 commences. The facilitator paces the discussion so the most relevant information for that group is brought out. Since many school districts require documentation for book studies, the facilitator could file the sheet with the appropriate person as well as distribute a copy to all group members for their notes.

Another possibility is to use the guiding questions for each chapter. You could have the same facilitator for all chapters. Perhaps this would be someone who read the book first and suggested it to the group. Or the facilitator role could rotate. It is suggested that the facilitator not only pace the group through the questions to hit on the most important information for the group's needs, but he or she should take notes for later distribution to group members and/or administrators if required for documentation.

The provided questions are meant to provoke discussion and might lead the group into areas not addressed in the questions. That is wonderful! The importance of a book study is to move the members along in their understanding of the book content. If time is limited, the facilitator might select certain questions from the list for the initial focus of the discussion, allowing other questions as time permits.

Of course, a third option is to combine the two structures. Select the format that best fits your group and the time frame you have set for completion of the book.

All book sessions should end with a purpose for reading the next chapter. It could be to generate questions the group still has, to find implications for each person's own teaching, or to identify new ideas. Purpose setting is a time-honored way to help readers (of any age) approach the text. If you are using the questions that accompany each chapter, direct the participants to read the questions prior to reading the chapter. This will provide a framework for processing the information in the chapter.

Book Study Questions for Each Chapter

chapter 1: Reading Achievement and Instruction in U.S. Schools

1. Allington sets out an argument that reading achievement in U.S. schools has not improved much over the past 30 years. At the same time, he notes that reading achievement is also not worsening. Think about the students you teach today: Are they better readers than your students used to be (or than you used to be if you are a new teacher)? Are they less able readers? Describe the differences you see.

2. The Reading First program of NCLB mandated a number of actions that schools had to accept. However, Congress has now ended funding for Reading First based on the findings that implementing the mandated requirements did not improve reading achievement and also because of the financial conflicts of interest that the Inspector General identified. What do you know about the impact of Reading First in your school?

3. Were you surprised by the effect the numbers of children living in low-income homes had on school reading achievement? Surprised that schools with few poor children (fewer than 25 percent) were ranked the best schools in the world? What factors other than wealth explain why some kids do so much better than others in schools?

4. Does your school do a better job of teaching kids to read than it does of developing children who do read? How would you explain the outcomes your school fosters?

5. Were you surprised to learn that research has found that "no one approach is so distinctly better in all situations" as to recommend its use? Were you surprised to find out that the federal What Works Clearinghouse found only one program of 153 studied had demonstrated "strong positive effects" on reading development? Or, were you more surprised that 148 programs had no evidence they improved reading performance?

6. As you read this book, it is even closer to 2014 than it was when Allington wrote this revision. What is the likelihood that all children in your school district will be reading on level in 2014? And, remember that 2014 gave your school district 12 years to put in place reading instruction to accomplish this.

7. Pupils with disabilities have been the AYP subgroup most likely to fail to meet reading standards. Why do you think so many schools have such a hard time bringing these children's reading performance up to grade level?

8. Does your school condone or even encourage holding children back who aren't reading on grade level? Has anyone ever examined the effects of this expensive option?

9. Summers are important but usually neglected by schools. Does your school have a program to ensure all children have easy access to books they can and want to read all summer long? Can you imagine how such a program might work in your school?

10. Does your school use commercial test preparation products (workbooks, computer-based drill and practice, etc.)? Since no research supports the use of these products, how is their use rationalized in your school?

11. Has RTI been implemented in your school? If so, is it funded with the special education dollars allowed? Is it viewed as a general education initiative? Has it resulted in fewer referrals to special education?

12. *Children differ.* This might be the best summary of what the research says about teaching children to read. Think of instances where you found a technique or teaching strategy that worked for only one child but it worked really well with that child. Can you understand why having teachers with big teaching toolboxes—filled with different instructional routines and strategies—is the best hope for achieving the goal of all children reading?

chapter 2: What Really Matters: Kids Need to Read a Lot

1. Think about how much reading your struggling readers do every day. Is it enough reading practice? Does the volume of reading your struggling readers do pale in comparison to your better readers?

2. How many hours of academic time do you have to teach every day? Is your school on the higher end (6 to 7 hours) or the lower end (2 to 3 hours) of the national continuum? Is there anything that you could do to improve the time you have available to teach and that kids have available to read?

3. Do your students spend more time each day doing worksheets than reading? If so, how could you change the time distributions?

4. Is scheduling of special area classes and support services well managed in your schools? Do you have almost all of your students the whole school day? Is there a way to improve the scheduling of special area classes and support services that you would like to try?

5. Are there any standards set for your school describing the volume of reading and writing activity students should do each day or week? Is there a reason not to propose that such standards be set? Would you then propose the 90 minutes of daily reading and 45 minutes a day of writing? Or would you propose more of each? Or less?

6. Are core programs (basal reader, science and social studies texts, etc.) restricting the reading volume of your students? Could you develop a two-day plan where these materials are used only on Monday and Tuesday and other relevant texts are made available on Wednesday, Thursday, and Friday? Does your school have sufficient material for your students to read on these days?

chapter 3: Kids Need Books They Can Read

1. Had it ever occurred to you that you don't like to read hard books? What was the last hard book you tried to read but finally quit reading because it was just too difficult and not at all enjoyable? Now ask yourself, Was this book selected by you or was it assigned to you? Imagine going through life never enjoying any book you read and never reading a book that was easy to read. That is the situation of too many struggling readers.

2. Are you surprised by what the research says about task difficulty? Are you surprised that learning and motivation are higher when tasks can be completed with a high degree of success? Talk with other teachers about this issue and see how many believe that difficult work produces better results. Try to figure out why anyone would believe that.

3. Reading with 98 to 99 percent accuracy sounds like easy reading, right? Allington notes that no adult would continue reading a book they could read only at 98 to 99 percent accuracy. In a John Grisham novel there are 300 to 400 words per page. Reading even at a 99 percent accuracy would still mean there would be 3 or 4 words on every page you couldn't pronounce and didn't know what they meant. In other words, there would be 75 to 100 words in every chapter that you wouldn't know. Have you ever read a book that difficult?

4. Accuracy seems to need to increase as children become better readers. Allington's hunch is that by grade 4, children should be reading most school material at an accuracy rate of 99.9 percent correct. That would be a single unknown word every 1,000 running words of text. Have a good, average, and struggling reader in your class read aloud for one minute from some randomly selected page of the science texts you are using. Can all of them read your science material at 99 or 99.9 percent accuracy?

5. Slightly lower levels of accuracy can be expected if the text is used in a small guided reading group (say, 5 to 7 children). For these instructional texts (instructional because you are there guiding their reading), it is the "before reading" teacher-led activity that is important. That is because it is during this step in the reading lesson that you typically work with students to develop word identification and word meanings for new words they will encounter. Monitor which words you preteach or at least expose the children to in this lesson segment. Were many of these words unknown to children?

6. Examine the list of motivating and unmotivating practices presented on pages 73–74. Put a check on each list by aspects that reflect your classroom. Do you have a classroom with more motivating or unmotivating practices when it comes to reading? Which unmotivating practices can you eliminate? Which motivating practices could you add or expand?

7. Select three texts your students use. Then select one of the methods for examining the readability of these texts. Calculate the readability of each of the three texts. Is each of the texts appropriate, given the reading levels of your struggling readers? Can you find alternative texts that do match their level of reading proficiency and present the same content?

8. Take a quick inventory of the books children can access in your classroom and school. Is your classroom library large enough? Are the texts at levels that all your students can locate appropriately difficult books? If not, which children can locate the fewest books they can read with 99 percent accuracy? How can you begin to change the situation for the better?

9. Do you have sets of series books in your classroom library? If not, how can you begin to acquire those?

10. Did you "bless" any books today? Develop a plan to begin blessing books every day. It doesn't take long and it pays big benefits.

chapter 4: Kids Need to Learn to Read Fluently

1. Normally developing readers overcome fluency problems usually before they end second grade. But struggling readers struggle with fluency forever, it seems. But do they struggle with fluency because we continue to give them "too hard" books to read? Examine children who present fluency problems and ask whether the books they are reading with little fluency are also books that they read at accuracy levels below 99 percent correct. If this is the case, the solution is to provide them with books they can read accurately first, then work on their fluency.

2. Look at the descriptions of struggling readers and developing readers on pages 105–106. Put a check next to each element of the description that is true in your classroom (Are struggling readers asked more often to read aloud?). If reading your instruction mimics what researchers have found as distinguishing the lessons offered to good and struggling readers, select one aspect that you will try to alter this week. Next week select another aspect to alter. Can you bring the reading lessons you offer to good and struggling readers closer together? Would someone be able to tell who was a good reader and who was not just by observing your teaching?

3. Try using the Pause-Prompt-Praise strategy when working with your struggling readers. Use it for three consecutive days. Do you see any changes in the struggling readers' behaviors?

4. Select one of the other strategies for fostering fluent reading. Use the strategy for a week with your struggling readers. Describe what differences you see in their reading behaviors by the end of the week.

5. It is now clear that expanding the amount of high-success reading of struggling readers not only solves fluency problems faster than other methods but more extensive reading also fosters both decoding and vocabulary skill development. For the next three weeks focus on providing your struggling readers with much high success reading. You could measure fluency at the beginning and at the end of these three weeks. If you don't observe improvements in fluent reading, write to the author. Really.

6. Remember that reading words fast is not fluency. *Fluency* is reading in phrases with appropriate expression and intonation. Work to move struggling readers to fluent reading and then watch them sprout!

chapter 5: Students Need to Develop Thoughtful Literacy

1. Have you ever quizzed a friend or loved one about their recall of a newspaper story? I think you should try it just to see how weird school "comprehension" questions are when applied to the majority of literate adults.

2. If we are preparing our students for the real adult world of work and life, what changes do we need to make in comprehension lessons/activities offered in our classrooms? Describe how you can make your classroom comprehension focus look more like what we expect adults to be able to do.

3. Observe a reading lesson with struggling readers. Note how much emphasis is placed on understanding the text being read. Note any activities that seem to reflect "thoughtful literacy." Note any that reflect a more interrogational emphasis, just the facts, please, approach. Would you classify the lesson you observed as comprehension focused?

4. Observe a classroom social studies lesson. Note whether the activities children are asked to do are focused on understanding. Or, are the activities more focused on remembering only with or without understanding?

5. Literate conversations about material that has been read are powerful for fostering understanding, perhaps more powerful than comprehension strategies lessons. Try engaging your students, struggling readers especially, in literate conversations. Don't be disappointed if they seem not to know how to engage in literate conversation initially. After years of interrogation they may need some time to develop their conversational skills.

6. Were you surprised that the results of skills-emphasis reading instruction were so weak? Were you surprised that more thoughtful reading lessons produced such consistently strong gains? How would you describe the sorts of reading intervention programs offered in your school? Skills- or meaning-emphasis? How would you describe the reading lessons you provide your readers?

7. How many of the strategy lessons featured on page 136 have you offered your students this year? Select one strategy lesson you have not featured and offer it to your students. After a few weeks do you see a change in your students proficiencies?

8. Struggling readers invariably know the meanings of fewer words than good readers. In part that is because they read less, and volume of reading is the key factor in vocabulary development. Describe the sorts of activities you use to foster vocabulary development. Are there other strategies you could be using?

9. Think about your reading lessons. Do you provide many opportunities for readers to think about what they are reading? Or do your lessons focus more on checking their recall of what they've read?

10. Did it surprise you to learn that researchers have found that almost nothing offered as comprehension instruction in core reading programs is supported by the research?

chapter 6: Where to Begin: Instruction for Struggling Readers

1. Were you aware of the emerging consensus among researchers that learning disabilities and dyslexia are largely caused by inadequate reading instruction, not by some mysterious neurological difference or deficit? In other words, we create children with LD and dyslexia by simply not providing some struggling readers with sufficient expert reading instruction. How many pupils with LD has your school identified? Can you document that they are receiving more and better reading instruction than anyone else in your building?

2. Has your school provided you with extensive professional development in teaching struggling readers? Maybe you are reading this text as part of such an initiative. Maybe not. Discuss professional development opportunities you have been provided.

3. Have you participated in something like the TAPER activity as professional development? If not, could you initiate such an activity in your school?

4. Are teachers in your school typically engaged in professional conversations with each other? Or, do you work in a school where teachers complain but rarely engage in professional discussions of teaching? How could you begin to change this?

5. Classroom teachers are the most important aspect of schools when it comes to teaching children to read. Some classroom teachers teach everyone to read, often with no help from anyone else. Other teachers fail to teach many students to read even with help. How many of each type of teacher are working in your school?

6. Does your school have a certified reading specialist on staff? If so, you are one of the few such schools. Discuss with your colleagues how you could increase the number of reading specialists working in your district.

7. Do professional support staff (reading specialists, learning disability teachers, special education teachers, etc.) in your school have the opportunity to work intensively with struggling readers? Or are they working nonintensively and solving the reading problems of few children? Can you imagine a different use of these staff to increase the numbers of struggling readers who receive intensive, expert reading instruction?

8. Do classroom teachers in your school offer struggling readers two guided reading lessons every day? If not, why not?

9. Does your school have an after-school program for students? For struggling readers? Is the program staffed by expert teachers of reading? If not, why not?

10. Does your school have a program to ensure children have easy access to books they can read and want to read every summer, all summer? If not, begin planning how to change this and make it easy for kids to have books in their hands all summer long.

11. Think about the high school(s) in your school district. Do they offer struggling readers intensive and expert reading instruction? Do they offer such instruction every year of high school? If not, what could you do to change the current situation?

Afterword

Thank you for reading this book and maybe even responding to the questions in this study guide. Remember: Teachers are the most important factor in how many struggling readers we have in our schools. Work to become a better teacher every year. And remember this: Change will never happen unless someone begins to push for it. So start pushing tomorrow.

Reading Reaction Sheet

Facilitator/Recorder (person who initiated the discussion): _____

Group reactants: _____

_____

Date of reaction/discussion: _____

Chapter title and author(s): _____

_____

Question #1: What ideas and information from this chapter could be used in classroom instruction?

Reactions:

Question #2: _____

_____

Reactions:

Question #3: _____

_____

Reactions:

Question #4: _____

_____

Reactions:

Bibliography

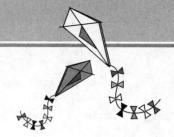

Achilles, C. M. (1999). *Let's put kids first, finally: Getting class size right.* Thousand Oaks, CA: Corwin Press.

Adams, G. L., & Englemann, S. (1996). *Research on direct instruction: Twenty-five years beyond DISTAR.* Eugene, OR: Educational Achievement Systems.

Alexander, K. L., Entwisle, D. R., & Olson, L. S. (2007). Lasting consequences of the summer learning gap. *American Sociological Review, 72*(2), 167–180.

Allington, R. L. (1977). If they don't read much, how they ever gonna get good? *Journal of Reading, 21,* 57–61.

———. (1980a). Poor readers don't get to read much in reading groups. *Language Arts, 57,* 872–877.

———. (1980b). Teacher interruption behaviors during primary grade oral reading. *Journal of Educational Psychology, 72,* 371–377.

———. (1983a). Fluency: The neglected goal. *Reading Teacher, 36,* 556–561.

———. (1983b). The reading instruction provided readers of differing abilities. *Elementary School Journal, 83,* 548–559.

———. (1984a). Content coverage and contextual reading in reading groups. *Journal of Reading Behavior, 16,* 85–96.

———. (1984b). Oral reading. In P. D. Pearson (Ed.), *Handbook of reading research* (pp. 829–864). New York: Longman.

———. (1987). Shattered hopes: Why two federal programs have failed to correct reading failure. *Learning, 13,* 60–64.

———. (1991). The legacy of "Slow It Down and Make It More Concrete." In J. Zutell & S. McCormick (Eds.), *Learner factors/teacher factors: Issues in literacy research and instruction* (40th Yearbook of the National Reading Conference, pp. 19–30). Chicago: National Reading Conference.

———. (1994a). The schools we have. The schools we need. *Reading Teacher, 48,* 2–16.

———. (1994b). What's special about special programs for children who find learning to read difficult? *Journal of Reading Behavior, 26,* 1–21.

———. (2001). Does state and federal reading policy-making matter? In T. Loveless (Ed.), *The great curriculum debate* (pp. 268–298). Washington, DC: Brookings.

———. (2002a). You can't learn much from books you can't read. *Educational Leadership, 60,* 16–19.

———. (2002b). *Big brother and the national reading curriculum: How ideology trumped evidence.* Portsmouth, NH: Heinemann.

———. (2002c). Research on reading/learning disability interventions. In A. E. Farstrup & S. J. Samuels (Eds.), *What research says about reading instruction* (3rd ed., pp. 261–290). Newark, DE: International Reading Association.

———. (2002d). What I've learned about effective reading instruction from a decade of studying exemplary elementary classroom teachers. *Phi Delta Kappan, 83,* 740–747.

———. (2004a). Setting the record straight. *Educational Leadership, 61,* 22–25.

———. (2004b). Federal intrusion in research and teaching and the medical model myth. In J. Carlson & J. R. Levin (Eds.), *Scientifically based educational research and federal funding agencies: The case of the No Child Left Behind legislation* (pp. 37–48). New York: Information Age.

———. (2005). Proven programs, profits and practice: Ten unprofitable but scientific strategies for improving reading achievement. In B. Altwerger (Ed.), *Reading for profit: How the bottom line leaves kids behind.* Portsmouth, NH: Heinemann.

———. (2006) Reading lessons and federal policymaking. *Elementary School Journal, 107*(1), 3–15.

———. (2007). Intervention all day long: New hope for struggling readers. *Voices from the Middle, 14*(4), 7–14.

————. (2009a). If they don't read much... 30 years later. In E. H. Hiebert (Ed.), *Reading more, reading better* (pp. 30–54). New York: Guilford.

————. (2009b). Literacy policies that are needed: Thinking beyond No Child Left Behind. In Y. Goodman & J. Hoffman (Eds.), *Changing literacies, changing times: A historical perspective on the future of reading research, public policy, and classroom practices* (pp. 266–281). New York: Routledge.

————. (2009c). *What really matters in response to intervention: Research-based designs.* Boston: Allyn & Bacon.

————, Boxer, N., & Broikou, K. (1987). Jeremy, remedial reading and subject area classes. *Journal of Reading, 30,* 643–645.

————, & Cunningham, P. M. (2006). *Schools that work: Where all children read and write* (3rd ed.). New York: Longman.

————, & Gabriel, R. (2009). *Middle-schoolers and magazines: Can they read interesting, self-selected texts.* Paper presented at the Literacy Research Association, Albuquerque, NM.

————, Guice, S., Michaelson, N., Baker, K., & Li, S. (1996). Literature-based curriculum in high-poverty schools. In M. Graves, P. van den Broek, & B. Taylor (Eds.), *The first R: Every child's right to read* (pp. 73–96). New York: Teachers College Press.

————, & Johnston, P. H. (Eds.). (2002). *Reading to learn: Lessons from exemplary 4th grade classrooms.* New York: Guilford.

————, & McGill-Franzen, A. (1989). School response to reading failure: Chapter 1 and special education students in grades 2, 4, and 8. *Elementary School Journal, 89,* 529–542.

————, & McGill-Franzen, A. (1992). Unintended effects of educational reform in New York State. *Educational Policy, 6,* 396–413.

————, & McGill-Franzen, A. (2003). The impact of summer loss on the reading achievement gap. *Phi Delta Kappan, 85,* 68–75.

————, & McGill-Franzen, A. (2009). Comprehension difficulties of struggling readers. In S. Israel & G. G. Duffy (Eds.), *Handbook of comprehension research* (pp. 551–568). New York: Guilford.

————, & McGill-Franzen, A. (2010). *Why so much oral reading?* In E. H. Hiebert & R. Reutzel (Eds.), Revisiting silent reading: New directions for teachers and researchers. Newark, DE: International Reading Association.

————, McGill-Franzen, A., Camilli, G., Williams, L., Graff, J., Zeig, J., Zmach, C., & Nowak, R. (2010). Addressing summer reading setback among economically disadvantaged elementary students. *Reading Psychology, 31*(5), 411–427.

————, & Nowak, R. (2004). "Proven programs" and other unscientific ideas. In C. C. Block, D. Lapp, E. J. Cooper, J. Flood, N. Roser, & J. V. Tinajero (Eds.), *Teaching all the children: Strategies for developing literacy in an urban setting* (pp. 93–102). New York: Guilford.

————, & Walmsley, S. A. (2007). *No quick fix: Rethinking literacy programs in American elementary schools: The RTI edition.* New York: Teachers College Press.

————, & Woodside-Jiron, H. (1998). Thirty years of research . . . : When is a research summary not a research summary? In K. Goodman (Ed.), *In defense of good teaching: What teachers need to know about the reading wars* (pp. 143–157). York, ME: Stenhouse.

————, & Woodside-Jiron, H. (1999). The politics of literacy teaching: How "research" shaped educational policy. *Educational Researcher, 28*(8), 4–13.

Almasi, J. F., Garas, K., & Shanahan, L. (2005). Qualitative research and the report of the National Reading Panel: No methodology left behind? *Elementary School Journal.*

Alvermann, D. E., Young, J. P., Green, C., & Wisenbaker, J. M. (1999). Adolescents' perceptions and negotiations of literacy practices in after-school read and talk clubs. *American Educational Research Journal, 36*(2), 221–264.

American Library Association. (1998). *Information power: Building partnerships for learning.* Chicago: Author.

Anderson, R. C., Wilson, P., & Fielding, L. (1988). Growth in reading and how children spend their time outside of school. *Reading Research Quarterly, 23*(3), 285–303.

Anderson, V., & Roit, M. (1993). Planning and implementing collaborative strategy instruction for delayed readers in grades 6–10. *Elementary School Journal, 94,* 121–137.

Applebee, A. N. (1991). Literature: Whose heritage? In E. Hiebert (Ed.), *Literacy for a diverse society: Perspective, practices, and policies.* New York: Teachers College Press.

———, Langer, J. L., Nystrand, M., & Gamoran, A. (2003). Discussion-based approaches to developing understanding: Classroom instruction and student performance in middle and high school English. *American Educational Research Journal 40*, 685–730.

Armbruster, B., Lehr, F., & Osborn, J. (2001). *Put reading first*. Washington, DC: National Institute for Literacy.

Au, K., & Jordan, C. (1980). Teaching reading to Hawaiian children: Finding a culturally appropriate solution. In H. T. Trueba, G. P. Guthrie, & K. Au (Eds.), *Culture and the bilingual classroom* (pp. 139–152). Rowley, MA: Newbury House.

Baumann, J. F., & Duffy, A. M. (1997). *Engaged reading for pleasure and learning*. Athens, GA: National Reading Research Center, University of Georgia.

Beck, I., McKeown, M., & Kucan, L. (2002). *Bringing words to life: Robust vocabulary instruction*. New York: Guilford.

Beck, I. L., McKeown, M. G., Hamilton, R. L., & Kucan, L. (1997). *Questioning the author*. Newark, DE: International Reading Association.

Beers, K. (2003). *When kids can't read: What teachers can do, a guide for teachers 6–12*. Portsmouth, NH: Heinemann.

Bembry, K. L., Jordan, H. R., Gomez, E., Anderson, M., & Mendro, R. L. (1998). *Policy implications of long-term teacher effects on student achievement*. Paper presented at the American Educational Research Association.

Berends, M., Bodilly, S., & Kirby, S. N. (2002). Looking back over a decade of whole-school reform: The experience of new American schools. *Phi Delta Kappan, 84*, 168–175.

Berger, A., & Shafran, E. (2000). *Teens for literacy*. Newark, DE: International Reading Association.

Bergman, J. L. (1992). SAIL—A way to success and independence for low-achieving readers. *Reading Teacher, 45*, 598–603.

Berliner, D. C. (1981). Academic learning time and reading achievement. In J. Guthrie (Ed.), *Comprehension and teaching: Research reviews* (pp. 203–225). Newark, DE: International Reading Association.

———, & Biddle, B. (1995). *The manufactured crisis*. New York: Longman.

Betts, E. A. (1946). *Foundations of reading instruction*. New York: American Book Co.

Biemiller, A. (1970). The development of the use of graphic and contextual information as children learn to read. *Reading Research Quarterly, 6*, 75–96.

———. (2010). Vocabulary development and implication for reading problems. In A. McGill-Franzen and R. L. Allington (Eds.), *Handbook of Reading Disability Research* (pp. 208–218). New York: Routledge.

Binkley, M., & Williams, T. (1996). *Reading literacy in the United States: Findings from the IEA Reading Literacy Study* (NCES 96-258). Washington, DC: U.S. Department of Education, Office of Educational Research and Improvement.

Birman, B. F., Desimone, L., Porter, A. C., & Garet, M. (2000). Designing professional development that works. *Educational Leadership, 57*, 28–32.

Block, C. C. (1993). Strategy instruction in a literature-based program. *Elementary School Journal, 94*, 139–151.

Block, J. H. (1980). Success rate. In C. Denham & A. Lieberman (Eds.), *Time to learn*. Washington, DC: National Institute of Education.

Bond, G. L., & Dykstra, R. (1967). The cooperative research program in first-grade reading instruction. *Reading Research Quarterly, 2*(4), 5–142.

Borman, G. D., Hewes, G. M., Overman, L. T., & Brown, S. (2003). Comprehensive school reform and achievement: A meta-analysis. *Review of Educational Research, 73*(1), 125–139.

Brabham, E. G., & Lynch-Brown, C. (2002). Effects of teachers' reading-aloud styles on vocabulary acquisition and comprehension of students in the early elementary grades. *Journal of Educational Psychology, 94*, 465–473.

Bracey, G. W. (2004). *Setting the record straight: Responses to misconceptions about public education in the United States*. Portsmouth, NH: Heinemann.

Brandt, R. (1986, October). On the expert teacher: A conversation with David Berliner. *Educational Leadership, 44*, 4–9.

Brenner, D., & Hiebert, E. H. (2010). If I follow the teachers' editions, isn't that enough? Analyzing reading volume in six core reading programs. *Elementary School Journal, 110*(3), 347–363.

Brophy, J. (2000). Beyond balance: Goal awareness, developmental progressions, tailoring to the context, and supports for teachers in ideal reading and literacy programs. In M. Graves, P. van den Broek, & B. Taylor (Eds.), *Reading for meaning: Fostering comprehension in the middle grades* (pp. 170–192). New York: Teachers College Press.

Brown, R. G. (1991). *Schools of thought: How the politics of literacy shape thinking in the classroom.* San Francisco: Jossey-Bass.

Brozo, W. G., Shiel, G., & Topping, K. (2008). Engagement in reading: Lessons learned from three PISA countries. *Journal of Adolescent and Adult Literacy, 51*(4), 304–315.

Bruer, J. T. (1994). *Schools for thought: A science for learning in the classroom.* Cambridge, MA: MIT Press.

Budiansky, S. (2001, February). The trouble with textbooks. *Prism,* 24–27.

Buly, M. R., & Valencia, S. W. (2002). Below the bar: Profiles of students who fail state reading assessments. *Educational Evaluation and Policy Analysis, 24,* 219–239.

Camilli, G., Vargas, S., & Yurecko, M. (2003). Teaching children to read: The fragile link between science and federal education policy. *Education Policy Analysis Archives, 11.* Retrieved May 20, 2003, from http://epaa.asu.edu/epaa/v11n15.

——, & Wolfe, P. (2004). Research on reading: A cautionary tale. *Educational Leadership, 61,* 26–29.

Campuzano, L., Dynarski, M., Agodini, R., & Rall, K. (2009). *Effectiveness of reading and mathematics software products: Findings from two student cohorts.* Washington, DC: National Center for Education Evaluation and Regional Assistance, Institute of Education Sciences, U.S. Department of Education.

Carpenter, R., & Pearson, P. D. (1999, December). *Estimating summer school reading achievement.* Paper presented at the National Reading Conference, Austin, TX.

Carter, L. (1984). The sustaining effects study of compensatory and elementary education. *Educational Researcher, 12,* 4–13.

Cazden, C. B. (1988). *Classroom discourse: The language of teaching and learning.* Portsmouth, NH: Heinemann.

Chall, J. S. (1983). *Stages of reading development.* New York: McGraw-Hill.

——. (1987). *Learning to read: The great debate* (updated ed.) New York: McGraw-Hill.

——, Bissex, G., Conard, S., & Harris-Sharples, S. (1996). *Qualitative assessment of text difficulty: A practical guide for teachers and authors.* Cambridge, MA: Brookline.

——, & Conard, S. S. (1991). *Should textbooks challenge students?* New York: Teachers College Press.

——, & Dale, E. (1995). *The Dale-Chall Readability Formula.* Brookline, MA: Brookline.

Chinn, C. A., Waggoner, M. A., Anderson, R. C., Schommer, M., & Wilkinson, I. (1993). Situated actions during reading lessons: A microanalysis of oral reading error episodes. *American Educational Research Journal, 30,* 361–392.

Chomsky, C. (1972). Stages in language development and reading exposure. *Harvard Educational Review, 42,* 1–33.

Cipielewski, J., & Stanovich, K. (1992). Predicting growth in reading ability from children's exposure to print. *Journal of Experimental Child Psychology, 54,* 74–89.

Clay, M. M. (1993). *An observation survey of early literacy achievement.* Portsmouth, NH: Heinemann.

——, & Imlach, R. H. (1971). Juncture, pitch, and stress as reading behavior variables. *Journal of Verbal Learning and Verbal Behavior, 10,* 133–139.

Coles, A. D. (1999, September 8). Gallup poll finds Americans committed to public schools. *Education Week,* 12.

Coles, G. (2003). *Reading, the naked truth: Literacy, legislation, and lies.* Portsmouth, NH: Heinemann.

Collins, C. (1991). Reading instruction that increases thinking abilities. *Journal of Reading, 34,* 510–516.

Collins, J. (1986). Differential instruction in reading groups. In J. Cook-Gumperz (Ed.), *The social construction of literacy* (pp. 117–137). New York: Cambridge University Press.

Connor, C. M., Morrison, F. J., Fishman, B. J., Schatschneider, C., & Underwood, P. (2007, January). Algorithm-guided individual reading instruction. *Science, 15,* 464–465.

Cooper, H., Charleton, K., Valentine, J. C., & Muhlenbruck, L. (2000). *Making the most of summer school: A meta-analytic and narrative review.* Ann Arbor, MI; Society for Research in Child Development.

——, Nye, B., Charlton, K., Lindsay, J., & Greathouse, S. (1996). The effects of summer vacation on achievement test scores: A narrative and meta-analytic review. *Review of Educational Research, 66* (3, Fall), 227–268.

————, Robinson, J. C., & Patall, E. A. (2006). Does homework improve academic achievement? *Review of Educational Research, 76*(1), 1–62.

Croninger, R. G., & Valli, L. (2009). "Where is the action?" Challenges to studying the teaching of reading in elementary classrooms. *Educational Researcher, 38*(2), 100–108.

Crowell, P. C., & Klein, T. W. (1981). Preventing summer loss of reading skills among primary children. *Reading Teacher, 34,* 561–564.

Cuban, L. (1993). *How teachers taught: Constancy and change in American classrooms, 1880–1990* (2nd ed.). New York: Longman.

Cunningham, A. E., & Stanovich, K. E. (1998). The impact of print exposure on word recognition. In J. Metsala & L. Ehri (Eds.), *Word recognition in beginning literacy* (pp. 235–262). Mahwah, NJ: Erlbaum.

Cunningham, J. W., Erickson, K. A., Spadorcia, S. A., Koppenhaver, D. A., Cunningham, P. M., Yoder, D. E., & McKenna, M. C. (1999). Assessing decoding from an onset-rime perspective. *Journal of Literacy Research, 31,* 391–414.

Cunningham, P. M. (2008). *Phonics they use: Words for reading and writing* (5th ed.). Boston: Allyn & Bacon.

————. (2008). *What really matters in vocabulary: research-based practices across the curriculum.* Boston: Allyn & Bacon.

————, & Allington, R. L. (2011). *Classrooms that work: They can all read and write* (5th ed.). Boston: Allyn & Bacon.

Cutting, L. E., & Scarborough, H. S. (2006). Prediction of reading comprehension: Relative contributions of word recognition, language proficiency, and other cognitive skills can depend on how comprehension is measured. *Scientific Studies of Reading, 10*(3), 277–299.

D'Agostino, J. V., & Murphy, J. A. (2004). A meta-analysis of reading recovery in United States schools. *Educational Evaluation and Policy Analysis, 26,* 23–38.

Dahl, K. L., & Freppon, P. A. (1995). A comparison of inner-city children's interpretations of reading and writing instruction in skills-based and whole language classrooms. *Reading Research Quarterly, 30,* 50–74.

Dahl, P. R. (1977). An experimental program for teaching high-speed word recognition and comprehension skills. In J. Button, T. Lovitt, & T. Rowland (Eds.), *Communications research in learning disabilities and mental retardation.* Baltimore: University Park Press.

Darling-Hammond, L. (1990). Instructional policy into practice: "The power of the bottom over the top." *Educational Evaluation and Policy Analysis, 12*(3), 233–241.

————. (1997). *Doing what matters most: Investing in quality teaching.* New York: National Commission on Teaching and America's Future.

————. (1998). Teachers and teaching: Testing policy hypotheses from a national commission report. *Educational Researcher, 27*(1), 5–15.

Datnow, A., & Castellano, M. (2000). Teachers' responses to Success for All: How beliefs, experiences, and adaptations shape implementation. *American Educational Research Journal, 37,* 775–799.

Davidson, J., & Koppenhaver, D. (1993). *Adolescent literacy: What works and why* (2nd ed.). Hamden, CT: Garland.

Delpit, L. (1995). *Other people's children: Cultural conflict in the classroom.* New York: Free Press.

Denham, C., & Lieberman, A. (1980). *Time to learn* (1980; 695–717). Washington, DC: U.S. Government Printing Office.

Dennis, D. (2008). Are assessment data really driving middle school reading instruction? *Journal of Adolescent and Adult Literacy, 51*(7), 578–587.

————. (2009). "I'm not stupid": How assessment drives (in)appropriate reading instruction. *Journal of Adolescent and Adult Literacy, 53*(4), 283–290.

Dewitz, P., Jones, J., & Leahy, S. (2009). Comprehension strategy instruction in core reading programs. *Reading Research Quarterly, 44*(2), 102–126.

Dickinson, D. K., & Smith, M. W. (1994). Long-term effects of preschool teachers' book readings on low-income children's vocabulary and story comprehension. *Reading Research Quarterly, 29*(2), 104–123.

Dole, J., Brown, K. J., & Trathen, W. (1996). The effects of strategy instruction on the comprehension performance of at-risk students. *Reading Research Quarterly, 31*(1), 62–88.

Donahue, P. L., Voelkl, K. E., Campbell, J. R., & Mazzeo, J. (1999). *NAEP 1998 reading report card for the nation and the states.* (NCES 1999; 500). Washington DC: National Center for Education Statistics, Office of Educational Research and Improvement, U.S. Department of Education.

Dowhower, S. L. (1987). Effects of repeated reading on second grade transitional readers' fluency and comprehension. *Reading Research Quarterly, 22,* 389–406.

Doyle, W. (1983). Academic work. *Review of Educational Research, 53,* 159–199.

Duffy, G. G. (1993). Teachers' progress toward becoming expert strategy teachers. *Elementary School Journal, 94*(2), 109–120.

———. (2003). *Explaining reading: A resource for teaching concepts, skills, and strategies.* New York: Guilford.

———. (2004). Teachers who improve reading achievement: What research says about what they do and how to develop them. In D. Strickland & M. Kamil (Eds.), *Improving reading achievement through professional development* (pp. 3–22). Norwood, MA: Christopher-Gordon.

———, & Hoffman, J. V. (1999). In pursuit of an illusion: The search for a perfect method. *Reading Teacher, 53*(1), 10–16.

———, Roehler, L., & Rackliffe, G. (1986). How teachers' instructional talk influences student understanding of lesson content. *Elementary School Journal, 87,* 3–16.

Duffy-Hester, A. (1999). Teaching struggling readers in elementary school classrooms: A review of classroom reading programs and principles for instruction. *Reading Teacher, 52*(5), 480–495.

Duke, N. K. (2000). For the rich it's richer: Print experiences and environments offered to children in very low- and very high-socioeconomic status first-grade classrooms. *American Educational Research Journal, 37,* 441–478.

———. (2004). The case for informational text. *Educational Leadership, 61,* 40–44.

Duthie, C. (1996). *True stories: Nonfiction in the primary classroom.* York, ME: Stenhouse.

Dweck, C. S. (1999). *Self-theories: Their role in motivation, personality, and development.* Philadelphia: Taylor & Francis.

Eder, D., & Felmlee, D. (1984). The development of attention norms in ability groups. In P. Peterson, L. Wilkinson, & M. Hallinan (Eds.), *The social context of instruction.* New York: Academic Press.

Egoff, S. (1972, October). If that don't do no good, that won't do no harm: The uses and dangers of mediocrity in children's reading. *School Library Journal.*

Ehri, L. C., Dreyer, L. G., Flugman, B., & Gross, A. (2007). Reading Rescue: An effective tutoring intervention model for language minority students who are struggling readers in first grade. *American Educational Research Journal, 44*(2), 414–448.

Eldredge, J. L., Reutzel, D. R., & Hollingsworth, P. M. (1996). Comparing the effectiveness of two oral reading practices: Round-Robin reading and the shared book experience. *Journal of Literacy Research, 28*(2), 201–225.

Elley, W. B. (1992). *How in the world do students read? IEA study of reading literacy.* The Hague, Netherlands: International Association for the Evaluation of Educational Achievement.

Elmore, R. F., Peterson, P. L., & McCarthy, S. J. (1996). *Restructuring in the classroom: Teaching, learning, and school organization.* San Francisco: Jossey-Bass.

Entwisle, D. R., Alexander, K. L., & Olson, L. S. (1997). *Children, schools, and inequality.* Boulder, CO: Westview.

Fawson, P. C., Reutzel, D. R., Ludlow, B. C., Sudweeks, R., & Smith, J. A. (2006). Examining the reliability of running records: Attaining generalizable results. *Journal of Educational Research, 100*(2), 113–126.

Ferguson, R. F. (1991). Paying for public education: New evidence on how and why money matters. *Harvard Journal on Legislation, 28,* 465–491.

Fiester, L. (2010). *Learning to read: Why reading by the end of third grade matters.* Baltimore, MD: Annie E. Casey Foundation.

Fisher, C. W., & Berliner, D. C. (1985). *Perspectives on instructional time.* New York: Longman.

Foertsch, M. A. (1992). *Reading in and out of school: Achievement of American students in grades 4, 8, and 12 in 1989–90.* Washington, DC: National Center for Educational Statistics, U.S. Government Printing Office.

Fountas, I. C., & Pinnell, G. S. (2001). *Guiding readers and writers, grades 3–6.* Portsmouth, NH: Heinemann.

———, & Pinnell, G. S. (2005). *Leveled book K–8: Matching texts to readers for effective teaching.* Portsmouth, NH: Heinemann.

Gallagher, K. (2009). *Readicide: How schools are killing reading and what you can do about it.* Portland, ME: Stenhouse.

Gambrell, L. B., & Marinak, B. A. (1997). Incentives and intrinsic motivation to read. In J. T. Guthrie & A. Wigfield (Eds.), *Reading engagement: Motivating readers through integrated instruction* (pp. 205–216). Newark, DE: International Reading Association.

———, Wilson, R. M., & Gantt, W. N. (1981). Classroom observations of task-attending behaviors of good and poor readers. *Journal of Educational Research, 74*(6), 400–404.

Gamse, B. C., Jacob, R. T., Horst, M., Boulay, B., & Unlu, F. (2009). *Reading First Impact Study Final Report* (NCEE 2009; 4038). Washington, DC: National Center for Education Evaluation and Regional Assistance, Institute of Education Sciences, U.S. Department of Education.

Garan, E. (2002). *Resisting reading mandates: How to triumph with the truth.* Portsmouth, NH: Heinemann.

Gartner, A., & Lipsky, D. K. (1987). Beyond special education: Toward a quality system for all students. *Harvard Educational Review, 57,* 367–395.

Gaskins, I. W., & Elliot, T. T. (1991). *Implementing cognitive strategy instruction across the school: The benchmark manual for teachers.* Cambridge, MA: Brookline.

Gaskins, R. W. (1996). "That's just how it was": The effect of issue related emotional involvement on reading comprehension. *Reading Research Quarterly, 31,* 386–405.

Gerber, S. B., Finn, J., Achilles, C., & Boyd-Zaharias, J. (2001). Teacher aides and students' academic achievement. *Educational Evaluation and Policy Analysis, 23*(2), 123–143.

Glass, G. V. (1983). Effectiveness of special education. *Policy Studies Review, 2,* 65–78.

Goatley, V. J., Brock, C. H., & Raphael, T. E. (1995). Diverse learners participating in regular education "book clubs." *Reading Research Quarterly, 30*(3), 352–380.

Goodlad, J. I. (1983). *A place called school: Prospects for the future.* New York: McGraw-Hill.

Graves, M., & Watts-Taffe, S. (2002). The place of word conciousness in a research-based vocabulary program. In A. Farstrup & S. J. Samuels (Eds.), *What research has to say about reading instruction* (pp. 140–165). Newark, DE: International Reading Association.

Grissmer, D. W., Kirby, S. N., Berends, M., & Williamson, S. (1994). *Student achievement and the changing American family.* Santa Monica, CA: RAND, Institute on Education and Training.

Guice, S., Allington, R. L., Johnston, P., Baker, K., & Michelson, N. (1996). Access?: Books, children, and literature-based curriculum in schools. *The New Advocate, 9*(3), 197–207.

Guthrie, J. T. (2002). Preparing students for high-stakes test taking in reading. In A. Farstrup & S. J. Samuels (Eds.), *What research has to say about reading instruction* (pp. 370–391). Newark, DE: International Reading Association.

———. (2004). Teaching for literacy engagement. *Journal of Literacy Research, 36*(1), 1–28.

———, & Anderson, E. (1999). Engagement in reading: Processes of motivated, strategic, knowledgeable, social readers. In J. T. Guthrie, & D. Alvermann (Eds.), *Engaged reading: Processes, practices, and policy implications* (pp. 17–45). New York: Teachers College Press.

———, & Humenick, N. M. (2004). Motivating students to read: Evidence for classroom practices that increase motivation and achievement. In P. McCardle & V. Chhabra (Eds.), *The voice of evidence in reading research* (pp. 329–354). Baltimore: Paul Brookes.

———, & Knowles, K. T. (2001). Promoting reading motivation. In L. Verhoeven & C. Snow (Eds.), *Literacy and motivation: Reading engagement in individuals and groups* (pp. 159–176). Mahwah, NJ: Erlbaum.

———, Van Meter, P., McCann, A., Wigfield, A., Bennett, I., Poundstone, C., Rice, M., Faibisch, F., Hunt, B., & Mitchell, A. (1996). Growth of literacy engagement: Changes in motivations and strategies during concept-oriented reading instruction. *Reading Research Quarterly, 31,* 306–322.

———, Wigfield, A., Barbosa, P., Perencevich, K., Taboada, A., Davis, M., Scaffidi, N., & Tonks, S. (2004). Increasing reading comprehension and engagement through concept-oriented reading instruction. *Journal of Educational Psychology, 96,* 403–423.

———, Wigfield, A., Metsala, J., & Cox, K. (1999). Motivational and cognitive predictors of text comprehension and reading amount. *Scientific Studies of Reading, 3*(3), 231–256.

———, Wigfield, A., & Von Secker, C. (2000). Effects of integrated instruction on motivation and strategy use in reading. *Journal of Educational Psychology, 92,* 331–341.

Halpern, R. (1999). After-school programs for low-income children: Promise and challenges. *The Future of Children, 9*(2), 81–95.

Harris, A. J., & Sipay, E. R. (1990). *How to increase reading ability* (8th ed.) New York: Longman.

Harvey, S., & Goudvis, A. (2000). *Strategies that work: Teaching comprehension to enhance understanding.* York, ME: Stenhouse.

Hayes, D. P., & Grether, J. (1983). The school year and vacations: When do students learn? *Cornell Journal of Social Relations, 17*(1), 56–71.

Haynes, M. C., & Jenkins, J. R. (1986). Reading instruction in special education resource rooms. *American Educational Research Journal, 23*(2), 161–190.

Herman, P. (1985). The effect of repeated readings on reading rate, speech pauses, and word recognition accuracy. *Reading Research Quarterly, 20,* 553–565.

Hidi, S., & Harackiewicz, J. M. (2000). Motivating the academically unmotivated: A critical issue for the 21st century. *Review of Educational Research, 70*(2), 151–179.

Hiebert, E. H. (1983). An examination of ability grouping for reading instruction. *Reading Research Quarterly, 18,* 231–255.

Hoerr, T. R. (2009). How book groups bring change. *Educational Leadership, 66*(5), 80–82.

Hoff, D. J., & Manzo, K. K. (1999, February 17). U.S. students bounce back in reading. *Education Week,* 16.

Hoffman, J. V., McCarthy, S. J., Elliott, B., Bayles, D., Price, D., Ferree, A., & Abbott, J. (1998). The literature-based basals in first-grade classrooms: Savior, satan, or same-old, same-old? *Reading Research Quarterly, 33*(2), 168–197.

———, O'Neal, S. F., Kastler, L., Clements, R., Segel, K., & Nash, M. (1984). Guided oral reading and miscue focused verbal feedback in second grade classrooms. *Reading Research Quarterly, 19,* 367–384.

Holdaway, D. (1979). *The foundations of literacy.* Sydney, Australia: Ashton-Scholastic.

House, E. R. (1991). Big policy, little policy. *Educational Researcher, 20,* 21–26.

———, Glass, G. V., McLean, L., & Walker, D. (1978). No simple answers: Critique of the follow through evaluation. *Harvard Educational Review, 48,* 128–160.

Howard, M. (2009). *RTI from all sides: What every teacher needs to know.* Portsmouth, NH: Heinemann.

Invernizzi, M., Rosemary, C., Juel, C., & Richards, H. (1997). At-risk readers and community volunteers: A three-year perspective. *Scientific Studies of Reading, 1*(3), 277–300.

Ivey, G. (1999). A multicase study in the middle school: Complexities among young adolescent readers. *Reading Research Quarterly, 34,* 172–193.

———. (2010). Texts that matter. *Educational Leadership, 67*(6), 18–23.

———, & Baker, M. I. (2004). Phonics instruction for older students? Just say no. *Educational Leadership, 61,* 35–39.

———, & Broaddus, K. (2001). Just plain reading: A survey of what makes students want to read in middle schools. *Reading Research Quarterly, 36,* 350–377.

James-Burdumy, S., Deke, J., Lugo-Gil, J., Carey, N., Hershey, A., Gersten, R., et al. (2010). *Effectiveness of selected supplemental reading comprehension interventions: Findings from two student cohorts.* Washington, DC: National Center for Educational Evaluation and Regional Assistance, Institute of Education Sciences, USDE.

Jenkins, C. B. (1999). *The allure of authors: Author studies in the elementary classroom.* Portsmouth, NH: Heinemann.

Jenkins, J. R., Fuchs, L. S., van den Broek, P., Esping, C., & Deno, S. L. (2003): Sources of individual differences in reading comprehension and reading fluency. *Journal of Educational Psychology, 95,* 719–729.

———, Peyton, J. A., Sanders, E. A., & Vadasy, P. F. (2004). Effects of reading decodable texts in supplemental first-grade tutoring. *Scientific Studies of Reading, 8*(1), 53–85.

———, Piuos, C., & Peterson, D. (1988). Categorial programs for remedial and handicapped students. *Exceptional Children, 55,* 147–158.

Johnston, P. (1985). Understanding reading failure: A case study approach. *Harvard Educational Review, 55*(2), 153–177.

———. (2000). *Running records.* York, ME: Stenhouse.

———. (2004). *Choice words: How our language affects children's learning.* York, ME: Stenhouse.

———. (2010). *RTI in literacy: Responsive and comprehensive.* Newark: DE: International Reading Association.

———. (in press). Response to intervention in literacy: Problems and possibilities. *Elementary School Journal.*

———, & Allington, R. L. (1991). Remediation. In P. D. Pearson (Ed.), *Handbook of reading research, vol. 2* (pp. 984–1012). New York: Longman.

———, Allington, R. L., Guice, S., & Brooks, G. W. (1998). Small change: A multi-level study of the implementation of literature-based instruction. *Peabody Journal of Education, 73*(3), 81–103.

Jordan, N. L. (2005). Basal readers and reading as socialization: What are children learning? *Language Arts, 82,* 204–213.

Juel, C. (1994). *Learning to read and write in one elementary school.* New York: Springer-Verlag.

———. (1996). What makes literacy tutoring effective? *Reading Research Quarterly, 31*(3), 268–289.

Kamil, M. L. (2004). Vocabulary and comprehension instruction. In P. McCardle and V. Chhabra (Eds.), *The voice of evidence in reading research* (pp. 213–234). Baltimore: Paul Brookes.

Keene, E. (2008). *To understand: New horizons in reading comprehension.* Portsmouth, NH: Heinemann.

Keene, E. O., & Zimmerman, S. (1997). *Mosaic of thought: Teaching comprehension in a reader's workshop.* Portsmouth, NH: Heinemann.

Keisling, H. (1978). Productivity of instructional time by mode of instruction for students at varying levels of reading skill. *Reading Research Quarterly, 13,* 554–582.

Kibby, M. W. (1995). *Student literacy: Myths and realities.* Bloomington, IN: Phi Delta Kappa Educational Foundation.

Kim, J. (2004). Summer reading and the ethnic achievement gap. *Journal of Education of Students at Risk, 9,* 169–189.

Kim, J. S., & White, T. G. (2008). Scaffolding voluntary summer reading for children in grades 3 to 5: An experimental study. *Scientific Studies of Reading, 12*(1), 1–23.

Klare, G. R. (1984). Readability. In P. D. Pearson (Ed.), *Handbook of reading research* (pp. 681–744). New York: Longman.

Knapp, M. S. (1995). *Teaching for meaning in high-poverty classrooms.* New York: Teachers College Press.

Kos, R. (1991). Persistence of reading disabilities: Voices of four middle-school students. *American Educational Research Journal, 28,* 875–895.

Koslin, B. L., Zeno, S., & Koslin, S. (1987). *The DRP: An effective measure in reading.* New York: College Entrance Examination Board.

Kovach, W., & Rosentiel, T. (1999). *Warp Speed: America in the age of mixed media.* New York: Century Foundation.

Kozol, J. (1991). *Savage inequalities: Children in America's schools.* New York: Crown.

Krashen, S. (2004a). *The power of reading: Insights from the research.* Englewood, CO: Libraries Unlimited.

———. (2004b). False claims about literacy development. *Educational Leadership, 61,* 18–21.

Kucan, L., & Beck, I. L. (1997). Thinking aloud and reading comprehension research: Inquiry, instruction, and social interaction. *Review of Educational Research, 67*(3), 271–299.

Kuhn, M. R. (2005). Helping students become accurate, expressive readers: Fluency instruction for small groups. *Reading Teacher, 58,* 338–344.

———, Schwanenflugel, P., Morris, R. D., Morrow, L. M., Woo, D., Meisinger, B., et al. (2006). Teaching children to become fluent and automatic readers. *Journal of Literacy Research 38*(4), 357–388.

———, Schwanenflugel, P. J., & Meisinger, E. B. (2010). Aligning theory and assessment of reading fluency: Automaticity, prosody, and definitions of fluency. *Reading Research Quarterly, 45*(2), 230–251.

———, & Stahl, S. A. (2003). Fluency: A review of developmental and remedial practices. *Journal of Educational Psychology, 95,* 3–21.

LaBerge, D., & Samuels, S. J. (1974). Toward a theory of automatic information processing in reading. *Cognitive Psychology, 6,* 293–323.

Langer, J. A. (1995). *Envisioning literature: Literary understanding and literature instruction.* New York: Teachers College Press.

———. (2002). *Effective literacy instruction: Building successful reading and writing programs.* Urbana, IL: NCTE.

Leach, J. M., Scarborough, H., & Rescorda, L. (2003). Late-emerging reading disabilities. *Journal of Educational Psychology, 95,* 211–224.

Leinhardt, G., & Pallay, A. (1982). Restrictive educational settings: Exile or haven? *Review of Educational Research, 52*(4), 557–578.

———, Zigmond, N., & Cooley, W. (1981). Reading instruction and its effects. *American Educational Research Journal, 18*(3), 343–361.

Lesesne, T. S. (2010). *Reading ladders: Leading students from where they are to where we'd like them to be.* Portsmouth, NH: Heinemann.

Lewis, M., & Samuels, S. J. (2004). Read more, read better? A meta-analysis of the literature on the relationship between exposure to reading and reading achievement. Unpublished paper, University of Minnesota.

Licopoli, L. (1984). The resource room and mainstreaming handicapped students: A case study. *Topics in Learning and Learning Disabilities, 3*(4), 1–15.

Linn, R. L. (2000). Assessments and accountability. *Educational Researcher, 29,* 4–16.

Lyon, G. R., & Moats, L. C. (1997). Critical conceptual and methodological considerations in reading intervention research. *Journal of Learning Disabilities, 30*(6), 578–588.

Lysynchuk, L. M., Pressley, M., D'Ailly, H., Smith, M., & Cake, H. (1989). A methodological analysis of experimental studies of comprehension strategy instruction. *Reading Research Quarterly, 24,* 458–470.

Mace, A. (1997). Organizing the instructional resource room. In M. Herzog (Ed.), *Inside learning network schools.* Katonah, NY: Richard C. Owen.

Malach, D. A., & Rutter, R. A. (2003). For nine months kids go to school, but in summer this school goes to kids. *Reading Teacher, 57*(1), 50–54.

Martinez, M. G., Roser, N. L., & Strecker, S. K. (1999). "I never thought I could be a star": A Readers Theater ticket to fluency. *Reading Teacher, 54,* 326–335.

Mastropieri, M. A., & Scruggs, T. E. (1997). Best practices in promoting reading comprehension in students with learning disabilities, 1976–1996. *Remedial and Special Education, 18*(4), 197–213.

Mathes, P. G., Denton, C. A., Fletcher, J. M., Anthony, J. L., Francis, D. J., & Schatschneider, C. (2005). The effects of theoretically different instruction and student characteristics on the skills of struggling readers. *Reading Research Quarterly, 40*(2), 148–182.

McBride-Chang, C., Manis, F., Seidenberg, M., Custodio, R., & Doi, L. (1993). Print exposure as a predictor of word reading and reading comprehension in disabled and nondisabled readers. *Journal of Educational Psychology, 85,* 230–238.

McGill-Franzen, A. (1993). "I could read the words!": Selecting good books for inexperienced readers. *Reading Teacher, 46,* 424–426.

———. (1996). Three children, three stories of school and literacy. *Language and Literacy Spectrum, 6,* 45–51.

———. (2000). Policy and instruction: What is the relationship? In M. Kamil, P. Mosenthal, P. D. Pearson, & R. Barr (Eds.), *Handbook of reading research, vol. III* (pp. 891–908). Mahwah, NJ: Erlbaum.

———. (2006) *Kindergarten literacy: Matching assessment and instruction in kindergarten.* New York: Scholastic.

———. (2009). Teachers using texts: Where we are and what we need. In E. H. Hiebert & M. Sailors (Eds.), *Finding the right texts: What works for beginning and struggling readers* (pp. 253–266). New York: Guilford.

———, & Allington, R. L. (1990). Comprehension and coherence: Neglected elements of literacy instruction in remedial and resource room services. *Journal of Reading, Writing, and Learning Disabilities, 6,* 149–182.

———, & Allington, R. L. (2008). Got books? *Educational Leadership, 65*(7), 20–23.

———, Allington, R. L., Yokoi, L., & Brooks, G. (1999). Putting books in the room seems necessary but not sufficient. *Journal of Educational Research, 93*(2), 67–74.

———, & Botzakis, S. (2009). Series books, graphic novels, comics, and magazines: Unauthorized texts, authorized literacy practices. In E. H. Hiebert (Ed.), *Reading more, reading better* (pp. 101–117). New York: Guilford.

———, & Lanford, C. (1994). Exposing the edge of the preschool curriculum: Teachers' talk about text and children's literary understandings. *Language Arts, 71,* 264–273.

———, Lanford, C., & Adams, E. (2002). Learning to be literate: A comparison of five early childhood programs. *Journal of Educational Psychology.*

———, Love, J. L., Zmach, C., & Solic, K. (2005). The confluence of two policy mandates: Core reading programs and 3rd grade retention. *Elementary School Journal.*

———, Ward, N., Goatley, V., & Machado, V. (2000). Teachers' use of the new standards frameworks and assessments: Local cases of New York state elementary grade teachers. *Reading Research and Instruction, 41,* 127–148.

———, Zmach, C., Solic, K., & Zeig, J. L. (2006). The confluence of two policy mandates: Core reading programs and third-grade retention in Florida. *Elementary School Journal, 107*(1), 67–91.

McQuillan, J. (1998). *The literacy crisis: False claims, real solutions.* Portsmouth, NH: Heinemann.

Mervar, K., & Hiebert, E. H. (1989). Literature-selection strategies and amount of reading in two literacy approaches. In S. McCormick & J. Zutell (Eds.), *Cognitive and social perspectives for literacy research and instruction* (pp. 529–535). Chicago: NRC.

Millin, S. K., & Rinehart, S. D. (1999). Some benefits of readers' theater participation for second grade Title I students. *Reading Research and Instruction, 39,* 71–88.

Morris, D., Ervin, C., & Conrad, K. (1996). A case study of middle school reading disability. *Reading Teacher, 49,* 368–377.

Morrow, L. M. (1992). The impact of a literature-based program on literacy achievement, use of literature, and attitudes of children from minority backgrounds. *Reading Research Quarterly, 27*(3), 250–275.

———, Pressley, M., Smith, J., & Smith, M. (1997). The effect of a literature-based program integrated into literacy and science instruction with children from diverse backgrounds. *Reading Research Quarterly, 32*(1), 54–76.

Nagy, W., & Anderson, R. C. (1984). How many words are there in printed school English? *Reading Research Quarterly, 19,* 304–330.

———, Anderson, R. C., & Herman, P. (1987). Learning word meanings from context during normal reading. *American Educational Research Journal, 24,* 237–270.

National Center for Education Statistics. (2004). *Who teaches reading in public elementary schools?* (Report no. NCES2004-034). Washington, DC: U.S. Department of Education, Institute for Education Sciences.

———. (2009). *The nation's report card: Reading 2009.* Washington, DC: U.S. Department of Education, Institute of Education Sciences.

National Center for Higher Education Management Systems. www.higheredinfo.org, retrieved October 18, 2010.

National Reading Panel. (2000). *Teaching children to read: An evidence-based assessment of the scientific research literature on reading and its implications for reading instruction.* (NIH Publication No. 00-4769). Washington, DC: U.S. Government Printing Office.

Neuman, S., & Celano, D. (2001). Access to print in low-income and middle-income communities. *Reading Research Quarterly, 36,* 8–26.

Nye, B., Konstantopoulos, S., & Hedges, L. V. (2004). How large are teacher effects? *Educational Evaluation and Policy Analysis, 26,* 237–257.

Nystrand, M. (2006). Research on the role of classroom discourse as it affects reading comprehension. *Research in the Teaching of English, 40,* 392–412.

———, Gamoran, A., Kachur, R., & Prendergast, C. (1997). *Opening dialogue: Understanding the dynamics of language and learning in the English classroom.* New York: Teachers College Press.

O'Connor, R. E., Bell, K. M., Harty, K. R., Larkin, L. K., Sackor, S. M., & Zigmond, N. (2002). Teaching reading to poor readers in the intermediate grades: A comparison of text difficulty. *Journal of Educational Psychology, 94,* 474–485.

Office of the Inspector General. (2006). *The Reading First program's grant application process: Final inspection report* (No. ED-OIG/I13-F0017). Washington, DC: U.S. Department of Education.

———. (2007). *RMC Research Corporation's adminstration of the Reading First program contracts.* (No. ED-OIG/A03F0022). Washington, DC: U.S. Department of Education.

Ohanian, S. (1999). *One size fits few.* Portsmouth, NH: Heinemann.

O'Shea, L. J., Sindelar, P. T., & O'Shea, D. J. (1985). The effects of repeated reading and attentional cues on reading fluency and comprehension. *Journal of Reading Behavior, 17,* 129–146.

O'Sullivan, P. J., Ysseldyke, J. E., Christenson, S. L., & Thurlow, M. L. (1990). Mildly handicapped elementary students' opportunity to learn during reading instruction in mainstream and special education settings. *Reading Research Quarterly, 25*(2), 131–146.

Palincsar, A. S., & Brown, A. (1984). Reciprocal teaching and comprehension-fostering and comprehension-monitoring activities. *Cognition and Instruction, 1*(2), 117–175.

Papay, J. P. (in press). The stability of teacher value-added estimates. *American Educational Research Journal.*

Paratore, J., Garnick, S., & Lewis, T. (1997). Watching teachers watch children talk about books. In J. Paratore & R. McCormack (Eds.), *Peer talk in the classroom: Learning from the research* (pp. 207–229). Newark, DE: International Reading Association.

Paris, S. G., Pearson, P. D., et al. (2004). Assessing the effectiveness of summer reading programs. In G. D. Borman & M. Boulay (Eds.), *Summer learning: Research, policies, and programs* (pp. 121–161). Mahwah, NJ: Erlbaum.

Patterson, W. A., Henry, J. J., O'Quin, K., Ceprano, M. A., & Blue, E. V. (2003). Investigating the effectiveness of an integrated learning system on early emergent readers. *Reading Research Quarterly, 38,* 172–207.

Pearson, P. D. (1993). Teaching and learning to read: A research perspective. *Language Arts, 70,* 502–511.

———. (2004). The reading wars. *Educational Policy, 18*(1), 216–252.

———, & Dole, J. (1987). Explicit comprehension instruction: A review of the research and a new conceptualization of instruction. *Elementary School Journal, 88,* 151–165.

———, & Fielding, L. (1991). Comprehension instruction. In M. Kamil, R. Barr, P. Mosenthal, & P. D. Pearson (Eds.), *Handbook of reading research, vol. 2* (pp. 815–860). New York: Longman.

Peterson, P. E., & Lastra-Anadon, C. X. (2010). State standards rising in reading but not math. *Education Next, 10*(4).

Phillips, G., & Smith, P. (2010). Closing the gaps: Literacy for the hardest to teach. In P. Johnston (Ed.), *RTI in literacy: Responsive and comprehensive.* Newark, DE: International Reading Association.

Phillips, L. M., Hayward, D. V., & Norris, S. P. (2010). Persistent reading disabilities: Challenging six erroneous beliefs. In A. McGill-Franzen & R. L. Allington (Eds.), *Handbook of Reading Disability Research.* New York: Routledge.

———, Norris, S., Osmond, W., & Maynard, A. (2002). Relative reading achievement: A longitudinal study of 187 children from first through sixth grade. *Journal of Educational Psychology, 94,* 3–13.

Pinnell, G. S., Pikulski, J. J., Wixson, K., Campbell, J. R., Gough, P. B., & Beatty, A. S. (1995). *Listening to children read aloud.* (No. ED-3788550). Washington, DC: National Center for Educational Statistics.

Pogrow, S. (1990). Challenging at-risk students: Findings from the HOTS program. *Phi Delta Kappan, 71,* 389–397.

———. (1993). Where's the beef? Looking for exemplary materials. *Educational Leadership, 50,* 39–45.

Pressley, M. (2002). Improving comprehension instruction: A path for the future. In C. C. Block, L. Gambrella, & M. Pressley (Eds.), *Improving comprehension instruction* (pp. 385–399). San Francisco: Jossey-Bass.

———. (2006). Reading instruction that works: *The case for balanced teaching* (3rd ed.). New York: Guilford.

———, & Allington, R. L. (1999). What should educational research be the research of? *Issues in Education: Contributions from Educational Psychology, 5*(1), 1–35.

———, Allington, R. L., Wharton-MacDonald, R., Block, C. C., & Morrow, L. (2001). *Learning to read: Lessons from exemplary first-grade classrooms.* New York: Guilford.

———, Dolezal, S., Raphael, L., Mohan, L., Roehrig, A., & Bogner, K. (2003). *Motivating primary grade students.* New York: Guilford.

———, El-Dinary, P. B., Gaskins, I., Schuder, T., Bergman, J., Almasi, L., & Brown, R. (1992). Beyond direct explanation: Transactional instruction in reading comprehension strategies. *Elementary School Journal, 92,* 511–554.

———, Hilden, K., & Shankland, R. (2006). *An evaluation of end-of-grade 3 Dynamic Indicators of Basic Early Literacy Skills (DIBELS): Speed reading without comprehension, predicting little.* East Lansing: Literacy Achievement Research Center, Michigan State University.

———, Johnson, C. J., Symons, S., McGoldrick, J., & Kurita, J. (1990). Strategies that improve memory and comprehension of what is read. *Elementary School Journal, 90,* 3–32.

———, Wharton-McDonald, R., Allington, R. L., Block, C. C., Morrow, L., Tracey, D., Baker, K., Brooks, G., Cronin, J., Nelson, E., & Woo, D. (2000). A study of effective first-grade reading instruction. *Scientific Studies of Reading, 5,* 35–58.

———, & Woloshyn, V. (1995). *Cognitive strategy instruction that really improves children's academic performance.* Cambridge, MA: Brookline.

Puma, M. J., Karweit, N., Price, C., Ricciuti, A., Thompson, W., & Vaden-Kiernan, M. (1997). *Prospects: Final report on student outcomes.* Washington, DC: U.S. Department of Education, Planning and Evaluation Services.

Purcell-Gates, V., McIntyre, E., & Freppon, P. (1995). Learning written storybook language in school. *American Educational Research Journal, 32*(3), 659–685.

Rashotte, C., & Torgeson, J. (1985). Repeated readings and reading fluency in learning disabled children. *Reading Research Quarterly, 20,* 180–189.

Rasinski, T. V. (1990). Effects of repeated readings and listening while reading on reading fluency. *Journal of Educational Research, 83,* 147–150.

———. (2000). Speed does matter in reading. *Reading Teacher, 54.*

Ravitch, D. (2010). *The death and life of the great American School system: How testing and choice are undermining education.* New York: Basic Books.

Reutzel, D. R., Hollingsworth, P. M., & Eldredge, J. L. (1994). Oral reading instruction: The impact on student reading development. *Reading Research Quarterly, 29*(1), 40–65.

Richardson, V. (Ed.). (1994). *Teacher change and the staff development process: A case in reading instruction.* New York: Teachers College Press.

Robinson, C. C., Larsen, J. M., & Haupt, J. H. (1996). The influence of selecting and taking picture books home on the at-home reading behaviors of kindergarten children. *Reading Research and Instruction, 35*(3), 249–259.

Rosenshine, B., & Meister, C. (1994). Reciprocal teaching: A review of the research. *Review of Educational Research, 64*(4), 479–530.

Roth, J., Brooks-Dunn, J., Linver, M., & Hofferth, S. (2002). What happened during the school day? Time diaries from a national sample of elementary school teachers. *Teachers College Record, 38*(2), 172–207.

Rothstein, R. (1998). *The way we were? The myths and realities of America's student achievement.* New York: The Century Foundation Press.

Rowan, B., & Guthrie, L. F. (1989). The quality of Chapter 1 instruction: Results from a study of twenty-four schools. In R. E. Slavin, N. Karweit, & N. Madden (Eds.), *Effective programs for students at risk* (pp. 195–219). Boston: Allyn & Bacon.

Ruddell, R. B., Draheim, M. E., & Barnes, J. (1990). A comparative study of the teaching effectiveness of influential and noninfluential teachers and reading comprehension development. In J. Zutell & S. MCormick (Eds.), *Literacy theory and research: Analyses from multiple paradigms* (pp. 153–162). Chicago: National Reading Conference.

Ryan, J. E. (2004). The perverse incentives of the No Child Left Behind Act. *New York University Law Review, 79,* 932–989.

Sailors, M., & Price, L. R. (2010). Professional development that supports the teaching of cognitive reading strategy instruction. *Elementary School Journal, 110*(3), 301–322.

Samuels, S. J. (2002). Reading fluency: Its development and assessment. In A. Farstrup & S. J. Samuels (Eds.), *What research has to say about reading instruction* (pp. 166–183). Newark, DE: International Reading Association.

———. (2007). The DIBELS tests: Is speed of barking at print what we mean by reading fluency? *Reading Research Quarterly, 42*(4), 563–566.

Scanlon, D. M., Gelzheiser, L. M., Vellutino, F. R., Schatschneider, C., & Sweeney, J. M. (2010). Reducing the incidence of early reading difficulties: Professional development for classroom teachers versus direct interventions for children. In P. H. Johnston (Ed.), *RTI in literacy—Responsive and comprehensive.* Newark, DE: International Reading Association.

———, & Vellutino, F. R. (1997). A comparison of the instructional backgrounds and cognitive profiles of poor, average, and good readers who were initially identified as at risk for reading failure. *Scientific Studies of Reading, 1,* 191–216.

———, Vellutino, F. R., Small, S., G, Fanuele, D. P., & Sweeney, J. M. (2005). Severe reading difficulties—Can they be prevented? A comparison of prevention and intervention approaches. *Exceptionality, 13*(4), 209–227.

Scharer, P. L. (1992). Teachers in transitions: An exploration of changes in teachers and classrooms during the implementation of literature-based reading instruction. *Research in the Teaching of English, 26*(4), 408–443.

Scharlach, T. D. (2008). These kids just aren't motivated to read: The influence of preservice teachers' beliefs on their expectations, instruction, and evaluation of struggling readers. *Literacy Research and Instruction, 47*(3), 158–173.

Schraw, G., Flowerday, T., & Reisletter, M. F. (1998). The role of choice in reader engagement. *Journal of Educational Psychology, 90,* 705–714.

Schrieber, P. A. (1980). On the acquisition of reading fluency. *Journal of Reading Behavior, 12,* 177–186.

Schweinhart, L. J., & Weikart, D. P. (1998, March). Why curriculum matters in early childhood education. *Educational Leadership, 55,* 57–60.

Seppanen, P. S., Love, J. M., deVries, D. K., & Bernstein, L. (1993). *National study of before- and after-school programs.* Washington, DC: U.S. Department of Education, Office of Policy and Planning.

Shanahan, T. (1998). On the effectiveness and limitations of tutoring. In P. D. Pearson & A. Iran-Nejad (Eds.), *Review of Research in Education: Vol. 23* (pp. 217–234). Washington, DC: American Educational Research Association.

Shanklin, N. L. (1990). Improving the comprehension of at-risk readers: An ethnographic study of four chapter I teachers, grades 4–6. *International Journal of Reading, Writing, and Learning Disabilities, 6*(2), 137–148.

Shany, M. T., & Biemiller, A. (1995). Assisted reading practice: Effects on performance for poor readers in grades 3 and 4. *Reading Research Quarterly, 30,* 382–395.

Share, D. L., & Stanovich, K. E. (1995). Cognitive processes in early reading development: Accommodating individual differences in a model of acquisition. *Issue in Education, 1*(1), 1–57.

Shepard, L. A., & Smith, M. L. (Eds.). (1989). *Flunking grades: Research and policies on retention.* Philadelphia: Falmer.

Showers, B., Joyce, B., Scanlon, M., & Schnaubelt, C. (1998). A second chance to learn to read. *Educational Leadership, 72,* 27–30.

Simmons, D. C., & Kame'enui, E. J. (2002). *A consumer's guide for evaluating core reading programs, K–3.* Eugene, OR: National Center to Improve the Tools of Educators.

Slavin, R. E., Cheung, A. C., Groff, C., & Lake, C. (2008). Effective reading programs for middle and high schools: A best evidence synthesis. *Reading Research Quarterly, 43*(3), 290–332.

———, Madden, N. A., Dolan, L. J., & Wasik, B. A. (1996). *Every child, every school: Success for all.* Thousand Oaks, CA: Corwin.

———, Madden, N. A., Karweit, B. L., Dolan, L. J., & Wasik, B. A. (1993). Success for all: A comprehensive approach to prevention and early intervention. In R. E. Slavin, B. L. Karweit, & B. A. Wasik (Eds.), *Preventing early school failure: Research, policy and practice* (pp. 175–205). Boston: Allyn & Bacon.

Smith, C., Constantino, R., & Krashen, S. (1997). Differences in print environment: Children in Beverly Hills, Compton and Watts. *Emergency Librarian, 24*(4), 8–9.

Smith, D. D. (1979). The improvement of children's oral reading through the use of teacher modeling. *Journal of Learning Disabilities, 12,* 39–42.

Smith, M. W., & Wilhelm, J. D. (2002). *Reading don't fix no Chevy's: Literacy in the lives of young men.* Portsmouth, NH: Heinemann.

Snow, C., Barnes, W., Chandler, J., Goodman, I. F., & Hemphill, L. (1991). *Unfulfilled expectations: Home and school influences on literacy.* Cambridge, MA: Harvard University Press.

———, Burns, M. S., & Griffin, P. (1998). *Preventing reading difficulties in young children: A report of the National Research Council.* Washington, DC: National Academy Press.

Stahl, S. A., Duffy-Hester, A., & Stahl, K. A. D. (1998). Everything you wanted to know about phonics (but were afraid to ask). *Reading Research Quarterly, 33*(3), 338–355.

———, & Heubach, K. (2005). Fluency oriented reading instruction. *Journal of Literacy Research, 37*(1), 25–60.

Stallings, J. (1980). Allocated academic learning time revisited, or beyond time on task. *Educational Researcher, 9*(11), 11–16.

Stanovich, K. E. (2000). *Progress in understanding reading: Scientific foundations and new frontiers.* New York: Guilford.

———, West, R. F., Cunningham, A. E., Cipielewski, J., & Siddiqui, S. (1996). The role of inadequate print exposure as a determinate of reading comprehension problems. In C. Cornoldi and J. Oakhill (Eds.), *Reading comprehension difficulties: Processes and intervention* (pp. 15–32). Mahwah, NJ: Erlbaum.

Stayter, F., & Allington, R. L. (1991). Fluency and comprehension. *Theory into Practice, 33,* 143–148.

Stenner, A. J. (1996). *Measuring reading comprehension with the Lexile Framework.* Durham, NC: Metametrics.

Stoll, D. R. (1997). *Magazines for kids and teens* (rev. ed.). Newark, DE: International Reading Association.

Strickland, D. S., & Walmsley, S. A. (1993). *School book clubs and literacy development: A descriptive study.* M. R. Robinson Foundation.

Swanson, H. L., & Hoskyn, M. (1998). Experimental intervention research on students with learning disabilities: A meta-analysis of treatment outcomes. *Review of Educational Research, 68*(3), 277–321.

———, Trainin, G., Necoechea, D. M., & Hammill, D. D. (2003). Rapid naming, phonological awareness, and reading: A meta-analysis of the correlational evidence. *Review of Educational Research, 73,* 407–440.

Taylor, B. M., Frye, B. J., & Maruyama, G. M. (1990). Time spent reading and reading growth. *American Educational Research Journal, 27*(2), 351–362.

———, Frye, B. J., Short, R., & Shearer, B. (1992). Classroom teachers prevent reading failure among low-achieving first-grade students. *Reading Teacher, 45,* 592–597.

———, Pearson, D., Clark, K., & Walpole, S. (2000a). *Beating the odds in teaching all children to read* (Report #2-006). East Lansing, MI: Center for Improving Early Reading Achievement.

———, Pearson, P. D., Clark, K., & Walpole, S. (2000b). Effective schools and accomplished teachers: Lessons about primary grade reading instruction in low-income schools. *Elementary School Journal, 101,* 121–165.

———, Pearson, P. D., Peterson, D. S., & Rodriguez, M. C. (2003). Reading growth in high-poverty classrooms: The influences of teacher practices that encourage cognitive engagement in literacy learning. *Elementary School Journal, 104*(1), 4–28.

———, Pearson, P. D., Peterson, D., & Rodriguez, M. (2005). The CIERA school change framework: An evidence-based approach to professional development and school reading improvement. *Reading Research Quarterly, 40,* 40–69.

Taylor, D. (1998). *Beginning to read and the spin doctors of science: The political campaign to change America's mind about how children learn to read.* Urbana, IL: National Council of Teachers of English.

Tharp, R. G., & Gallimore, R. (1989). Rousing schools to life. *American Educator, 13*(2), 20–25, 46–52.

Therrien, W. J. (2003). Fluency and comprehension gains as a result of repeated reading: A meta-analysis. *Remedial and Special Education, 25*(4), 252–261.

Thurlow, M., Gaden, J., Ysseldyke, J., & Algozzine, R. (1984). Student reading during reading class: The lost activity in reading instruction. *Journal of Educational Research, 77*(5), 267–272.

Tierney, R. J., & Shanahan, T. (1991). Research on reading-writing relationships: Interactions, transactions and outcomes. In R. Barr, M. Kamil, P. Mosenthal & P. D. Pearson (Eds.), *Handbook of Reading Research* (Vol. 2, pp. 246–280). New York: Longman.

Timar, T. B., & Kirp, D. L. (1987). Educational reform and institutional competence. *Harvard Educational Review, 57,* 308–330.

Topping, K. (1987). Peer tutored paired reading: Outcome data from ten projects. *Educational Psychology, 7,* 604–614.

———, & Ehly, S. (1998). *Peer assisted learning.* Mahwah, NJ: Erlbaum.

Torgeson, J. K. (2000). Individual differences in response to early interventions in reading: The lingering problem of treatment resisters. *Learning Disabilities Research and Practice, 15,* 55–64.

———. (2002). The prevention of reading difficulties. *Journal of School Psychology, 40,* 7–26.

———, & Hecht, S. A. (1996). Preventing and remediating reading disabilities. In M. Graves, P. van den Brock, & B. Taylor (Eds.), *The first R: Every child's right to read* (pp. 133–159). New York: Teachers College Press.

Tovani, C. (2001). *I read it, but I don't get it: Comprehension strategies for adolescent readers.* Portland, ME: Stenhouse.

———. (2004). *Do I really have to teach reading?* Portland, ME: Stenhouse.

Troia, G. A. (1999). Phonological awareness intervention research: A critical review of the experimental methodology. *Reading Research Quarterly, 34,* 28–53.

Turner, J. C. (1995). The influence of classroom contexts on young children's motivation for literacy. *Reading Research Quarterly, 30*(3), 410–441.

U.S. Department of Education. (2002). *No Child Left Behind Act: A desktop reference.* Office of Elementary and Secondary Education. Retrieved from www.ed.gov/admins/lead/account/nclbreference/page.html.

Valencia, S. W., Place, N. A., Martin, S. D., & Grossman, P. L. (2006). Curriculum materials for elementary reading: Shackles and scaffolds for beginning teachers. *Elementary School Journal, 107*(1), 94–120.

Valli, L., Croninger, R. G., & Walters, K. (2007). Who (else) is the teacher? Cautionary notes on teacher accountability systems. *American Journal of Education, 113*(4), 635–662.

Vaughn, S., & Linan-Thompson, S. (2003). What is special about special education for students with learning disabilities? *Exceptional Children, 69*(4), 391–409.

Vaughn, S., Moody, S. W., & Schumm, J. (1998). Broken promises: Reading instruction in the resource room. *Exceptional Children, 64,* 211–225.

Vellutino, F. R., & Fletcher, J. M. (2005). Developmental dyslexia. In M. Snowling & C. Hulme (Eds.), *The science of reading: A handbook* (pp. 362–378). Malden, MA: Blackwell.

———, Scanlon, D. M., Sipay, E. R., Small, S. G., Pratt, A., Chen, R., et al. (1996). Cognitive profiles of difficult-to-remediate and readily remediated poor readers: Early intervention as a vehicle for distinguishing between cognitive and experiential deficits as basic causes of specific reading disability. *Journal of Educational Psychology, 88*(4), 601–638.

Venezky, R. L. (1998). An alternate perspective on success for all. In K. K. Wong (Ed.), *Advances in educational policy* (vol. 4, pp. 145–165). Greenwich, CT: JAI Press.

Walmsley, S. A. (1981). On the purpose and content of secondary reading programs: An educational ideological perspective. *Curriculum Inquiry, 11*(1), 73–93.

Wang, J. H., & Guthrie, J. T. (2004). Modeling the effects of intrinsic motivation, extrinsic motivation, amount of reading, and past reading achievement on text comprehension of U.S. and Chinese students. *Reading Research Quarterly, 39,* 162–186.

Waples, D. (1937/1972). *Social aspects of reading in the depression.* New York: Arno Press.

Wasik, B. A. (1998). Volunteer tutoring programs in reading: A review. *Reading Research Quarterly, 33*(3), 266–293.

———, & Slavin, R. E. (1993). Preventing early reading failure with one-to-one tutoring: A review of five programs. *Reading Research Quarterly, 28*(2), 178–200.

Weber, R. M. (1970). A linguistic analysis of first grade reading errors. *Reading Research Quarterly, 5,* 427–451.

What Works Clearinghouse. (2007). Beginning reading: Reading Recovery. Institute of Education Sciences, U.S. Department of Education. (Available at www.whatworks.ed.gov)

Wigfield, A. (1997). Children's motivations for reading and reading engagement. In J. T. Guthrie & A. Wigfield (Eds.), *Reading engagement: Motivating readers through integrated instruction* (pp. 14–33). Newark, DE: International Reading Association.

Wilhelm, J. D. (1997). *"You gotta be the book": Teaching engaged and reflective reading with adolescents.* New York: Teachers College Press.

Wilkinson, I., Wardrop, J., & Anderson, R. C. (1988). Silent reading reconsidered: Reinterpreting reading instruction and its effects. *American Educational Research Journal, 25*(1), 127–144.

Williams, L. M. (2008). Book selections of economically disadvantaged Black elementary students. *Journal of Educational Research, 102*(1), 51–63.

Willman, A. T. (1999). "Hello, Mrs. Williams, it's me!": Keeping kids reading over the summer by using voice mail. *Reading Teacher, 52,* 788–789.

Wolk, S. (2010). What should students read? *Phi Delta Kappan, 91*(7), 9–16.

Wong, K. K., Anagnostopoulos, D., Rutledge, S., & Edwards, C. (2003). The challenge of improving instruction in urban high schools: Case studies of the implementation of the Chicago academic standards. *Peabody Journal of Education, 78*(3), 39–97.

Worthy, J., & McCool, L. S. (1996). Students who say they hate to read: The importance of opportunity, choice, and access. In D. Leu, C. Kinzer, & K. Hinchman (Eds.), *Literacies for the 21st century* (pp. 245–256). Chicago: National Reading Conference.

Ysseldyke, J. E., Thurlow, M. L., Mecklenberg, C., & Graden, J. (1984). Opportunity to learn for regular and special education students during reading instruction. *Remedial and Special Education, 5,* 29–37.

Zigmond, N., Vallecorsa, A., & Leinhardt, J. (1980). Reading instruction for students with learning disabilities. *Topics in Language Disorders, 1,* 89–98.

Zill, N., & West, J. (2001). *Entering kindergarten: A portrait of American children when they begin school: Findings from The Condition of Education 2000.* Washington, DC: National Center for Education Statistics, U.S. Department of Education.

Index